The Impact of Inflation
on Internal Planning and Control

by

Allen H. Seed, III
Arthur D. Little, Inc.
Cambridge, Mass.

A study carried out on behalf of the
National Association of Accountants
New York, N.Y.

Published by

National Association of Accountants

919 Third Avenue, New York, N.Y. 10022

NAA Publication Number 81131
ISBN 0-86641-010-4

Foreword

A basic and rather obvious aspect of inflation is its differential impact on various individuals, organizations and groups. The impact of inflation on an economic entity, such as a business enterprise, is conditioned by its relative standing with respect to the nature and direction of the prevailing inflationary pressures. During the course of any inflationary process, however, the impact of inflation varies considerably with the ability of a business enterprise to adjust its economic behavior to inflation and thus to place itself into a more favorable position in an inflationary environment.

Presented here are the results of a study commissioned by the National Association of Accountants to provide assistance to business enterprises in their efforts to cope with inflation. The main objective was to identify and examine internal planning and control practices that are suitable as means of dealing with the issues pertinent to a variety of inflationary settings. Giving recognition to the diversity of situations regarding the impact of inflation, the research design called for in-depth coverage of internal planning and control practices in selected companies. An overall view of the state of the art was obtained through a mail survey.

Guidance in the preparation of this research report was kindly and generously provided by the Project Committee:

Geraldine F. Dominiak, *Chairman*
Texas Christian University
Fort Worth, Texas

Dwight H. Davis
A.O. Smith Corporation
Kankakee, Illinois

Richard F. Bebee
Alexander Grant and Company
Chicago, Illinois

Joseph J. McCann
Ryan Homes, Inc.
Pittsburgh, Pennsylvania

The report reflects the views of the researchers and not necessarily those of the Association, the Committee on Research or the Project Committee.

Stephen Landekich
Research Director
National Association of Accountants

About the Author

Allen H. Seed, III, has a broad background in finance and accounting. He is a senior consultant with Arthur D. Little, Inc., Cambridge, Mass., where he specializes in the areas of business planning and management control.

He was previously a vice president for corporate development at The Gillette Company, a group and division controller of International Paper Company, chief financial executive of Munsingwear, Inc., and Farmhand, Inc. He has been active as a volunteer in the National Association of Accountants and has served as a national vice president, chairman of the Research Committee and chairman of the Education Committee. He is the author of several articles on financial business planning and accounting subjects. His research study, *Inflation: Its Impact on Financial Reporting and Decision Making,* was published by the Financial Executives Research Foundation in 1978.

Acknowledgments

The author wishes to express his appreciation to his hard-working colleagues, Mr. Ernest Arvai, Mr. Jeffrey Traenkle, and Mrs. Maureen Hammond of Arthur D. Little, Inc. Mr. Arvai was a co-researcher on this project. He compiled and analyzed the responses to the questionnaire and prepared the N.V. Philips and General Electric case studies. Mr. Traenkle reviewed the results of our work and contributed to our conclusions and recommendations. Mrs. Hammond processed and assembled the many drafts and redrafts that were required.

Special thanks go to Dr. Geraldine F. Dominiak, chairman of the Department of Accounting of the M. J. Neeley School of Business, Texas Christian University. Dr. Dominiak, who was chairman of the Project Committee, is an extremely knowledgeable accounting professional and a demanding taskmaster. She critiqued and edited all of this material and made innumerable suggestions for improving the product. In the view of the author, Dr. Dominiak's pursuit of excellence is in no small measure responsible for whatever quality the end product may contain.

Mr. Stephen Landekich, research director of the National Association of Accountants, provided invaluable advice and guidance. His direction and encouragement were most appreciated.

Several executives from five leading companies opened their doors, contributed their time, and reviewed the case studies contained in this research. While all of the persons interviewed in each company cannot be listed, the author is especially indebted to these individuals, and the principal points of contact in each company who are identified below:

- Duane R. Borst, comptroller, Inland Steel Company
- Fernando Braga Hilsenbeck, controller, Acos Villares S.A.
- William J. Ihlanfeldt, assistant controller, Shell Oil Company
- J.N. Weezenberg, manager of Bureau Administrative Directivas, N.V. Philips Company
- Bernard R. Doyle, manager, General and Cost Accounting Operations, General Electric Company

Finally, we thank the 282 anonymous persons who responded to our questionnaire and provided the data upon which much of this research is based.

Table of Contents

Page

Foreword iii

About the Author v

Acknowledgments vii

Section I—Introduction and Background 1

Chapter 1—Introduction 3
Purpose and Scope of Research 3
Methodology 4
Literature Search 4
Analysis of Inflation-Adjusted Results 4
Questionnaire 5
Company Case Studies 6
Organization of Report 6
Summary of Findings 8

Chapter 2—Inflation: Roots, Prescriptions and Implications 13
Causes of Inflation 13
Prescriptions and Policies 14
Worldwide Implications 15
The Measurement Problem 15
Factors Influencing Accounting Measurements 19
Type of Business 20
Inventory Valuation Methods and Turnover Rates 20
Business Maturity 21
Composition of Expenditures 22
Capital Structure 22
Strategic Implications of Inflation 22
Capital Formation Impairment 22
Increased Uncertainty 23

Chapter 3—Accounting Alternatives for Coping With Inflation   25
    Definitions of Terms   26
    Origin of Concepts   26
    Where LIFO Fits In   27
    Experimentation, Consideration and Debate   28
    Practices in Other Countries   31
        Great Britain   31
        Canada   32
        Brazil   32
        Argentina   34
        The Netherlands   34

Chapter 4—Requirements of FASB Statement No. 33   37
    Information Requirements   37
    Objectives of Statement   40
    Constant Dollar Application   41
        Discussion of Indices   41
        Minimal Financial Data Requirements   42
        Calculation Methodology   43
    Current Cost Application   47
        Calculation Methodology   48

Chapter 5—Results of Applying FAS No. 33   51
    Effect on Income Statement   51
    Monetary Gains and Losses   52
    Holding Gains   54
    Variations by Industry and Company   54
    Income Tax Implications   55
    Capital Formation   55
    A Comment on Methodology   63

Section II—Management Accounting Issues and Practices   65

Chapter 6—Strategic Planning and Budgeting Issues   67
    Scope of Resource Allocation   67
    Business Unit Analysis   68
    Financial Projections   69
    Portfolio Analysis   70
    Financial Strategies   71
    Capital Expenditure Evaluations   73
    Increased Cost of Capital   75
    Operating Planning and Budgeting   76
    Summary of Key Issues and Options   78

Chapter 7—Management Control Issues 79
    Product Pricing 79
    Standard Costing 81
    Inventory Valuation 81
    Management Reporting and Performance Evaluation 83
        Trend Analyses 84
        Profitability Reporting 84
        Variance Analysis 86
        Funds Management 88
        Productivity Measurements 90
    Management Incentive Compensation 93
    Summary of Key Issues and Options 95

Chapter 8—Planning and Control Practices 97
    Profile of Respondents 97
    Inflation Expectations 98
    Financial Strategies 100
    Management Incentive Compensation 101
    Planning and Budgeting 102
    Capital Expenditures 104
    Standard Costs 105
    Inventory Valuation 105
    Management Reporting and Performance Evaluation 106

Section III—Company Case Studies 109

Chapter 9—Inland Steel Company 111
    Industry Situation 111
    Background of Company 112
    Organization 113
    Status of Management Accounting Systems 115
    Resource Allocation 116
    Capital Expenditures 117
    Flexible Budgeting and Cost Control Reporting
        at Works Level 121
    Standard Cost System 122
    Inventory Valuation and Management 122
    Productivity Measurement 123
    Key Measurements 125
    Budgeting and Profitability Accounting 125
    Funds Management 128
    Experimentation with Inflation Accounting 129

Chapter 10—Acos Villares, S.A. 131
Background of Company 132
Organization 133
Planning and Budgeting Systems 133
Capital Expenditures 136
Cost Systems 137
Product Pricing 138
Top Management Reporting 141
Structure of Profit-and-Loss Statement 141
Computation of Return on Invested Capital 143
Funds Statement 143
Cost-of-Production Statement 144
Productivity Measurements 145

Chapter 11—Shell Oil Company 147
Background of Company 147
Organization 148
Strategic Planning 152
Corporate Financial Strategies 154
Capital Expenditures 155
Financial Reporting 159
Productivity Measurement 164
Profitability and Performance Measurement 164

Chapter 12—N.V. Philips 167
Company Background 167
Organization and Management Philosophy 169
Planning at Philips 173
Strategic Planning—The Four-Year Plan 174
Operating Planning and Budgeting 175
Transfer Pricing 175
Capital Expenditure Planning and Evaluation 177
Management Reporting 178

Chapter 13—General Electric Company 183
Company Background 183
Management Philosophy 184
Organization 185
Management Practices 188
Management Education 188
Strategic Planning 191
Capital Expenditure Evaluations 194
Calculation of Inflation-Adjusted Results 194

Planning and Budgeting   196
Performance Reporting   198
Productivity Measurement   198
Six "P's" of Management in an Inflationary Environment   200

Section IV—Conclusions and Recommendations   201

Chapter 14—Conclusions and Recommendations   203
Significant Focal Points   204
Management Education   204
Strategic Management   206
Forecasting   207
Monitoring Actual Results   208
Productivity Measurements   210
Budgeting and Standard Costs   210
Management Reporting   211
Summary   211

Selected Bibliography   213
Management and Management Accounting Issues   215
LIFO Inventory Valuation   220
Productivity Measurement   220
Inflation Accounting Concepts   221
FASB Statement No. 33   222
Practices in Other Countries   223

Appendix   227
Questionnaire   231

Section I

Introduction and Background

Chapter 1

Introduction

Purpose and Scope of Research

Worldwide inflation's distortions of traditional measurements of economic activities have raised fundamental questions concerning the adequacy of existing accounting concepts. The purchasing power of the dollar has declined, and historical measures of cost are regarded as inadequately reflecting economic reality.

Conceptual accounting and external reporting issues resulting from inflation have been addressed by extensive research and a number of bodies including the Accounting Principles Board, U.S. Securities and Exchange Commission, Financial Accounting Standards Board, and several international organizations. Little, however, has been published concerning the internal planning and control issues associated with inflation. These issues are as significant to management as those relating to external financial reporting. This study is intended to help fill the gap.

The thrust of our research was to find out how inflation has actually affected internal planning and control practices in leading corporations. The main objective of our report is to describe the state of the art and how companies are coping with management accounting problems associated with inflation.

For purposes of our study, "internal planning and control" was considered to include:

- Strategic planning and long-range financial forecasting
- Capital expenditure and investment planning and evaluations
- Profit planning and financial budgeting
- Standard cost development and product pricing
- Inventory accounting
- Variance analysis and business unit performance evaluation
- Management reporting

Our research was undertaken and our report written primarily for the management accountant who is searching for better ways to deal with the planning and control issues pertaining to inflation in his particular business. Therefore, we were more concerned with the "how to's" and the application of accounting in an inflationary environment than we were in the theoretical considerations involved.

Methodology

Our research consisted of four tasks:

1. A search of the articles, books and other publications that pertain to the issues associated with management accounting in an inflationary environment
2. An analysis of the inflation-adjusted results of 29 of the 30 companies that constitute the Dow Jones Industrial Average
3. Distribution of a questionnaire covering the effect of inflation on planning and control practices and analysis of the results
4. On-site, in-depth case studies of the internal planning and control practices of five leading industrial companies

The methodology employed in each task is described in the sections that follow.

Literature Search

We conducted a search of the articles, books, and publications that contain material pertinent to various categories related to our subject matter. These categories are:

- Management and management accounting issues
- LIFO inventory valuation
- Productivity measurement
- Inflation accounting concepts
- FASB Statement No. 33
- Practices in other countries

Some of the more relevant and useful publications we viewed in the course of our literature search are listed by category in the bibliography appended to this report. For the most part, information obtained in the course of our search is found in those chapters that deal with the inflation accounting background and management accounting issues.

Analysis of Inflation-Adjusted Results

We prepared an analysis of the 1979 and 1980 inflation-adjusted results of 29 of the 30 companies that constitute the Dow Jones Industrial Average. [1] This sample, though small, provided a picture of the impact of the constant dollar and current cost methodologies on the results reported by one of the most referred-to segments of American industry. These companies are representative of the leaders of U.S. industry, and their stock prices constitute the well-known stock price index.

Most of the patterns of financial relationships that emerged from this analysis were confirmed by a broader study of 409 companies in 49 major industries conducted by Peat, Marwick, Mitchell & Co. [2], and a study of 300 companies conducted by Arthur Young & Company. [3] These studies differed from ours in that they were largely oriented towards earnings and data related to return on investment. While our analysis covered the effect on the income statement, monetary gains or losses, holding gains, and income tax implications, we were also concerned with the capital formation issues. Consequently we analyzed the funds available for growth for the companies included in our sample. These analyses are contained in Chapter 5.

Questionnaire

A questionnaire covering topics related to the impact of inflation on internal planning and control was mailed, with a self-addressed, stamped envelope, to the chief financial executives of the *Fortune* 1,000 companies on March 31, 1980. The questionnaire and a summary of responses is included in the Appendix, pages 227–239.

The following topics were addressed:

- Company background
- Assumptions about U.S. inflation
- Corporate financial strategies
- Planning or budgeting
- Capital expenditures
- Standard costs
- Inventory valuation
- Management reporting and other management practices

The researchers received 282 responses (28% response rate) from this

---

[1] The 30th company, General Foods (fiscal year on March 31), was omitted because its fiscal year annual report was not available at the time of our analysis.

[2] Peat, Marwick, Mitchell & Co., *The New Inflation Data: A Survey of Annual Reports*, June 1980.

[3] Arthur Young & Company, *Financial Reporting and Changing Prices: A Survey of How 300 Companies Complied with FAS No. 33*, August 1980.

mailing between April 3 and May 12, 1980. Results were tabulated and analyzed by:

- Type of business
- Size of business measured by:
  Revenues—over and under median ($590 million)
  Total assets—over and under median ($385 million)
- Total assets—over and under median ($385 million)
- Capital turnover rate—over and under median (1.5 times)
- Percent revenues and assets outside U.S.—30% or more; less than 30%

Written comments and responses to the open-ended questions were also reviewed.

Company Case Studies

We conducted case studies of internal planning and control at five companies. These case studies, which constituted about half of our research effort, are intended to provide the reader with a true-to-life picture of what managements are doing to cope with inflation in their own businesses.

The practices of the five companies are not offered as typical. These companies are the leaders. Indeed, we seriously doubt that many other companies have reached the levels of sophistication exhibited by these leaders. Nevertheless, we thought our research would be more meaningful if it included some undisguised examples of what companies are doing. Because of their "real world" setting, we believe these studies can be used as vehicles for management accounting instruction and classroom discussion.

The companies that we selected for the case studies and some of the reasons for their selection are tabulated in Exhibit 1–1.

We spent two to three days at each location. In each case, we received the enthusiastic cooperation of top financial accounting management, and we interviewed between 10 and 30 persons. Successive drafts of our manuscripts were reviewed by the management of each company for factual accuracy and completeness, but management allowed us to pinpoint what we perceived to be the issues and problems.

Organization of Report

Because we believe internal planning and control techniques are often linked to external events and reporting practices we thought it would be useful to preface our exposition of internal practice by tracing the roots and implications of inflation. We explore prescriptions for its cure, discuss the accounting alternatives for coping with inflation and the requirements of

EXHIBIT 1–1

Reasons for Selection of Case Studies

Company	Reasons for Selection
Inland Steel Company Chicago, Illinois	• Regarded as one of the best controlled businesses in the steel industry. • All steel-making facilities are in a single location. • Controller actively experimenting with inflation accounting techniques.
Acos Villares, S.A. Sao Paulo, Brazil	• Well-managed Brazilian steel company. • Has coped with inflation at 50–100% annual rate and regulatory constraints associated with Brazilian economy. • Modern management accounting employed.
Shell Oil Company Houston, Texas	• Capital-intensive business that has benefited from inflation. • Well-managed business with effective controls. • Was pioneer in price level adjusted external reporting.
N.V. Philips Eindhoven, Netherlands	• Acknowledged leader in development of replacement cost accounting. • Large, multinational, multi-division company that deals with several currencies and inflation rates.
General Electric Company Fairfield, Connecticut	• Acknowledged leader in adopting inflation accounting techniques to internal planning and control. • Strong management education program of special interest. • In forefront of developing strategies for coping with inflation.

FASB Statement No. 33, and evaluate the effect of inflation on various companies from applying FAS No. 33.

This background material is contained in the first section of our report, "Introduction and Background" (Chapters 1–5). Readers who are familiar with inflation accounting concepts and their impact on financial statements may want to skip this section and proceed directly to Chapter 6.

The second section of our report, "Management Accounting Issues and Practices" (Chapters 6–8), contains a core discussion of the strategic planning and budgeting issues, management control issues, and planning and control practices that are associated with inflation. Our aim was to frame the issues and provide factual data of the practices that are in place.

The third section of our report (Chapters 9–13) contains case studies that describe how these five leading corporations are coping with inflation-oriented management accounting issues.

The final section of our report (Chapter 14) contains our conclusions and recommendations. While the opinions expressed are those of the researchers, we hope that they will be of use to management accountants who are concerned with how to deal with inflation in their own businesses.

Summary of Findings

Despite the substantial effect of inflation on the transactional values and yardsticks used by American businesses, most companies are not applying constant dollar or current cost techniques internally. Instead, traditional historical cost accounting techniques are being adapted to deal better with the cost changes and unpredictability associated with an inflationary environment.

Constant dollar and current cost data contained in the 1979 statements of large corporations in accordance with FAS No. 33 show that inflation can have an important effect on key financial results. Irrespective of whether the constant dollar or current cost methodology is applied, certain events seem to occur:

- Cost of sales (exclusive of depreciation) increases—especially for those companies who value inventories on a FIFO basis.
- Depreciation increases significantly—capital-intensive companies are most affected.
- Reported profits are greatly reduced.
- Effective tax rates shoot up from a level of 50% of income, or less, to over 60% of income.
- Much of the reported decrease in profits is often offset by monetary gains on the purchasing power of net amounts owed. However, the usefulness of this information is still an issue of dispute to many preparers and users of financial statements.
- Dividend payout ratios increase dramatically and capital available for growth is seriously impaired in many cases.
- Effects of inflation differ among industries, even for companies within the same industry.

The prospects of continuing inflation at the 5% to 20% level and the magnitude of the preceding effects raise significant internal planning and control as well as external reporting issues. More specifically, planning, budgeting and capital expenditure issues—and our key findings related to these issues—include:

1. *Assumptions about inflation.* Most financial managers surveyed thought that inflation will range between 10% and 15% in 1981, but will drop to the 5% to 9% range by 1985. Most think that selling prices will lag behind the CPI-U, that energy costs increases will exceed increases in the CPI-U, but that other costs will increase at about the same rate as the CPI-U. Practices vary as to who is responsible for developing inflation assumptions within each company. The most common practice seems to be to look to the planning manager or corporate economist for this information.

2. *Effect of price changes on plans, budgets and standard costs.* As a result of inflation, many companies are updating plans, budgets and standards more frequently to assure that current costs are used for profit margin analysis, performance measurement and inventory valuation. Many companies update budgets quarterly although long-range plans and standard costs are usually prepared annually. Price change expectations are commonly reflected in budgets and standard costs. Plans and budgets are being subjected to more intensive reviews as a result of inflation.

3. *Statements and measurements included in plans and budgets.* An overwhelming number of companies now include funds statements, and a significant number include productivity measurements as part of their plans and budgets.

4. *Preparation of forecasts.* Strategic plans are prepared in constant dollars, nominal dollars or both constant and nominal dollars, but most companies appear to prepare forecasts in nominal dollars. Many of the more sophisticated companies, however, prepare forecasts in both nominal and constant dollars and apply sensitivity analyses to test the effect of different inflation rate assumptions.

5. *Effect of inflation on capital expenditure hurdle rates.* Most companies that use capital expenditure hurdle rates have increased these rates because of inflation. Whereas 10% to 15% hurdle rates were common ten years ago, hurdle rates in the 15% to 20% range seem to be more common today. Moreover, capital expenditures for cost reduction are commonly emphasized because this is one of the ways that inflationary increases in wages, energy and other operating costs can be minimized.

6. *Reflecting inflation in capital expenditure evaluations.* Most companies make some kind of allowance for inflation in capital expendi-

ture requests, forecast in nominal dollars, and compare internal rates of return with or compute net present values using a cost of capital adjusted for inflation. However, inflation is not usually taken into consideration in computing residual values. Some companies, such as Inland Steel and Shell Oil, have developed internal indices for predicting future construction costs.

7. *Dealing with differences between local and U.S. currency and local and U.S. tax rates in capital expenditure evaluations for overseas expenditures.* The most common practice is to forecast future cash flows in both the local currency and U.S. dollars and to apply both the local and U.S. income tax rates.

Our findings related to methods of inventory valuation, management reporting and other management control issues include:

1. *Inventory valuation method.* LIFO now seems to be the predominant method of inventory valuation. Sixty-one percent of the companies surveyed use LIFO as the predominant method of inventory valuation in the U.S., and 19% indicated that continued inflation either may, or probably will, lead to a switch to LIFO.

2. *Management reporting.* Most companies are placing emphasis on funds flow and productivity reporting as a result of inflation. Funds flow reporting focuses on cash rather than reported profits. Productivity measurements often are not at all affected by inflation.

3. *Tracking price level changes.* Many companies have devised methods for tracking price level changes. These methods include formal reconciliations of successive estimates, price level adjusted flexible budgeting, variance analyses that isolate the effect of price level changes, and supplemental reporting. However, in each case historical cost accounting concepts are used for this purpose.

4. *Internal use of constant dollars and current costs.* A few companies are using constant dollar and current cost measurements internally, and a few others are investigating using these measurements. Many managers are plagued by the uncertainty of inflation, and some companies are tracking real growth in constant dollars. N.V. Philips is using replacement cost accounting, but constant dollar and current cost accounting have not caught on in most companies. Most managers either do not understand constant dollar and current cost accounting techniques or do not see how they can be applied in their businesses.

5. *Management education*. One company, General Electric, has mounted a major effort to educate its managers about the effects of inflation, inflation accounting techniques and the implications of inflation in the selection of business strategies. GE appears to be the leader in teaching executives how to manage in an inflationary environment. GE reports supplemental constant dollar and current cost information by business unit.

Chapter 2

Inflation: Roots, Prescriptions and Implications

United States consumers are painfully aware that a 1981 dollar buys less than half the goods and services that could be purchased by a 1972 dollar. Many other countries have seen the purchasing power of their currencies decline even more.

Inflation has far-reaching effects on business enterprises. Measurements are distorted, larger amounts of money are required to maintain productive capacity, capital formation is impaired, and uncertainty intensifies. Inflation pervades the entire business structure and has broad financial reporting, internal planning and control implications.

This chapter provides a sketch of some of the theories as to the causes of inflation and the prescriptions that have been suggested or tried to deal with the problem. The measurement problem, factors influencing accounting measurements, and the strategic implications on business are also discussed. Such information is offered as background to the management accountant or other reader who wishes to review the nature and scope of the underlying malady in connection with considering its planning and control implications.

Causes of Inflation

"Inflation has one cause and one cause alone—government," President Ronald Reagan contends, "and therefore, less government is the only cure."[1] It would be expedient to accept this statement at face value and end the discussion of causes of inflation here. Nevertheless, while this particular campaign rhetoric may have appeal and may indeed be substantially correct, renowned economists, central bankers and national politicians have debated the causes of inflation over the decades without reaching agreement.

---

[1]*Newsweek*, March 31, 1980, p. 26.

An identification of the causes of inflation depends on whether one accepts Keynesian, monetarist or neo-Keynesian theories. Prescriptions for the problem also stem from these theories and the social and political persuasions of the policymakers concerned.

In the 1930's, English economist John Maynard Keynes and many of his contemporaries, including Sir John Hicks, identified two major causes of inflation: "demand-pull" and "cost-push." Demand-pull inflation takes place when excess demand for goods and services pulls prices upward. Cost-push inflation results from wage and costs increases in excess of productivity increases. Views differ as to which cause is the most significant.

Keynesian theories were challenged in the '60s by the monetarists, including Milton Friedman of the University of Chicago. The essence of the monetarist theory is that inflation is caused when too much money is available to bid up prices on existing goods and services. Monetarists see U.S. inflation over the last 15 years as clearly associated with quite identifiable surges of growth in the money supply.

Neo-Keynesians tend to use a mixture of both Keynesian and monetarist theories. They maintain that inflation is caused by changes in supply and demand and not solely by monetary causes. They argue that inflation results from a variety of factors: resource, social, and political. For example, neo-Keynesians would point out that resource limitations, coupled with the expanding demand we have experienced during the Vietnam war and in the current oil shortage, lead to higher prices. Similarly, they would argue that a higher standard of living without accompanying productivity increases contributes to inflation and that deficit spending, monetary expansion, and unfavorable balances of trade all add fuel to the fire.

Prescriptions and Policies

Prescriptions to cure inflation depend on the economic school involved and the policies of the government.

Keynes called for government involvement in the economy—not to control inflation, which at the time was minimal, but rather to cure unemployment. This view led to the practice of regulating the economy through the application of fiscal policies and deficit spending. Such practices worked quite well for a while, but by the end of the 1960's stagflation developed. Some observers began to question whether Keynesian approaches to managing the economy stimulated inflation rather than growth as expected. Moreover, economic policies to reduce inflation in one period may cause it to increase in another. Because Keynesian approaches did not produce the results that were desired, the policies of the monetarists were more widely applied.

Monetarist solutions to inflation are directed to controlling the money supply because they believe that aggregate demand depends on the supply of money. They consider the rate at which money circulates and multiplies itself (velocity of money) to be constant and hold that inflation can be controlled by matching the supply of money with the quantity of output.

Neo-Keynesians still maintain that government can indeed regulate, stimulate, and dampen the economy, but that it does so in response to social and political pressures and international events. In their view these forces must be dealt with within a framework of economic capacity and a finite supply of natural resources. When the cost of responding to social and political forces exceeds the capacity (resources and productivity) of the economy, excess costs are redistributed throughout the economy as inflation.

Minimizing inflation in the long run, therefore, depends on either limiting demands on the economy or expanding the economy (supply) to meet demand. Restraining demand means either capping social aspirations, restraining the growth of government, or transferring consumption from one segment of the society to another. Economic expansion (increasing supply) requires increased capital formation and resultant productivity improvements, more output from the labor force, and new sources of energy and other natural resources.

Worldwide Implications

Inflation is a worldwide phenomenon, and many industrial countries are more severely affected by it than the United States. Highlights of the extent of inflation in selected industrial countries are tabulated in Exhibit 2–1.[2] The inflation record for 1970–79 is calculated as a change in the consumer price index. Special characteristics of each economy and actions taken to combat inflation also are shown.

Exhibit 2–1 is not purported to be a comprehensive tabulation but rather an informal indication of the scope and diversity of some of the circumstances and responses behind the inflation record of each country. Characteristics of each economy and actions taken to combat inflation constitute an ever-moving tableau. The ten-year record shows that inflation rates have varied over time, and policies designed to cope with inflation tend to respond to these variations. Exhibit 2–1, therefore, must be regarded as simply a snapshot of highlights that prevailed at the time of our research.

The Measurement Problem

The decline in the value of the dollar and the uneven changes in spe-

---

[2]Reproduced and updated, with permission, from *Inflation: Its Impact on Financial Reporting and Decision Making*, Financial Executives Research Foundation, 1978, pp. 8–10.

EXHIBIT 2-1

Highlights of Extent of Inflation in Selected Industrial Countries

Inflation Record 1970–79 (% Change Consumer Price Index)[3]

United States		Canada		United Kingdom	
1979	12.1	1979	9.6	1979	15.8
1978	7.7	1978	9.0	1978	12.1
1977	6.5	1977	8.0	1977	15.9
1976	5.8	1976	7.5	1976	16.5
1975	9.1	1975	10.8	1975	24.2
1974	11.0	1974	10.8	1974	16.0
1973	6.2	1973	7.6	1973	9.2
1972	3.3	1972	4.8	1972	7.1
1971	4.3	1971	2.9	1971	9.5
1970	5.9	1970	3.3	1970	6.4

Special Characteristics of Current Economy

United States	Canada	United Kingdom
• World's largest free economy	• Extensive ties to U.S. economy	• Heavy reliance on foreign trade
• Growing dependence on imported oil	• Policy setting constrained by desire to maintain competitiveness of Canadian products in U.S. marketplace	• Older plant and equipment
• Low productivity increases	• High imported inflation	• Low productivity
• Re-emergence of pressures of protectionism		• Strong commitment to full employment and welfare

Actions Taken to Combat Inflation

United States	Canada	United Kingdom
• Money supply curtailed by Federal Reserve Board	• Anti-inflation Board established	• Mandated wage and price controls
• Interest rate and credit regulation	• Mandated wage and price controls	• Value-added and other indirect taxes imposed
• Voluntary wage and price controls	• Personal income taxes indexed	• Consumer credit restricted

[3] OECD, *Economic Outlook*, No. 26, December 1979.

Inflation Record 1970–79 (% Change Consumer Price Index)

Year	France	Netherlands	West Germany
1979	11.0	3.9	5.3
1978	9.1	4.1	2.6
1977	9.4	6.4	3.9
1976	9.6	8.8	4.5
1975	11.8	10.2	6.0
1974	13.7	9.6	7.0
1973	7.3	8.0	6.9
1972	6.0	7.8	5.5
1971	5.5	7.5	5.3
1970	4.8	3.6	3.4

Special Characteristics of Current Economy

France	Netherlands	West Germany
• Strong wage pressures caused by leftist unions, class antagonisms, and geographic dislocations of labor force • Emphasis placed on minimizing unemployment	• Heavy reliance on foreign trade (50–60% GNP) • High tax rates in comparison with other European countries • Active workers' councils	• Growing economy with relatively new plant • Higher worker productivity • Diversified export markets • Workers' councils participate in management • Substantial public anti-inflation sentiment

Actions Taken to Combat Inflation

France	Netherlands	West Germany
• Use of revalued asset base to increase borrowing power (Barre Plan)	• Monetary policy focused on providing liquidity from balance of payment surplus • Wage and price controls established • Currency (Guilder) revalued	• Tight money supply by Bundesbank • Currency (Deutschemark) revalued

EXHIBIT 2–1 (continued)
Highlights of Extent of Inflation in Selected Industrial Countries

Inflation Record 1970–79 (% Change Consumer Price Index)

Brazil		Japan				Australia			
1979	77.2	1979	3.1	1974	24.5	1979	9.2	1974	15.1
1978	40.8	1978	3.8	1973	11.7	1978	7.9	1973	9.5
1977	44.0	1977	8.1	1972	4.5	1977	12.3	1972	5.8
1976	41.7	1976	9.3	1971	6.1	1976	13.5	1971	6.1
1975	29.0	1975	11.8	1970	7.7	1975	15.1	1970	3.9

Special Characteristics of Current Economy

Brazil
- Relatively undeveloped growth economy
- Rapid population growth
- Relatively low per capita income
- Stable political environment since 1964
- Strong central control by government

Japan
- Heavy reliance on foreign trade
- Highly leveraged corporate financial structures
- Strong monetary control by central bank
- High productivity of work force
- Tradition of lifetime employment

Australia
- Population growth through immigration
- Heavy reliance on commodity trade
- Economy with large underdeveloped natural resources
- High imported inflation

Actions Taken to Combat Inflation

Brazil
- Financial transactions indexed (monetary correction)
- Tight control over, and extensive taxation of, imports
- Exchange rates stringently managed
- Wages and prices indexed to reflect cost of living adjustment and productivity gains. (Oil not included in index)

Japan
- Money supply adjusted to balance of payments
- Government support provided industry to stimulate exports

Australia
- Extensive system of wage controls
- Income taxes indexed
- Monetary and fiscal constraints applied

cific prices bend the meaning of historical measurements of economic and business performance. Revenues, costs, earnings, assets and liabilities for 1981 are not comparable with corresponding figures recorded ten years, five years, or even one year ago.

Distortions caused by inflation have created several thorny accounting issues. The adequacy and accuracy of conventional accounting methods are being seriously challenged. A worldwide debate is under way which focuses on questions of measurement standards and valuation. The debate examines the function of accounting, probing the question of whether accounting is purely a record-keeping operation or whether it should address subjective issues of economic valuation.

The measurement problem can be viewed from at least three alternative perspectives that lead to distinctly different conceptual accounting solutions.

A first perspective holds that accounting should provide consistent measurements in terms of general purchasing power. The mission of accounting information is to measure what the dollar will buy. When general price levels are rising, larger amounts of money are required to maintain a fixed amount of purchasing power. Thus a consistent yardstick is required to measure the economy and business. A perceived need for consistent measurements has led to the development of the price level and constant dollar concepts that are discussed in Chapter 3.

A second perspective suggests that accounting should reflect the current value of assets and liabilities of the enterprise and the resultant changes in value caused by changes in specific prices. Accounting's role is to state the value of an enterprise in terms of current dollars irrespective of changes in the purchasing power of the dollar. A perceived need for such reflections of value led to the replacement cost, current value and current cost concepts which are also discussed in Chapter 3.

A third perspective, articulated by Richard F. Vancil[4] and others, suggests that accounting should not only provide a consistent unit of measure, but that it should also reflect changes in specific prices. There is a need to provide data for both the general purchasing power and the physical capacity of the firm. A perceived need for both kinds of information leads to the restatement of current values into units of constant purchasing power.

Factors Influencing Accounting Measurements

The five business and financial characteristics listed below will influ-

[4]Richard F. Vancil, "Inflation Accounting—The Great Controversy," *Harvard Business Review,* March/April 1976, pp. 58–67.

ence the degree of distortion caused by inflation in addition to the accounting methodology that is employed.

1. Type of business
2. Inventory valuation method and turnover rate
3. Maturity of business and age of assets
4. Types of expenditure, costs involved and the inflation rate applicable to each type
5. Capital structure of business

These factors are discussed in the sections that follow.

Type of Business

The type of business determines the proportion of assets to revenues employed in cash, receivables, inventories, and fixed assets (with various lives). For example, some capital-intensive businesses, such as utilities, steel, chemical and paper companies, require substantial investments in fixed assets in relation to revenues whereas consumer product manufacturers and financial service companies have more modest fixed-asset requirements.

The effect of inflation on financial institutions is different from the effect on manufacturing enterprises. Property, plant and equipment constitute a relatively small proportion of the total assets of financial institutions; the financing of large capital expenditures for new equipment is not one of their major concerns. For example, Manufacturers Hanover Corporation's 1979 annual report states,

'The impact of inflation on financial institutions differs significantly from that exerted on industrial concerns. Since financial institutions are not heavily involved in making large capital expenditures or in the acquisition, processing or sale of consumable products, the direct results of more costly goods and services are limited. However, the indirect effects are considerable. Since consumers and producers require additional funds to maintain a fixed level of assets, inventory or consumption, inflation has the effect of increasing the level of loan demand on financial institutions. . . . The increased demand for money can be met by obtaining more and more funds in the form of deposits . . . or by raising additional funds in the capital market." [5]

Inventory Valuation and Turnover Rates

Inventory valuation methods and turnover rates can have an important impact on how inflation affects reported profits. The use of LIFO tends to decrease the impact of inflation on the income statement but increases the

---

[5] Financial Accounting Standards Board, *Examples of the Use of FASB Statement No. 33, Financial Reporting and Changing Prices*, November 1980, p. 5.

impact on the balance sheet. The FIFO valuation method has the opposite effect.

Exhibit 2–2 shows the effect of inventory profits caused by inflation on a manufacturing company with varying turnover and inflation assumptions. This table shows that FIFO inventory profits represent a substantial percentage (over 2%) of cost when the inflation rate is at or over 6% if inventory turnover drops below three turns per year.

EXHIBIT 2–2

FIFO Inventory Profit as a Percent of Cost of Sales[6]

Inventory Turnover Rate	Annual Inflation Rate Assumed				
	0%	6%	12%	18%	24%
1.0	0	6.2	12.7	19.8	27.2
1.5	0	4.1	8.3	12.6	17.0
2.0	0	3.0	6.0	9.0	12.0
2.5	0	2.4	4.7	7.1	9.4
3.0	0	1.9	4.0	5.8	7.6
3.5	0	1.7	3.3	4.9	6.5
4.0	0	1.5	2.9	4.3	5.7

Business Maturity

Business maturity is likely to have an important bearing on the age of the assets employed and the need for funds reinvestment. The earnings of new businesses and growth businesses in their early years are often only moderately affected by inflation because of the relatively recent vintage of much of their plant and equipment.

Inflation can distort the reported results of mature businesses in different ways depending on whether the fixed assets involved are going to be replaced. Some mature businesses, such as steel companies and utilities, have major requirements to reinvest their cash flows in their existing business in order to remain competitive or serve customer needs. Many of these companies have a large stock of old fixed assets, and the distortions to earnings caused by inflation can be quite significant. Other mature businesses, such as a coal mine, for example, may go out of business after their resources are depleted. Price level adjusted or current cost depreciation does not mean much in such cases.

---

[6] Reproduced, with permission, from *Inflation: Its Impact on Financial Reporting and Decision Making,* Financial Executives Research Foundation, 1978, p. 50.

Composition of Expenditures

It is axiomatic that inflation does not affect all types of expenditures in the same way. The construction cost index, for example, has increased by 119% from 79.1 to 173.0 between 1970 and 1979. During the same period the consumer price index (CPI-U) increased by 87% from 116.2 to 217.4. Similarly, the energy costs of many companies have increased at a rate that far outstrips the growth in CPI. Unit computational costs, on the other hand, have decreased because of technological advances by computer and electronic companies. Thus, the extent of distortions depends on how much of each type of cost (labor, materials, energy, services, etc.) each business consumes and the inflation rate that applies to each type.

Capital Structure

The capital structure of the business is significant because firms are hurt by inflation if their monetary assets[7] exceed liabilities. Theoretically, firms benefit from inflation if monetary liabilities exceed monetary assets.

While highly leveraged firms (with substantial debt) tend to benefit from inflation on an arithmetic basis, this benefit may be short-lived if the debt becomes due and must be refinanced at interest costs that exceed the earning power of the enterprise's assets. Liquidity can quickly become impaired, and the house of cards can tumble down. Penn Central has been referred to by critics of the monetary adjustment concept as an extreme example of a company that reported big losses and became illiquid while showing monetary gains. Chrysler Corporation's monetary gains may also prove to be a case in point although at this writing the outcome of Chrysler's travails remains to be seen.

Strategic Implications of Inflation

In addition to distorting accounting measurements, inflation has two adverse strategic implications that can have a serious effect on many businesses. The first, and possibly most important, strategic implication is that inflation tends to impair the rate of capital formation. The second implication is that inflation tends to increase uncertainty. These two implications are discussed below.

Capital Formation Impairment

Capital is, of course, the wherewithal that is used to purchase the ma-

---

[7] "A monetary asset is money or a claim to receive a sum of money the amount of which is fixed or determinable without reference to future price goods or services." FAS No. 33, p. 16.

chinery and equipment needed to increase productivity and replace and expand productive capacity. The formation of capital depends on the savings of individuals and the retention of earnings by corporations. Inflation has raised the cost of improving productivity, replacing old capacity and adding new capacity, which means that capital requirements have increased. It has also dampened the rate of capital formation because corporate and personal income taxes are based on stated nominal profits rather than inflation-adjusted profits. Increasing cost, coupled with what amounts to taxation on capital, has impaired the corporate sector's ability to finance itself internally.

This deterioration in the rate of capital formation raises the philosophical issue as to whether or not each company should provide for the replacement of its own capital stock. We note that many chief executive officers and chief financial officers state that they must eventually replace their plant and equipment. Nevertheless, the life cycle theory suggests that many assets are not replaced, and that some companies should pay dividends out of their capital stock, become "cash cows," and allow the shareholder to reinvest his or her funds as he or she sees fit.

In a letter to *Business Week*, W. W. Brown, assistant comptroller of AT&T, said, "The data required by the Financial Accounting Standards Board's Statement 33 is not an accurate representation of inflation's effects. It is based on a faulty premise—that the funds recovered through 'depreciation expense' will provide for the replacement of assets being depreciated. Only to a limited extent will such funds ever be used for this purpose. . . ." [8]

Irrespective of which point of view prevails, corporations or individuals must form capital if existing assets are to be replaced and productivity is to be improved. If inflation squeezes the individual's ability to save and at the same time cuts the corporate sector's ability to form capital, eventually capital will not be available to invest in the productivity improvements and capacity expansion that neo-Keynesians say are needed to curb inflation.

Increased Uncertainty

When we conducted our research for the Financial Executives Research Foundation in 1977, we asked 35 preparers and 23 users of financial statements what their expectations were as to the U.S. inflation rates in the next five years (1978–1983). Ninety-five percent of the participants in that study said that they expected inflation to fluctuate in the 4%–8% range. *None* thought that inflation was going to dip below 4%, and none was looking to a return to double digit rates. [9] The participants in the earlier study were so-

---

[8] *Business Week*, July 7, 1980, pp. 4–5.

[9] *Inflation: Its Impact on Financial Reporting and Decision Making*, Financial Executives Research Foundation, 1978, p. 14.

phisticated, experienced financial and accounting executives and investors from leading institutions.

How wrong the expectations were proven to be! No one anticipated the actions of the OPEC nations. U.S. inflation climbed to 7.7% in 1978, 12.1% in 1979, and, at this writing, 1980, is running at a 13% rate.

The point that we make here is not that the individuals involved were not astute. On the contrary, they represented the best in their trade. What we are saying is that predicting international and economic events is inherently uncertain and that inflation magnifies the uncertainty. Business risk is increased, which translates to a higher cost of capital.

The current research project also includes a question about inflation expectations (to be discussed more fully later) from 282 financial executives for the years 1980, 1981, and 1985. Again, it remains to be seen how accurate these forecasts will be.

It should be emphasized that much of the underlying problem is not the rate of inflation itself but, rather, the *unpredictability* of the inflation rate. If financial and accounting executives were reasonably certain that inflation would continue at a 15%–20% rate they would tend to adjust their financial strategies and management accounting systems. However, uncertainties about inflation, coupled with the hope that it will decrease in time, may aggravate swings in the financial markets and slow the adaptation of planning and control systems to cope with the probability of ongoing inflation.

Chapter 3

Accounting Alternatives for Coping with Inflation

"Shall I count them pure with the wicked balances, and with the bag of deceitful weights?" Bible: Micah 6:11.

As indicated in Chapter 2, conceptually different alternatives have emerged as solutions to the problems of reflecting changes in general purchasing power and accounting for changes in specific prices. They are "constant dollar" and "current cost" accounting. Both concepts are embodied in Financial Accounting Standards Statement No. 33, "Financial Reporting and Changing Prices," which was issued by the Financial Accounting Standards Board in September 1979. Varying applications of these concepts, or combinations thereof, have been advocated for many years.

Constant dollar accounting is the concept of restating all dollars to units of constant general purchasing power. Elements of the income statement and balance sheet are adjusted by an inflation index so that the dollars shown in preceding years will be roughly comparable to current year dollars.

Current cost accounting, on the other hand, updates balance sheet items to their current replacement value and adjusts the income statement to reflect these changes in input values caused by inflation. Thus, constant dollar accounting is oriented towards what a historical dollar will *buy,* while current cost accounting is oriented toward determining the input or output values of assets and liabilities in terms of nominal dollars.

Constant dollar and current cost accounting are referred to by different names and are applied in different ways in the accounting literature. Despite differences in terminology and application, however, specific approaches can be classified as either constant dollar or current cost.

Constant dollar accounting includes:
• Price level adjusted accounting
• General purchasing power accounting
• Stabilized accounting

Current cost accounting includes:
- Current value accounting
- Value accounting
- Replacement cost accounting

The combination of constant dollar and current cost accounting is referred to as price level adjusted current cost reporting (PLACC) or price level adjusted replacement cost reporting (PLARC).

Two general approaches have been developed for determining current cost within the framework of the current cost accounting concept: entry prices (input values) and exit prices (output values). Entry prices are the current cost to repurchase or reproduce the asset or its productive capacity. Exit prices are the net realizable values or the economic values, such as the present value of future cash flows, that can be obtained from disposing of the asset. [1]

Definitions of Terms

The terms "nominal dollars," "constant dollars" and "inflation-adjusted dollars" are used in this study.

Nominal dollars are the units of measurement that were actually recorded or the units that are expected to be recorded in the future. Nominal dollars may, of course, be derived from the application of either historical or current cost accounting concepts.

Constant dollars are dollars of uniform purchasing power and are computed for every period except the base period.

Inflation-adjusted dollars is a broader term that has different meanings depending on the context in which it is used. It may mean that nominal dollars have been converted to constant dollars, as in the case of FAS No. 33, or that constant dollars have been converted to nominal dollars, as in the case of certain forecasts. It may also mean that forecasts in nominal dollars have been adjusted to reflect changes in specific price levels. Thus, we have attempted to use the more specific terms, "nominal dollars" or "constant dollars" wherever they are appropriate.

Origins of Concepts

Constant dollar accounting is not a new subject by any means. In 1918 Livingston Middleditch, Jr. noted the fluctuating value of the dollar and pointed out that conventional accounting, with historical costs as its basis, has the effect of mixing dollars of different value. He said that "to mix these

---

[1] Elwood L. Miller, *Inflation Accounting*, Van Nostrand Reinhold Company, 1980, p. 125.

units is like mixing inches and centimeters or measuring a field with a rubber tape line."[2]

In the early 1930's, Henry W. Sweeney, a New York accountant, contended in his doctoral thesis that such inconsistency makes historical cost accounting inaccurate: "It is obvious, therefore, that if quantities . . . are to be correctly combined or compared, the unit of measurement must be homogeneous."[3]

Current cost accounting also had an early start. In 1918 accounting giant Professor William Paton said that the principal function of accounting is to aid management decision making and that management's needs are best served by furnishing replacement cost data.

"It is not the cost of the building or power unit or machine which is significant to the manager interested in a wise utilization of available resources. It is rather the *cost of replacement* which must form the basis of his reckoning."[4]

Sweeney attempted to link constant dollar and current cost accounting concepts, while retaining historical cost conventions. He advocated the use of replacement costs in the balance sheet, but wanted to retain the concept of net income realization. Sweeney recommended that the unrealized segment of net income be used as a connecting link between the balance sheet and the income statement. He believed that the use of replacement costs on the balance sheet furnished values that many users had begun to expect from financial statements.

The year 1961 marked the appearance of *The Theory & Measurement of Business Income* by Edwards and Bell.[5] Monroe Ingberman observes that Edwards and Bell developed theoretic support and systematic procedures for replacement cost accounting. Their book has been regarded as the inspiration for much that has been written on the subject since then and is the culmination of developments initiated by Paton in 1918.

Where LIFO Fits In

LIFO inventory valuation techniques are used as a partial substitute for current costing. LIFO is not current cost, nor does it adjust the financial

[2]Livingston Middleditch, Jr., "Should Accounts Reflect the Changing Value of the Dollar?" *The Journal of Accountancy*, February 1918, pp. 114–115.

[3]Henry W. Sweeney, *Stabilized Accounting*, Harper & Brothers, 1936. Revised by Holt, Rinehart & Winston, Inc., 1964, p. 11.

[4]Monroe Ingberman, "The Evolution of Replacement Cost Accounting," *Journal of Accounting, Auditing and Finance*, Winter, 1980, pp. 101–112.

[5]Edgar O. Edwards and Philip W. Bell, *The Theory and Measurement of Business Income*, University of California Press, Berkeley, 1961.

statements to current cost; LIFO attacks (with varying success) a single part of the current cost problem. Nevertheless, as FAS No. 33 states, cost of goods sold measured on a LIFO basis may provide an acceptable approximation of cost of goods sold measured at current cost, provided that the effect of any decrease in inventory layers is excluded.[6]

The LIFO method was conceived in the late 1930's to minimize taxation in an inflationary environment. The Internal Revenue Code pertaining to LIFO requires that LIFO be used for financial reporting in order to be acceptable for tax accounting purposes. While the related conceptual underpinnings of LIFO have been the subject of controversy, LIFO is being more and more widely used as a principal method of inventory valuation for historical purposes as well as a surrogate for current cost information for compliance with FAS No. 33.

LIFO became widely accepted after the dollar-value method was allowed to any taxpayer for valuing inventory for income tax purposes. The method was conceived in 1941 in order to accomplish the objective of charging against current operations the increased costs of carrying required continuous inventory investments. It provides for dealing with inventory as a composite in terms of dollars and computing an index of price change contained in the ending inventory compared to the beginning-of-year costs. Treasury Decision No. 5756 was issued in November 1949, permitting the use of the dollar-value LIFO method by any taxpayer.[7]

Experimentation, Consideration and Debate

Since inflation spurted ahead following World War II several companies and accounting organizations have explored aspects of providing meaningful financial measurements in an inflationary environment.

The United States Steel Corporation pioneered reporting depreciation on an accelerated basis in order to offset the effect of the steady rise in the general price level on the company's capital replacement program. Accelerated depreciation was controversial when it began in 1947, and it was not until 1954 that it was allowed for Federal income tax purposes.

United States Steel also called for depreciation based on replacement costs following World War II. However, such reporting was not allowed at the time by the SEC.

The subject of changes in general prices was extensively studied by the Accounting Principles Board (APB) and its predecessor, the Committee on

---

[6]FAS No. 33, p. 20.

[7]Herbert T. McAnly, "How LIFO Began," *Management Accounting,* May 1975, pp. 1–3.

Accounting Procedure. In 1947, 1948, and 1953, the Committee, and in 1965, the APB, considered accounting problems related to sharp increases in the general level of prices. [8] "Several of these pronouncements were particularly concerned with the amount of depreciation to be charged against current income for facilities acquired in the past at lower prices. The Committee concluded that depreciation charges should be based on historical cost, but gave full support to the use of supplementary financial schedules, explanations, or footnotes by which company management might explain the need for retention of earnings because of the effects of inflation." [9]

The APB issued Statement No. 3, *Financial Statements Restated for General Price Level Changes,* in June 1969. Statement No. 3 recommended that historical dollar financial statements be supplemented by general price level information, but very few companies followed the recommendation. [10]

The FASB supported the price level approach to inflation accounting in 1974 when it issued its exposure draft, *Financial Reporting in Units of General Purchasing Power.* This exposure draft embodied concepts similar to those in APB Statement No. 3. Both, in effect, required a comprehensive restatement of historical cost financial statements to a historical cost/constant dollar basis. (The terms "general price level changes" and "general purchasing power" have similar meanings and have been used more or less interchangeably in accounting literature.) The 1974 exposure draft, and the field test that followed, met with a ho-hum response from many users and preparers of financial statements. U.S. inflation subsided to single-digit rates in 1975, and many accounting executives and practitioners may have expected that the problem of inflation would go away.

In March 1976, the Securities & Exchange Commission, under the prodding of then Chief Accountant John Burton, called for the current value (cost) approach to inflation accounting with Accounting Series Release No. 190. This document required certain publicly-held companies to disclose replacement cost information about inventories, cost of sales, productive capacity, and depreciation. According to Burton, in an interview with the author, "It was a beginning . . . there is a time when you have to do something. . . ." However, the consensus of the preparers and users of financial statements we interviewed during the previous research for the Financial Executives Research Foundation was that the information required by ASR No. 190 was either misleading or useless. [11] The SEC, nevertheless, did not

---

[8] In APB Opinion No. 6, *Status of Accounting Research Bulletins.*

[9] FAS No. 33, p. 35, par. 71.

[10] FAS No. 33, p. 36, par. 72.

[11] *Inflation: Its Impact on Financial Reporting and Decision Making,* Financial Executives Research Foundation, 1978, pp. 46–47 and Appendix C.

rescind ASR No. 190, but rather encouraged the FASB to produce a more palatable alternative.

The FASB deferred action on its exposure draft on general purchasing power in 1976 and undertook a major project for developing a conceptual framework for accounting and reporting. Public hearings were conducted in early 1977, and several points of view were expressed with respect to inflation accounting in the context of a conceptual framework. These points of view can be roughly categorized as follows:

Alternative approaches:

1. Retain historical cost concept—*do nothing* else
2. Retain historical cost concept—*supplement* reports with inflation-adjusted data on an *optional* basis
3. Retain historical cost concept—*supplement* reports with inflation-adjusted data on a prescribed basis
4. *Substitute* inflation-adjusted information for the historical cost information

At the public hearings there was not much support for the fourth approach, and most of the discussion centered around the first three alternatives.

Several alternative methodologies for showing inflation-adjusted information were presented to the FASB. However, as previously discussed, these methodologies can be roughly classified into two categories although several variations on the theme exist in each: the constant dollar (price level) approach and the current cost approach.

Both methodologies had their advocates. The constant dollar approach was favored by some preparers of financial statements because of its relative simplicity and objectivity. However, the current cost approach was favored by the SEC, many educators, and financial analysts because of its specificity.

The FASB issued an exposure draft, *Financial Reporting and Changing Prices,* in December 1978. This draft called for supplemental inflation accounting information and allowed for flexibility in the choice of methodologies applied. However, it is reported that the SEC's price for withdrawing ASR No. 190 was the mandatory inclusion of supplemental current cost information in the annual reports of large publicly-held companies. Hence FAS No. 33, as issued, requires the disclosure of both supplemental constant dollar information in 1979 annual reports and current cost information beginning in 1980.

As a result, *both* methodologies have received official recognition within the accounting profession for external reporting purposes. Because external reporting is a product of internal accounting systems and external reporting concepts are used for many internal reports, both methods might reasonably be considered for measuring the impact of inflation on internal planning and control.

Practices in Other Countries

Other countries have also addressed concepts of inflation accounting and financial reporting methodologies. Because of the breadth of influence of its business and accounting practices and the authoritative position taken by the FASB, the U.S. is probably considered to be the leader at this time. Nevertheless, Great Britain, Canada, Brazil, and other countries have taken different approaches to this problem, and many positions are still necessarily of an experimental nature.

Great Britain

Great Britain has embraced the current cost approach and has introduced the concepts of "gearing" holding gains based on the relationship of monetary assets to monetary liabilities. Use of current cost statements is required for all listed companies for periods beginning January 1, 1980, under SSAP No. 16, issued by the United Kingdom Accounting Standards Committee. Under this Standard, three adjustments must be made to income statements computed on a historical basis:

1. *Depreciation:* An adjustment should be made for the difference between depreciation based on the current cost of fixed assets (based on published indices) and depreciation charged in computing the historical cost result.
2. *Inventory Costs:* An adjustment should be made for the difference between the cost of inventories at the date of sale (computed by a variety of methods) and the amount charged on a historical cost basis.
3. *Gearing for monetary items:* Different treatment is called for in each of two situations: If total liabilities (including preference share capital) exceed total monetary assets (so that part of operating capital is effectively financed by net monetary liabilities), an adjustment should be made to reflect the extent to which depreciation and inventory cost adjustments do not need to be provided from current revenues; and if total monetary assets exceed total liabilities, an adjustment should be made to reflect the increase in net monetary assets needed to maintain its scale of operations. [12]

---

[12] Accounting Standards Committee, "Inflation Accounting—An Interim Recommendation," November 4, 1977.

The Standard may be complied with by presenting current cost statements with supplemental historical cost statements, only current cost statements with adequate historical cost disclosure, or historical cost statements with supplemental current cost statements prominently displayed. A current cost balance sheet is also required, including all assets and liabilities on a current cost basis to the degree practical.

The application of these current cost adjustments to the income statement reported by the John Brown Company in its annual report for 1980 is shown in Exhibit 3–1.

Canada

Canada is also embracing the current cost approach. "An exposure draft issued by the Canadian Institute of Chartered Accountants would require companies to report the effects of changing prices as supplementary information on the basis of current cost. The proposal would require a 'net productive monetary items' adjustment to historical cost income to provide for the effect of specific price changes during the period, and the amount of the tax provision in the current cost income statement must be the same amount in the historical cost income statement."[13]

Brazil

Accounting in Brazil, with inflation running at an annual rate of near 100%, is based on a combination of historical and current cost accounting concepts. Brazilian corporation law of December 1976 maintains the concept of the lower of cost (FIFO or average cost basis) or market in valuing inventories, but provides for the monetary correction of certain business transactions and plant and equipment. The terms of purchase agreements, contracts, leases and loan agreements are periodically adjusted to reflect inflation through the application of an "ORTN" index and other specific indices published by the government. The ORTN (National Treasury Adjustable Bond) is based on the bond redemption rate and is used as a monetary unit to express the updated value of Brazil's currency.

At the end of each year, plant, equipment, all permanent assets (excluding land) and net equity accounts are revalued based on indices. Depreciation (monetary adjustment) is then recalculated for income tax and book purposes based on this determination of current replacement cost of plant and equipment. The inflation components of the increase in gross plant, equipment and other items are offset by reserves in the capitalization section of the balance sheet. Liabilities are also adjusted to reflect changes

---

[13]Robert F. Randall, "Data Sheet," *Management Accounting*, May 1980, p. 5.

EXHIBIT 3–1

Consolidated Current Cost Statement
for the year ended 31st March 1980

	Notes	1980		1979	
		£000	£000	£000	£000
Profit before taxation			21,132		28,370
Current cost adjustments					
Depreciation	2	3,515		3,101	
Cost of sales	3	5,426		3,845	
		8,941		6,946	
Gearing	4	3,652	5,289	1,347	5,599
Current cost profit before taxation			15,843		22,771
Taxation and minorities	5		7,680		8,652
Current cost profit after taxation			8,163		14,119
Extraordinary item	5		31		960
			8,132		13,159
Dividends			4,174		3,527
Current cost profit retained			3,958		9,632

Notes

1. Basis. — The statement has been prepared in accordance with the interim recommendations of the Accounting Standards Committee (Hyde guidelines).

2. Depreciation. — The depreciation adjustment represents the additional charge which would be required if the fixed assets of the group were revalued on a current cost basis.

3. Cost of sales. — The cost of sales adjustment, computed mainly on the averaging method, reflects the difference between the actual cost of products sold and their replacement cost. No adjustments have been made by the contracting companies.

4. Gearing. — The gearing adjustment, computed on a group basis, reflects the extent to which the depreciation and cost of sales adjustments have been financed other than by ordinary stockholders' funds.

5. Taxation and extraordinary items. — No adjustments have been made to taxation and extraordinary items set out in the historical cost accounts.

6. Indices. — The calculations have been made, in the main, by using the indices issued by the Central Statistical Office, and in other cases by those internally constructed.

in price level. Principal and interest on Brazilian National Development Bank (BNDE) loans, for example, are always calculated on constant ORTN's and are converted to cruzeiros at the date due for accounting and payment purposes. The intended effect of these adjustments is to provide for the maintenance of capital and to tax each enterprise on operating rather than inflated profits. [14]

Argentina

In Argentina, where the inflation rate outstrips that in Brazil, historical accounting records are used for legal purposes. The government has sporadically allowed write-ups of fixed assets. However, current costs are used for internal purposes. "Each month, we adjust the historical figures to produce inflation accounts—a balance sheet and income statement to guide management. We revalue the assets with indices of replacement costs. These yield current depreciation charges. The cost of goods sold is computed from the last available invoice price." [15]

The Netherlands

Inflation accounting in the Netherlands has been strongly influenced by the practices of N.V. Philips Gloeilampenfabrieken, who participated in this research as a case study. Philips' system was initiated for internal use in the late 1930's, but has also been used for external reporting since 1951. Their approach is based on the replacement value theory of Professor T. Limperg. [16]

The theory states that a business firm needs to maintain its capital (in terms of its physical assets) in order to assure its continuity, and no business income would result from operations unless current revenues are charged with the "sacrifice value" of physical assets used or sold. Sacrifice value is said to be best measured by current replacement cost. Specific price indices are constructed to measure the price changes of inventories and fixed assets.

Two accounting adjustments are required:

1. Inventories are adjusted from a historical cost to a replacement (current)

---

[14] *Inflation: Its Impact on Financial Reporting and Decision Making*, Financial Executives Research Foundation, p. 35.

[15] W.T. Baxter, "Coping with High Inflation in Argentina," *The Accountant*, November 4, 1976, pp. 526–527.

[16] A. Mey, "Theodore Limperg and His Theory of Values and Costs," *Abacus*, September 1966, pp. 3–23.

cost basis through the use of an index on inventory price changes. At the time of sale, cost of sales is computed on a replacement cost basis. The excess of replacement cost over historical cost is charged to cost of sales and ending inventory accounts and is credited to a "revaluation capital" account. The ending inventory is thus stated on a year-end replacement cost basis in the balance sheet.

2. Plant and equipment are adjusted from a historical cost to a replacement cost basis through the use of an index on fixed asset price changes. Accumulated depreciation is adjusted to maintain the same proportion to related plant and equipment. The excess of replacement cost over historical cost is charged to plant and equipment and credited to accumulated depreciation and revaluation capital accounts. Depreciation expense for the year is computed on the new replacement cost basis. [17]

The diversity of international practices illustrates varying techniques for reflecting the impact of inflation that might be applied in management accounting issues involved in the internal planning process.

---

[17] John C.H. Woo, "Accounting for Inflation: Some International Models," *Management Accounting*, February 1978, pp. 39–40.

Chapter 4

Requirements of FASB Statement No. 33

In September 1979, the Financial Accounting Standards Board issued its long awaited and hotly debated Statement No. 33, *Financial Reporting and Changing Prices.* Statement No. 33 is the latest step taken in the United States to reflect the impact of inflation in external financial reports.

> In the Statement Summary the Board said it "believes that this Statement meets an urgent need for information about the effects of changing prices. If that information is not provided: resources may be allocated inefficiently; investors' and creditors' understanding of the past performance of an enterprise and their ability to assess future cash flows may be severely limited; and people in government who participate in decisions on economic policy may lack important information about the implications of their decisions. The requirements of the Statement are expected to promote a better understanding by the general public of the problems caused by inflation. Statements by business managers about those problems are unlikely to have sufficient credibility until financial reports provide quantitative information about the effects of inflation." [1]

Statement No. 33 is directed towards external reporting requirements while this book deals with internal planning and control. Furthermore, Statement No. 33 is of an experimental nature and is still the subject of controversy. Despite these limitations, the Statement embodies much of the alternative inflation accounting methodology that has been seriously considered and officially recognized, and provides a basis for a potential linkage between external and internal reporting. Thus, it seems appropriate to review the objectives of the Statement, its key requirements, and its methodology. Chapter 5 contains an analysis of the results of the application of FAS No. 33 by companies that constitute the Dow Jones Industrial Average.

Information Requirements

Approximately 1,300 publicly-held companies are required to report

---

[1]Statement of Financial Accounting Standards No. 33, *Financial Reporting and Changing Prices,* Financial Accounting Standards Board, September 1979, p. ii.

constant dollar and current cost information in accordance with FAS No. 33. These companies have either inventories and property, plant and equipment before deducting accumulated depreciation, depletion and amortization amounting in aggregate to more than $125 million or total assts amounting to more than $1 billion after deducting accumulated depreciation. [2]

Two financial reports are required:

1. A comparison of information for the current year as reported in the traditional statements, adjusted for general inflation (constant dollars), and adjusted for changes in specific prices (current costs).
2. A five-year summary of historical cost and current cost information in constant dollars.

This information is published as supplementary data in the annual report together with appropriate notes and explanations. Illustrations of these two reports (Exhibit 4–1) follow. They are reproduced with permission from General Electric Company's 1979 annual report.

EXHIBIT 4–1

Supplementary Information—Effect of Changing Prices

(In millions, except per-share amounts)

For the year ended December 31, 1979	As reported in the traditional statements	Adjusted for general inflation	Adjusted for changes in specific prices (current cost)
Sales of products and services to customers	$22,461	$22,461	$22,461
Cost of goods sold	15,991	16,093	16,074
Selling, general and administrative expense	3,716	3,716	3,716
Depreciation, depletion and amortization	624	880	980
Interest and other financial charges	258	258	258
Other income	(519)	(519)	(519)
Earnings before income taxes and minority interests	2,391	2,033	1,952
Provision for income taxes	953	953	953
Minority interest in earnings of consolidated affiliates	29	16	13
Net earnings applicable to common stock	$ 1,409	$ 1,064	$ 986
Earnings per common share	$ 6.20	$ 4.68	$ 4.34
Share owners' equity at year-end (net assets)	$ 7,362	$10,436	$11,153

[2] FAS No. 33, p. 10, par. 23.

EXHIBIT 4–1 (continued)

Supplementary Information—Effect of Changing Prices

(In millions, except per-share amounts)

Current cost information in dollars of 1979 purchasing power
(All amounts expressed in average 1979 dollars)

	1979	1978	1977	1976	1975
Sales of products and services to customers	$22,461	$21,867	$20,984	$20,015	$19,022
Cost of goods sold	16,074	15,548	14,793	14,145	13,914
Selling, general and administrative expense	3,716	3,566	3,606	3,360	3,018
Depreciation, depletion and amortization	980	1,000	986	979	1,006
Interest and other financial charges	258	249	238	222	251
Other income	(519)	(466)	(467)	(350)	(235)
Earnings before income taxes and minority interests	1,952	1,970	1,828	1,659	1,068
Provision for income taxes	953	995	926	853	620
Minority interest in earnings and consolidated affiliates	13	13	20	26	26
Net earnings applicable to common stock	$ 986	$ 962	$ 882	$ 780	$ 422
Earnings per common share	$ 4.34	$ 4.22	$ 3.88	$ 3.45	$ 1.88
Share owners' equity at year-end (net assets)	$11,153	$11,020	$10,656	$10,526	$10,056
Other inflation information					
Average Consumer Price Index (1967 = 100)	217.4	195.4	181.5	170.5	161.2
(Loss)/gain in general purchasing power of net monetary items	$ (209)	$ (128)	$ (61)	$ (20)	$ 19
Dividends declared per common share	2.75	2.78	2.52	2.17	2.16
Market price per common share at year-end	47⅞	50½	58¼	69⅜	60¼

GE's annual report also includes a discussion of the impact of inflation on the individual and company. Capital formation, taxation and productivity improvement are covered. In addition, the report contains an explanation of the inflation accounting methodology that has been applied in accordance with FAS No. 33.

Objectives of Statement

FAS No. 33 was promulgated to help users of financial reports understand the effects of changing prices on a business enterprise to help their decisions on investment, lending and other matters. In the section on objectives, FAS No. 33 says that the Statement is intended to assist users in the following specific ways:

"a. *Assessment of future cash flows.* Present financial statements include measurements of expenses and assets at historical prices. When prices are changing, measurements that reflect current prices are likely to provide useful information for the assessment of future cash flows.

b. *Assessment of enterprise performance.* The worth of an enterprise can be increased as a result of prudent timing of asset purchases when prices are changing. That increase is one aspect of performance even though it may be distinguished from operating performance. Measurements that reflect current prices can provide a basis for assessing the extent to which past decisions on the acquisition of assets have created opportunities for earning future cash flows.

c. *Assessment of the erosion of operating capability.* An enterprise typically must hold minimum quantities of inventory, property, plant and equipment and other assets to maintain its ability to provide goods and services. When the prices of those assets are increasing, larger amounts of money investment are needed to maintain the previous level of output. Information on the current prices of resources that are used to generate revenues can help users to assess the extent to which and the manner in which operating capability can be maintained.

d. *Assessment of the erosion of general purchasing power.* When general price levels are increasing, larger amounts of money are required to maintain a fixed amount of purchasing power. Investors typically are concerned with assessing whether an enterprise has maintained the purchasing power of its capital. Financial information that reflects changes in general purchasing power can help with that assessment. The needs described in the preceding paragraphs are important to investors, creditors, and also to the users. If information about the effects of changing prices is not available, the cost of capital may be excessive for enterprises that can use capital most effectively. Resources may be allocated inefficiently and all members of society may suffer. Furthermore, people in government who participate in decisions on economic policy may not obtain the most relevant information on which to base their decisions." [3]

---

[3] FAS No. 33, pp. 1 and 2.

40

While the needs alluded to in the text of FAS No. 33 apply only to *external* financial reports, General Electric has used this vehicle to refer to management accounting needs. In the section of its 1979 report to stockholders, required by FAS No. 33, the company includes in its discussion on the impact of inflation:

"An area receiving special attention by management is experimentation with the use of inflation-adjusted measurements at the individual business level for capital budgeting. Since 1973, your company (GE) has been experimenting with various techniques to measure the impact of inflation, to incorporate the perspectives provided by such measurements into decision making, and to stimulate awareness by all levels of management of the need to develop constructive business strategies to deal with inflation. The objective is to ensure that investments needed for new business growth, productivity improvement and capacity expansions earn appropriate *real rates of return* commensurate with the risks involved. Such supplemental measurements can assist in the entire resource allocation process, starting with initial project approval, implementation and subsequent review." [4]

Few large companies have developed the internal planning and control approach to inflation to the degree General Electric has. Indeed, as our research indicates and will be subsequently discussed, many companies are struggling with the problem of what to do, and many other companies are ignoring the impact of inflation.

Constant Dollar Application

The constant dollar (general price level) approach requires restating historical data in units of constant general purchasing power. It is an attempt to provide a consistent yardstick to replace the "rubber tape line" referred to by Middleditch. Put more precisely, constant general purchasing power is a measure of the ability of a unit of money to purchase a specified market basket of goods and services during a period of changing prices.

Discussion of Indices

In the United States the price level of this market basket is currently measured by two indices:

1. Consumer Price Index, All Urban Consumers (CPI-U)
2. Gross National Product (GNP) implicit price deflator

The CPI-U, published by the U.S. Department of Labor, Bureau of Labor Statistics, utilizes a predetermined (base period) market basket. It is

---

[4] *1979 Annual Report,* General Electric Company, p. 29.

the most widely known index and is prescribed by FAS No. 33. Thus the CPI-U is probably the most relevant—though not necessarily the best—constant dollar measurement from an accounting point of view.

The CPI-U is based on prices of food, clothing, shelter, fuels, transportation fares, charges for doctors' and dentists' services, drugs, and other goods and services that people buy for day-to-day living. "All urban consumers" include wage earners and clerical workers, the self-employed, short-term workers, the unemployed, retirees and others not in the labor force. In total, approximately 80% of the population is covered under the definition of "all urban consumers."

The index measures price changes from a designated reference date—at present, 1967—which equals 100.0. An increase of 22%, for example, is shown as 122.0. This change can also be expressed in dollars as follows: The price of a base period market basket of goods and services in the CPI has risen from $10 in 1967 to $12.20.[5]

The CPI-U is an average-for-the-month index. It is calculated monthly and quarterly and annual averages are also available. For purposes of application under FAS No. 33, however, average-for-the-year or end-of-year dollars are normally used for computations relating to the current year.[6]

The GNP implicit price deflator, published by the Department of Commerce, is regarded by many economists to be a better measurement of inflation than the CPI because it encompasses the entire economy rather than a predetermined market basket. The GNP deflator is a weighted average of the detailed price indices used in the deflation of GNP.

"In each period, weights are based on the composition of the constant dollar output in that period. In other words, the price index for each item is weighted by the ratio of the quantity of the item valued in 1972 prices to the total output in 1972 prices. Changes in the implicit price deflator reflect both changes in prices and changes in the composition of output. Accordingly, comparisons over any time span reflect only changes in prices."[7]

Minimal Financial Data Requirements

The following minimal financial data in units of current purchasing power are required to comply with FAS No. 33:

1. Net sales and other operating revenue (CPI applied to historical sales)

---

[5] CPI Detailed Report—Bureau of Labor Statistics, U.S. Department of Labor, as contained in *Financial Reporting & Changing Prices,* Deloitte Haskins & Sells, 1979.

[6] FAS No. 33, p. 14, par. 40.

[7] *Survey of Current Business,* United States Department of Commerce, Bureau of Economic Analysis, February 1980, p. 11.

2. Earnings (loss) from continuing operations (CPI applied to inventory, and property, plant and equipment)
3. Earnings (loss) per common share from continuing operations
4. Net assets (shareholders' equity) at year-end (CPI applied to inventories, and property, plant and equipment)
5. Purchasing power gain or loss on net monetary items (CPI applied to elements of net monetary assets and liabilities)
6. Cash dividends declared per common share (CPI applied to dividends)
7. Market price per common share at fiscal year-end (CPI applied to market price)

The derivation of these elements is shown schematically in Exhibit 4–2.

Calculation Methodology

Measurements of constant dollar amounts for purposes of FAS No. 33 are computed by multiplying the components of historical cost measurement by the average level of the CPI for the current fiscal year and dividing by the level of the index at the date on which the associated asset was established.[8]

The underlying formula is:

Constant dollar amount = historical cost amount × (average index for period ÷ index at measurement date).

For example:

Cost of machine purchased February 1973	$10,000
CPI-U 1979 average (current fiscal year)	217.4
CPI-U February 1973	128.6

Then the 1979 constant dollar amount of this cost would be:

$$\$10,000 \times (217.4 \div 128.6) = \$16,905.$$

The current year may be selected as the base year or some similar year may be selected for this purpose. Accordingly, the constant dollar amount may be rolled forward or rolled back.

The FASB also permits the use of end-of-year dollars if the reporting firm undertakes a comprehensive restatement of its financial statements.

The application of this approach to inventory (valued on a FIFO basis) is illustrated next. Note that cost of sales is determined by adding constant dollar purchases to constant dollar beginning inventories and subtracting constant dollar ending inventories. This illustration assumes that purchases were made evenly throughout the year.

---

[8] FAS No. 33, p. 15, par. 43.

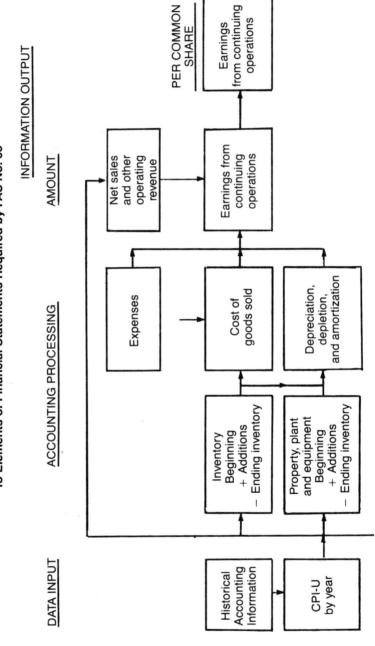

EXHIBIT 4-2

**Overview of Application of Constant Dollar Accounting
To Elements of Financial Statements Required by FAS No. 33**

44

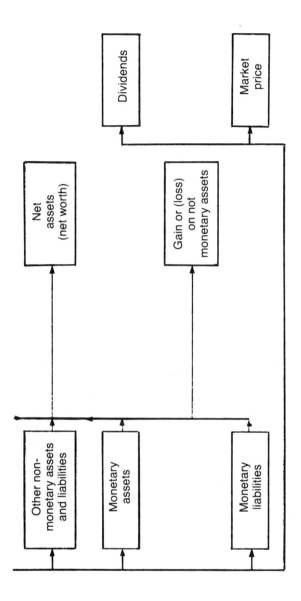

45

	Historical Dollars	1978 Restatement Factor	1978 Constant Dollars
Beginning Inventory:			
October 1977	20,000	195.4/184.5	21,180
November 1977	40,000	195.4/185.4	42,160
December 1977	60,000	195.4/186.1	63,000
Total	120,000		126,340
Purchases	500,000	1.00	500,000
Goods available for sale	620,000		626,340
Ending Inventory:			
September 1978	10,000	195.4/199.3	9,800
October 1978	20,000	195.4/200.9	19,450
November 1978	30,000	195.4/202.0	29,020
December 1978	50,000	195.4/202.9	48,150
Total	110,000		106,420
1978 cost of sales	510,000		519,920

While the preceding example assumes that inventories are aged by month, an average age can also be estimated based on inventory turnover rates.

The same approach is applied to property, plant and equipment and to net monetary items. Assets are restated to constant dollars by year of acquisition. Depreciation is then computed in constant dollars for that year, and the reserve for depreciation is recalculated on a constant dollar basis. These calculations are illustrated in the table below:

Machine Purchase Date	Cost of Machine			Annual Depreciation[9]	
	Historical Cost	1978 Restatement Factor	1978 Constant Dollars	Historical Cost	1978 Constant Dollars
Feb. 1973	10,000	195.4/128.6	15,190	1,000	1,519
March 1974	15,000	195.4/143.1	20,470	1,500	2,047
June 1978	12,000	195.4/195.3	12,010	1,200	1,201
	37,000		47,670	3,700	4,767

	Reserve for Depreciation		Net Book Value–1978	
	Historical Cost	1978 Constant Dollars	Historical Cost	1978 Constant Dollars
Feb. 1973	5,500	8,355	4,500	6,835
March 1974	6,750	9,212	8,250	11,258
June 1978	600	601	11,400	11,409
	12,850	18,168	24,150	29,502

---

[9] Assume straight-line, 10-year life, 1/2 year of depreciation in year of acquisition, no salvage value.

The purchasing power gain or loss on net monetary items is (similarly) equal to the net gain or loss found by restating in constant dollars the opening and closing balances of, and transactions in, monetary assets and liabilities.[10]

Current Cost Application

Current costs are based on the current values of the elements of financial statements normally expressed in historical dollars. Reported profits, therefore, stem from operations, changes in the replacement cost of specific items, and changes in the purchasing power of the dollar. Put another way, profits consist of "operating" profits and "holding gains" (resulting from changes in specific price levels and changes in general purchasing power).

As discussed in Chapter 3, several methods for calculating current costs are described in accounting literature and have been applied in different circumstances. Three of the principal alternatives are:

1. Replacement cost—the cost of replacing an asset
2. Current exit values—what an asset can be sold for
3. The present values of future cash flows—a measure of economic worth

FAS No. 33 provides rather broad definitions of current cost which embodies all three of the preceding concepts:

The current cost of inventory has been defined as "the current (replacement) cost of purchasing the goods concerned or the current cost of the resources (material, labor and overhead) to produce the goods concerned (including an allowance for the current overhead costs according to the allocation bases used under generally accepted accounting principles) whichever would be appropriate in the circumstances."[11] As previously noted, LIFO inventory values can be used as a surrogate for current costs in the income statement.

"The current cost of property, plant, and equipment owned by an enterprise is the current cost of acquiring the same service potential (indicated by operating costs and physical output capacity) as embodied by the asset owned."[12] This definition differs from the definition used in the SEC's replacement cost requirements. Under ASR 190 replacement (current) cost is the cost of maintaining current productive capacity by replacing the assets in

---

[10]FAS No. 33, p. 16, par. 50.

[11]FAS No. 33, p. 19, par. 57.

[12]FAS No. 33, p. 19, par. 58.

use with new assets, utilizing the latest available processes and technology. Under the FASB approach to current cost, assets are valued at the cost of acquiring or reproducing essentially the same assets as those currently in use.

Calculation Methodology

Current costs are measured for purposes of complying with FAS No. 33 by direct reference to current prices of comparable assets by four methods including indexing, direct pricing, unit pricing, or functional pricing.

Indexing, generally regarded as the most common approach, is the restatement of the base cost of an asset or group of assets by an appropriate index which may be either internally or externally generated. Well-known U.S. indices include the composite construction cost index published by the U.S. Department of Commerce, the construction industry cost indices published in *Engineering News Record*, the Marshall & Stevens index published in *Chemical Engineering*, and the producer price index published by the Bureau of Labor Statistics. Several indices are also available for assets in other countries.

Direct pricing is based on using current invoice prices, vendors' price lists or quotations, appraisals, or updated standard manufacturing costs that reflect current costs. While this method may be more objective than the others, it usually involves substantial detail.

Unit pricing is based on the determination of the current cost of providing a unit of service embodied in the asset owned, such as the current cost per square foot of different classes of floor space. Total current cost is determined by multiplying the unit cost by the appropriate number of service units.

Functional pricing is based on providing the current cost of an integrated production process, with results expressed as a cost per unit of output. It would be used to determine the current cost of a processing function rather than for specific assets. Costs are classified by allocating them to the various functions performed.[13] This method is especially useful for determining the current cost of specialized functions or processes that involve rapid changes in technology.

FAS No. 33 requires that "if current cost is measured in a foreign currency, the amount shall be translated into U.S. dollars at the current exchange rate. . . ."[14]

---

[13]Touche Ross and Co., *Financial Reporting and Changing Prices*, 1979, p. 90.

[14]FAS No. 33, p. 20, par. 59.

48

The Statement also requires that current costs be used to measure value unless a lower recoverable amount is more appropriate. Recoverable amounts may be measured by considering the net realizable values or values in use of the assets concerned. Net realizable value is the amount of cash, or its equivalent, expected to be derived from the sale of an asset, net of selling costs. Value in use is the present value of future cash flows expected to be derived from the use of an asset.[15]

In the next chapter we analyze the differences between historical financial information, and the constant dollar and current cost financial information required by FAS No. 33, for companies that constitute the Dow Jones Industrial Average.

---

[15]FAS No. 33, p. 21–22, par. 63.

Chapter 5

Results of Applying FAS No. 33

The application of the constant dollar and current cost financial reporting requirements prescribed by FAS No. 33 can have a significant effect on costs, profitability and funds available for growth. This chapter provides an indication of the magnitude of this impact.

In order to quantify the amounts involved, we analyzed the 1979 and 1980 historical cost, constant dollar and current cost results reported by 29 of the 30 companies that constitute the Dow Jones Industrial Average. These data were obtained from the primary statements and the supplementary information required by FAS No. 33 and contained in the annual reports of the 29 companies. The 30th company, General Foods, fiscal year ended on March 31, 1981, was omitted because its annual report was not available in time for our analysis. Similar patterns emerged from our analysis of both the 1979 and 1980 data so we will only refer to 1980 data in this chapter.

We point out that the companies that constitute the Dow Jones Industrial Average are large industrial companies and retailers.

Smaller companies, transportation companies, banks and other financial service institutions are not represented in the sample. While we suspect that smaller companies are affected by inflation no differently from larger companies, we do not have any evidence to support this hypothesis.

Effect on Income Statement

Exhibit 5–1 provides a summary of some of the data reported by the 29 companies. Data and percentage relationships to sales are shown in the form of an abbreviated aggregate income statement on a historical cost (as reported), constant dollar, and current cost basis. These 29 companies reported aggregate sales of $543 billion, assets of $458 billion, and net income of $29 billion. The largest company in this sample is Exxon with 1980 sales of $110 billion, assets of $57 billion and net income of $5.7 billion. The smallest company is Johns-Manville with sales of $2.3 billion, assets of $2.3 billion and net income of $81 million. General Motors re-

51

ported a loss of $763 million, which because of its size, tended to depress the results in the Consumer Products Manufacturers' Group.

The summary shows that cost of sales for 29 companies increased from 71.6% to 72.4% of sales when computed on a constant dollar basis and to 72.1% of sales when computed on a current cost basis. The relatively small percentage increase may be attributed to the wide application of LIFO inventory valuation practices. (Of the 29 companies included in the sample, 25 used LIFO.)

Depreciation expense is substantially affected by the application of constant dollar and current cost accounting. It increased from 4.4% of sales on a historical basis to 6.7% of sales on a constant dollar basis and to 6.8% of sales on a current cost basis. This is the area of cost where inflation causes the most significant distortions as a percentage of sales or as a percentage of historical costs.

Net income is greatly reduced as a result of the application of both constant dollar and current cost reporting. It dropped by 58% from 5.4% of sales to 2.3% of sales on a constant dollar basis and by 54% to 2.5% of sales on a current cost basis. Income before income taxes dropped 34% on a constant dollar basis and by 32% on a current cost basis. The after-tax decrease is more pronounced than the pre-tax decline because the amount of the provision for income taxes is not affected by the rules prescribed for the different accounting methods. Holding taxes constant in dollars leverages the effect on net (after-tax) income.

Monetary Gains and Losses

The monetary gain (loss) on purchasing power of net amounts owed offsets much of the earnings decline. This amount is shown as a separate figure in Exhibit 5-1 because these gains are considered to be unrealized. However, if depreciation based on replacement costs is deducted from earnings, it may be equally appropriate to include these gains or losses in this calculation.

Duane R. Kullberg, chairman of Arthur Andersen & Co., says: "The purchasing power gain or loss is a very real reflection of one effect of inflation. . . . This separate reporting makes constant dollar statements more difficult to explain and to understand and seems to raise some doubt as to whether such gains and losses are 'real'." [1] Some companies, such as Shell Oil, Exxon, and Trans Union Corporation, added purchasing power gains to income from continuing operations in their annual reports. However, most companies reported these gains separately. The issue is still the subject of debate.

---

[1] Duane R. Kullberg, *Inflation and Its Impact on Financial Executives*, Arthur Andersen & Co., 1980, p. 4.

EXHIBIT 5-1

Summary of Aggregate 1980 Results Reported by
29 of 30 Companies Included in the Dow Jones Industrial Average

Income Statement

	($ Billions)				(Percentage of Sales)		
	Historical (As Reported)	Constant Dollar	Current Cost		Historical (As Reported)	Constant Dollar	Current Cost
Sales	542.5	542.5	542.5		100.0	100.0	100.0
Costs and Expenses:							
Cost of sales	388.7	392.8	390.9		71.6	72.4	72.1
Depreciation	23.9	36.6	37.2		4.4	6.7	6.8
Other costs and expenses	80.0	80.3	80.3		14.8	14.8	14.8
Total costs and expenses	492.6	509.7	508.4		90.8	93.9	93.7
Income before income taxes	49.9	32.8	34.1		9.2	6.0	6.3
Provision for income taxes	20.5	20.5	20.5		3.8	3.8	3.8
Net income	29.4	12.3	13.6		5.4	2.3	2.5
Gain on purchasing power of net amounts owed		11.4				2.1	
Estimated increase in value of inventories and property, plant and equipment held during the year (holding gains)			43.5				8.0

Source: Data contained in company annual reports.

53

Holding Gains

The aggregate estimated increase in value of inventories and property, plant and equipment held during the year was $44 billion, or 8.0% of sales, before giving effect to taxation. This increase more than offsets the 2.9% of sales difference between historical cost and current cost income before income taxes. Holding gains are seldom referred to in the text of annual reports but may be one of the most important, though unpublicized, financial effects of inflation on many companies. For example, the three oil companies as a group reported estimated holding gains of $15 billion (7.4% of sales) and AT&T reported holding gains of $14 billion (27.5% of revenues!).[2]

Twenty-five companies in the sample reported increases in specific prices: current cost of inventories and property, plant and equipment held during the year. Four companies reported only the excess of the increase in specific prices over the increase in the general price level (as required by FAS No. 33). For these four companies, (General Motors, International Harvester, Union Carbide, and SOCAL), we estimated the effect of the increase in the general price level and added or subtracted the amount of the reported excess to this estimate to determine the increase in specific prices.

Variation by Industry and Company

The effect of inflation on reported results varies widely by industry group and by company within each industry. Exhibit 5–2 shows the percentage change in 1980 cost of sales, depreciation and net income by company and industry group for the 29 companies included in the sample.

In general, the cost of sales of the three companies (American Brands, IBM, and Minnesota Mining & Manufacturing) that continue to value their inventories on a FIFO or average cost basis increased more, on both a constant dollar and current cost basis, than the cost of sales of the companies that valued inventories on a LIFO basis.

Increases in depreciation are most pronounced among the capital-intensive oil companies; steel, metal, and paper companies; and AT&T. For example, oil company constant dollar depreciation is 72% higher than historical cost, and current cost depreciation is up 110%. Steel, metal and paper company depreciation is up 71% on a constant dollar basis and 79% on a current cost basis. AT&T's depreciation is up 73% and 58% respectively. Consumer Product Manufacturer depreciation, on the other hand, increased by only 18% on a constant dollar basis and by 27% on a current

---

[2] AT&T's holding gains are probably academic in terms of creating values for stockholders because most regulators allow only historical costs for rate-making purposes.

54

cost basis although these latter percentages are heavily weighted by General Motors.

Net income turned into losses for six companies (American Can, Goodyear, Bethlehem Steel, INCO, U.S. Steel, and Woolworth on a constant dollar basis). General Motors and International Harvester reported losses on a historical cost basis, and these losses were increased on a constant dollar and current cost basis. Net income of three companies (Eastman Kodak, Merck and IBM) was much less affected by inflation than that of the other companies in the sample.

Income Tax Implications

The application of the concepts of constant dollar and current cost accounting causes the effective income tax rate for our sample to increase from 41% on a historical cost basis to 63% on a constant dollar basis and 60% on a current cost basis. Effective tax rates are compared by company in Exhibit 5–3.

In their discussion of the effects of inflation, many 1979 and 1980 annual reports make the point that taxes based on historical earnings, in effect, tax capital.[3] This conclusion is based on the premise that each corporation exists in perpetuity, and each business should provide for replacing its own plant and equipment. The premise behind historical accounting, on the other hand, is that depreciation should be assigned to the cost of the goods produced by the plant and equipment; current replacement costs are relevant for expenditures for new plant and equipment decisions but are irrelevant for the evaluation of existing operations. Whether or not inflation taxes capital, therefore, depends on how the corporation is viewed and the accounting concepts are applied.

Capital Formation

The impact of inflation as measured on a constant dollar and current cost basis on the aggregate formation of capital of the 29 companies is shown in Exhibit 5–4. In the analysis we have subtracted the provision for plant and equipment replacement (depreciation, depletion and amortization) and dividends from funds provided by continuing operations to determine funds available for growth. (Constant dollar or current cost depreciation is used as a measure of the funds needed to replace existing plant and equipment.) The dividend payout ratio is also shown.

---

[3] Fifty-nine percent of the sample showed comparative effective tax rates or discussed the effect of inflation on taxation in their 1980 annual reports.

EXHIBIT 5–2

Percent Change in 1980 Cost of Sales, Depreciation and Net Income Caused by Constant Dollar and Current Cost Accounting Methods for 29 of 30 Companies Included in Dow Jones Industrial Average

	Principal Inventory Valuation Method	Cost of Sales		Depreciation		Net Income	
		Constant Dollar	Current Cost	Constant Dollar	Current Cost	Constant Dollar	Current Cost
Consumer Products Manufacturers							
American Brands	FIFO	3.3	1.2	46.7	68.0	(58.3)	(28.6)
Eastman Kodak	LIFO	0.2	2.4	29.8	44.6	(11.4)	(16.4)
General Motors	LIFO	2.3	0.7	14.0	21.6	NA	NA
Merck	LIFO	3.4	(1.3)	45.1	53.8	(18.1)	(8.7)
Proctor and Gamble	LIFO	1.7	0.9	62.2	77.6	(38.1)	(33.4)
Total Group		2.1	0.7	18.3	26.9	NA	(99.4)
Industrial Product Manufacturers							
American Can	LIFO	1.5	1.7	74.5	66.7	NA	NA
General Electric	LIFO	0.9	0.8	48.8	54.5	(32.0)	(33.9)
Goodyear	LIFO	2.7	1.7	69.1	74.8	NA	NA
IBM	Avg.	3.0	(0.7)	28.7	11.7	(30.0)	(10.2)
International Harvester	LIFO	2.0	0.5	45.4	63.8	NA	NA
Johns-Manville	LIFO	0.7	0.7	46.8	40.5	(60.5)	(64.3)
Minnesota Mining & Mfg.	FIFO	4.8	1.2	44.3	45.5	(40.7)	(25.2)
Owens-Illinois	LIFO	1.6	1.7	58.1	55.9	(79.9)	(81.9)
United Technologies	LIFO	0.9	0.7	22.1	25.2	(33.6)	(20.8)
Westinghouse Electric	LIFO	1.6	1.3	42.7	50.3	(45.2)	(41.4)
Total Group		1.7	0.8	38.0	30.8	(44.1)	(30.1)
Chemical Companies							
Allied	LIFO	1.4	0.7	45.8	42.8	(61.6)	(49.5)
DuPont	LIFO	1.2	1.4	43.8	37.9	(66.9)	(62.7)
Union Carbide	LIFO	2.3	0.8	79.8	54.9	(59.1)	(32.3)
Total Group		1.6	1.1	52.5	42.8	(62.8)	(48.0)

Oil Companies

Exxon	LIFO	0.2	0.2	68.5	103.3	(30.4)	(44.5)
Standard Oil of California	LIFO	0.1	0.1	66.6	125.0	(22.3)	(41.0)
Texaco	LIFO	0.1	0.3	83.3	113.6	(36.1)	(52.8)
Total Group		0.1	0.2	72.1	110.1	(30.0)	(45.8)

Steel, Metal and Paper Companies

Alcoa	LIFO	1.1	1.8	67.8	70.1	(62.8)	(69.4)
Bethlehem Steel	LIFO	1.0	2.0	63.7	68.5	NA	NA
INCO	LIFO	7.0	3.7	85.5	93.9	NA	NA
International Paper	LIFO	1.7	1.5	68.4	65.1	(67.5)	(62.7)
U.S. Steel	LIFO	1.9	2.3	73.9	90.6	NA	NA
Total Group		1.9	2.1	70.9	78.6	NA	NA

Retailers

Sears Roebuck	LIFO	0.9	0.2	61.6	50.9	(64.9)	(32.3)
Woolworth	LIFO	3.1	0.9	70.2	47.9	NA	(63.4)
Total Group		1.3	0.3	64.3	50.0	(82.8)	(38.9)

American Telephone & Telegraph	NA	—	—	72.9	58.1	(84.4)	(67.3)
Total 29 Companies		1.0	0.6	53.5	56.0	(58.2)	(53.8)

( ) denotes decrease
NA data not applicable (loss)

Source: Data contained in company annual reports

EXHIBIT 5-3

Percent Change in 1980 Effective Income Tax Rates of 29 of 30 Companies Included in Dow Jones Industrial Average

	Historical (As Reported)	Constant Dollar	Current Cost
Consumer Products Manufacturers			
American Brands	38.6	60.1	46.9
Eastman Kodak	41.2	44.2	45.7
General Motors	NA	NA	NA
Merck	36.4	41.2	38.6
Proctor and Gamble	40.6	52.5	50.7
Total Group	42.3	178.8	99.1
Industrial Product Manufacturers			
American Can	32.8	NA	NA
General Electric	38.8	48.2	48.9
Goodyear	34.4	605.0	170.4
IBM	39.6	48.5	42.2
International Harvester	NA	NA	NA
Johns-Manville	48.4	70.4	67.3
Minnesota Mining & Mfg.	43.3	56.3	50.5
Owens-Illinois	41.1	77.6	79.4
United Technologies	48.8	58.9	57.5
Westinghouse Electric	27.4	40.8	40.2
Total Group	39.4	53.8	48.2
Chemical Companies			
Allied	68.8	85.2	81.4
DuPont	36.0	62.9	60.1
Union Carbide	33.6	55.4	42.8
Total Group	45.0	68.7	61.1
Oil Companies			
Exxon	49.0	58.0	63.4
Standard Oil of California	44.1	50.4	57.3
Texaco	41.5	52.6	60.1
Total Group	48.7	55.1	61.3
Steel, Metal and Paper Companies			
Alcoa	34.8	58.9	63.5
Bethlehem Steel	NA	NA	NA
INCO	52.1	136.8	107.2
International Paper	21.3	45.5	42.1
U.S. Steel	24.4	616.7	NA
Total Group	30.5	114.2	158.5
Retailers			
Sears Roebuck	12.3	28.5	17.2
Woolworth	21.1	NA	42.2
Total Group	14.3	49.2	21.4
American Telephone & Telegraph	35.4	77.8	62.7
Total 29 Companies	41.1	62.5	60.1

Source: Data contained in company annual reports
(Provision for income taxes divided by income before income taxes as shown; this computation may differ from the effective tax rate reported by the company.)

NA: Data not available (loss)

58

EXHIBIT 5-4

Summary of Aggregate 1980 Results of Funds Available for Growth of 29 of 30 Companies Included in the Dow Jones Industrial Average

	($ Billions)			(Percentage of Funds from Continuing Operations)		
	Historical (As Reported)	Constant Dollar	Current Cost	Historical (As Reported)	Constant Dollar	Current Cost
Sources of funds:						
Net Income	29.4	12.3	13.6	48.1	21.7	23.2
Depreciation	23.9	36.7	37.2	39.1	64.6	63.5
Other non-cash items	7.8	7.8	7.8	12.8	13.7	13.3
Funds provided by operations	61.1	56.8	58.6	100.0	100.0	100.0
Requirements for funds:						
Provision for plant and equipment replacement	23.9	36.7	37.2	39.1	64.6	63.5
Dividends	14.0	14.0	14.0	22.9	24.6	23.9
Funds available for growth	23.2	6.1	7.4	38.0	10.8	12.6
Dividend payout ratio	47.6	113.8	102.9			

Source: Data contained in company annual reports

59

This summary of sources and funds available for growth shows an aggregate funds flow from continuing operations of $61 billion on a historical basis, $57 billion on a constant dollar basis, and $59 billion on a current cost basis. (Funds provided by continuing operations are considered to be a more appropriate measure of funds available for capital formation than net income because it is a better measure of the cash that a company has at its disposal and is unaffected by the depreciation rates that are used.) The constant dollar and current cost funds provided by continuing operations are lower than the historical dollar figure because the former amounts reflect the general or specific price level adjusted value of all inventories whereas the latter is based on the historical valuation methods used.

The percentage of funds available for growth shown in Exhibit 5–4 is slashed from 38% of funds from continuing operations to either 11% to 13%, depending on which methodology is considered. This decrease is largely caused by the increased cost of plant and equipment replacement which, by the process of elimination, must be offset by decreased dividends or funds available for growth.

The dividend payout ratio (dividends ÷ net income) is increased from 48% on a historical basis to 114% on a constant dollar basis, and 103% on a current cost basis. In short, when aggregate reported results are adjusted for inflation, net income does not cover the dividend requirements of the companies in the sample.[4] Much of the high payout ratio on a constant dollar and current cost basis, it should be noted, was caused by General Motors which reported a constant dollar loss of $2.5 billion, a current cost loss of $2.0 billion, and dividends of $874 million.

Exhibit 5–5 shows the effect of the current cost methodology on each of the industry groups and the companies included in the sample. The total percentages shown are computed on aggregations of the underlying dollar amounts.

Exhibit 5–5 shows a wide variation of impacts. Ten companies (General Motors, American Can, Goodyear, International Harvester, Johns-Manville, DuPont, Bethlehem Steel, INCO, U.S. Steel, and Sears Roebuck) presumably did not generate enough funds from continuing operations in 1980 to provide for the replacement of their plant and equipment (as computed on a current cost basis) and pay dividends. Even AT&T squeaked by with just 3% of funds from continuing operations available for growth. General Motors, International Harvester, and Bethlehem Steel paid dividends out of capital even on a historical cost basis, but the other companies all showed that they were adding to their capital stock.

---

[4] Ten percent of the sample showed comparative dividend payout ratios or discussed the effect of inflation on dividends in their 1980 annual reports.

EXHIBIT 5–5

Distribution of 1980 Funds Provided by Operations

29 of 30 Companies Included in Dow Jones Industrial Average

	(Percentage of Funds) Reported on a Historical Basis			(Percentage of Funds) Reported on a Current Cost Basis		
	Replace	Divs.	Growth	Replace	Divs.	Growth
Consumer Product Manufacturers						
American Brands	16.2	40.2	43.6	31.7	46.7	21.6
Eastman Kodak	25.7	33.2	41.1	37.4	33.5	29.1
General Motors	120.5	25.2	(45.7)	164.7	28.3	(93.0)
Merck	17.4	34.0	48.6	26.1	33.1	40.8
Proctor and Gamble	22.2	31.8	46.0	42.4	34.3	23.3
Total Group	71.7	29.5	(1.2)	98.3	31.9	(30.2)
Industrial Product Manufacturers						
American Can	42.1	24.4	33.5	95.5	33.5	(29.0)
General Electric	30.2	28.6	41.2	49.4	30.3	20.3
Goodyear	52.8	21.3	25.9	122.9	28.4	(51.3)
IBM	33.6	28.6	37.8	38.1	29.0	32.9
International Harvester	NA	NA	NA	NA	NA	NA
Johns-Manville	43.6	37.6	18.8	65.7	40.2	(5.9)
Minnesota Mining & Mfg.	26.0	33.8	40.2	40.1	35.9	24.0
Owens-Illinois	36.7	11.6	51.7	75.2	15.2	9.6
United Technologies	35.3	27.5	37.2	48.8	30.3	20.9
Westinghouse Electric	34.2	22.2	43.6	59.5	25.7	14.8
Total Group	35.8	29.6	34.6	49.5	31.3	19.2
Chemical Companies						
Allied	45.6	15.7	38.7	68.3	16.4	15.3
DuPont	49.2	25.3	25.5	74.4	27.7	(2.1)
Union Carbide	26.9	17.0	56.1	43.4	17.7	38.9
Total Group	40.7	20.7	38.6	62.1	22.1	15.8

EXHIBIT 5-5 (continued)
Distribution of 1980 Funds Provided by Operations
29 of 30 Companies Included in Dow Jones Industrial Average

	(Percentage of Funds) Reported on a Historical Basis			(Percentage of Funds) Reported on a Current Cost Basis		
	Replace	Divs.	Growth	Replace	Divs.	Growth
Oil Companies						
Exxon	21.1	14.2	64.7	43.7	14.4	41.9
Standard Oil of California	19.3	15.5	65.2	43.7	15.6	40.7
Texaco	28.0	17.0	55.0	61.9	17.7	20.4
Total Group	22.2	15.1	62.7	47.5	15.3	37.2
Steel, Metal and Paper Companies						
Alcoa	35.5	15.9	48.6	74.9	19.7	5.4
Bethlehem Steel	84.5	15.8	(0.3)	195.7	21.7	(117.4)
INCO	43.2	20.4	36.4	106.0	25.8	(31.8)
International Paper	35.5	23.5	41.0	65.1	26.0	8.9
U.S. Steel	52.6	14.0	33.4	130.1	18.2	(48.3)
Total Group	48.7	17.3	34.0	108.8	21.6	(30.4)
Retailers						
Sears Roebuck	31.2	47.1	21.7	50.2	50.2	(0.4)
Woolworth	42.5	19.6	37.9	74.3	23.2	2.5
Total Group	34.0	40.5	25.5	55.6	44.2	0.2
American Telephone & Telegraph	45.8	24.5	29.7	72.4	24.5	3.1
Total 29 Companies	39.1	22.9	38.0	63.5	23.9	12.6

Source: Data contained in company annual reports.
NA: Not applicable; negative funds provided by operations

A Comment on Methodology

Several companies stated in their 1980 annual reports that they view current cost information, while imprecise, to be more meaningful than constant dollar information. Other companies said that they regard neither the constant dollar nor current cost methodology to be particularly relevant. No company in our sample said that it prefers the constant dollar methodology.

Our analysis suggests that the overall message delivered by constant dollar accounting may not really be much different from the message delivered by current cost accounting. In each case, cost of sales is increased moderately, depreciation is increased substantially, and net earnings are decreased by approximately the same proportions. However, important differences between the effects of the two methodologies were reported on a company-by-company basis. We will, of course, leave it to the FASB to ponder the issue of which methodology to apply because complete analysis of the arguments for each of the approaches is beyond the scope of this book.

Section II

Management Accounting Issues and Practices

Chapter 6

Strategic Planning and Budgeting Issues

A number of issues pertaining to the methodologies used for planning resource allocation have emerged as a result of the prospective changes in the
value of the dollar, changes in specific prices, and uncertainty as to the
amount and/or timing of these changes. Such issues have an important effect
on the practice of strategic planning including business unit analysis, the
preparation of financial projections, portfolio analysis, the selection of financial strategies and the evaluation of capital expenditures. This effect is
heightened because of the three- to twenty-year time spans encompassed by
most strategic plans. Inflation-related issues also affect operating planning
and budgeting, although perhaps to a lesser extent than strategic planning,
because the latter activities usually entail a much shorter time frame, usually
one or two years, than strategic plans.

As GE points out in its 1979 annual report, investments for new business
growth, productivity improvements and capacity expansion need to earn appropriate *real* rates of return.[1] This statement illustrates the challenge posed to
the management accounting profession: How to fashion or modify its resource
allocation planning tools to assure that the objective of earning "appropriate
real rates of return" will be achieved in an inflationary environment.

To provide a framework for discussion of inflation-related management
accounting practices, this chapter identifies the principal strategic planning
and budgeting issues involved and our perception of some of the options for
dealing with these issues.

Scope of Resource Allocation

For the purposes of this discussion, strategic planning and budgeting
resource allocation will include the management planning and decision-
making process that determines where and how a company's capital resources are invested. In some companies resource allocation planning is

---

[1] 1979 Annual Report, General Electric Company, p. 29.

carried on in a sophisticated, formal manner, while other companies act more opportunistically, entrepreneurially, or informally. Budgeting systems are often more formal than strategic planning systems because of their typically longer tenure and their emphasis on quantification. Irrespective of where a company is in the spectrum of management style, however, the same management accounting fundamentals apply to the quantification of decisions.

Business Unit Analysis

Business unit analysis entails the selection of information to be analyzed and the measurement methods to be applied. Arthur D. Little, Inc.'s strategy center profiling format is shown in Exhibit 6–1 as an example of the kinds of ratios and other measurements that are gathered in the process of preparing analysis by business unit. Our example is a two-edged sword. While it illustrates the current state-of-the-art practices in business unit analysis, it may also illustrate some of the potential deficiencies of these practices in an inflationary environment.

EXHIBIT 6–1

Strategic Business Unit Indices and Ratios

INDICES (Base Year = 100)

- Industry throughput (units)
- Business unit's product throughput (units)
- Business unit's sales (dollars)
- Profit after taxes
- Net assets

COST & EARNINGS (per $ Sales)

- Cost of goods sold
- Research and development
- General administration
- Other income and expenses
- Profit before taxes
- Profit after taxes
- Return on net assets

INVESTMENT (per $ Sales)

- Receivables
- Inventories
- Current liabilities
- Working capital and other assets
- Total net assets

FUNDS GENERATION & DEPLOYMENT

- Operating cash flow (per $ sales)
- Change in assets (per $ sales
- % internal deployment (change in assets ÷ operating funds flow)

Source: Arthur D. Little, Inc.

Most of the measurements in Exhibit 6–1 are currently determined on a historical cost basis. The issue is, should they be? Should dollar amounts be translated into units of constant purchasing power or current costs, or are nominal dollars sufficient for purposes of analyzing the performance of business units? Would an analysis of a particular business unit benefit from separating the inflation-generated (holding gain or loss) component of profit from the operating component, or are the results reported all part of a single, integrated and indivisible business undertaking?

The advantages of using historical (nominal) dollars are that they are available in the records, are also used by competitors, and are more easily understood by management. The disadvantage of this approach is that historical dollars do not necessarily reflect what economists would call "real" rates of return. Return on net assets (RONA) is based on profits after taxes (based on historical costs) divided by historical (not current) net assets. This disadvantage, however, is mitigated by the fact that emphasis is placed on funds (operating cash) flow as well as profit after taxes. Because operating cash flow is computed before depreciation, the amount is not affected by the depreciation method that is used.

According to William MacAvoy of William E. Hill & Company,

"Specific businesses that appear attractive from a profitability and growth standpoint are not necessarily so, once performance is adjusted for inflation. Analysis of the performance of companies or company units against the aggregate performance of the businesses in which they participate—one of the fulcrums of strategic planning— is by itself meaningless without such adjustment.

As a case in point, consider a firm with a huge, expensive, new plant and high depreciation rates competing against a rival with a low-cost, older plant and equipment and low depreciation rates. How can two business activities such as these be compared, even in businesses where technological change is slow? How can strategy decisions be made in the absence of true information regarding absolute and relative profit performance?" [2]

To comply with FAS No. 33 large corporations must develop a current cost data base. FAS No. 33 also requires the use of the CPI-U for comparative purposes. Now that this information is available, perhaps it will also be used internally for business unit analysis. FAS No. 33 also "encouraged" presentation of inflation-adjusted information by business segment. [3] However, none of the reports that we reviewed (including 27 of the 30 Dow Jones companies) contained such information.

Financial Projections

Strategy selection entails dealing with financial forecasts rather than

---

[2] Robert E. MacAvoy, "Business Strategy & Inflation: Finding the Real Bottom Line," *Management Review,* January, 1978, pp. 17–24.

[3] FAS No. 33, p. 11.

historical results. Prospective results are ordinarily shown in the form of income statements, balance sheets or statements of net assets, funds statements and other supporting information.

In trying to develop information for use in selecting a strategy, some of the inflation-oriented management accounting issues are:

1. Given the unpredictable record of inflation, how often should forecasts of the impact of strategic actions be updated? Forecasts can rapidly become obsolete as a result of unanticipated price changes.
2. What forms of statements and measurements should be used? For example, should greater emphasis be placed on prospective cash flows than on forecasted profit contribution? How should prospective holding gains (losses are seldom anticipated) be reflected? Solutions to this problem will depend on the accounting concepts that are applied.
3. Should sales and earnings estimates consist of single numbers, prospective high and low results, or multiple forecasts? While single number forecasts may be easier to prepare than "hi-low" forecasts, they are probably less useful in an inflationary environment.
4. Should financial forecasts be shown in nominal dollars, constant dollars, or in both nominal and constant dollars? Forecasts in nominal dollars entail making assumptions about inflation rates.
5. Should inflation rate assumptions be determined centrally, be determined by the local business unit or not be considered in the planning process? Who should make these assumptions? Assumptions determined by local business units may be more accurate than those determined centrally, but they are also subject to distortion by local business unit managers to support a desired conclusion.
6. For foreign affiliates, should plans be submitted in local currencies only, U.S. dollars only, or both local currencies and U.S. dollars? Should the currency exchange rates used be determined centrally or by the local business unit? How does the interaction of these two factors affect the placement of responsibility of forecasting rates used for planning purposes? Because of the fluctuating value of the dollar in relation to other currencies caused by relative rates of inflation and monetary practices, the exchange rate must be considered in conjunction with the inflation rate.

Portfolio Analysis

Portfolio analysis at the corporate level leads to the development of corporate business and financial policies, and corporate strategies. This type of analysis is conducted on a systematic basis in some companies while in many other companies it evolves on an informal, ad hoc basis. The issues involved in portfolio analysis typically concern: (1) What do we have? (2) What is our appetite for risk? (3) What can we support? and (4) Which businesses do we invest in and which do we divest?

The management accounting alternatives that are applicable to analyses made at the business unit level are also applicable to analyses at the corporate level. For example, current costs or historical costs can be used in portfolio analysis. If historical costs are used to determine replacement requirements without adjusting for inflation, the capital required to replace assets will clearly be understated.

Inflation may also have added a new dimension to the strategic planning process. Strategic planning methodology has customarily been concerned primarily with industry maturity and competitive position. Inflation, however, suggests that capital replacement requirements measured in real terms should be considered. Moreover, firms are offered the strategic choice of investing resources in capital-intensive businesses with rapidly escalating replacement costs or in less capital-intensive businesses that are likely to be less directly affected by inflation. Thus inflation can affect the evaluation of new investment opportunities as well as the replacement of existing assets.

Real estate offers a potential investment hedge in an inflationary environment provided that such investment can be financed with debt that costs less after taxes than the underlying inflation rate. It should also be noted that measurements in real estate are usually cash-flow-oriented rather than net-profit-oriented. Because cash flow is roughly equivalent to net income before depreciation, inadequacies of historical depreciation are less likely to affect the evaluation of investments when cash flow is used than when investment decisions are based on net earnings.

Assuming that funds are available for expansion, the cost of capital is an important concept that can be used in portfolio analysis. The cost of capital customarily includes the anticipated impact of inflation on historical dollars. Thus businesses offering a prospective, risk-adjusted, nominal dollar future cash flow with a present value in excess of the corresponding nominal dollar cost of capital offer a financial advantage. Consistency of measurement, of course, is important in making this determination. Cost of capital will be explored later, in connection with capital expenditure evaluations.

Financial Strategies

Inflation also affects financial strategies in different ways in different companies. If plant and equipment replacement costs call for an increasing share of cash flow, one, or a combination of three, consequences follow:

1. Some replacements must be deferred.

2. External financing must be increased.
3. Other uses of funds such as dividend payments or acquisition activity must be reduced.

External financing can be provided by short-term borrowing, long-term borrowing, leasing or equity financing. Two illustrations of strategies that have been described in the literature follow:

AMAX's strategy, according to Vice President & Controller Martin Alonzo, has been "to invest more than our cash flow each year and to cover the cash deficit with long-term borrowing and equity when necessary."[4]

This strategy was based on the conclusion that inflation would be a long-term structural problem facing the world. AMAX does not defer capital investment because it thinks that interest rates may be too high or that they may go down in a year or two. Moreover, AMAX has "avoided the temptation to borrow Swiss francs or Deutschemarks at lower interest rates than U.S. dollar borrowings and, as a result, has probably saved some money over the long run." This policy results from AMAX's views of the extent to which the political and social forces in the United States are debasing the value of the dollar.[5]

Alonzo suggests the following strategies for beating inflation:

"Investment
- Explore, buy and develop natural resources and build capital facilities as a hedge.
- Take advantage of recessionary periods and negotiate better engineering, construction and labor contracts.
- Be prepared to buy used facilities.
- Look for 'buys' in the stock market.
- Forecast higher future selling prices to justify new investment.

Financing
- Borrow as much long-term debt as you can for as long as you can.
- In lease-finance transactions, retain residual equipment values.

Operating
- Use LIFO inventory valuation method.
- During periods of over-supply increase inventory.
- Negotiate long-term purchase contracts.

---

[4]Martin V. Alonzo, "Corporate Strategy for Combating Inflation," *Management Accounting*, March 1978, pp. 57–58.

[5]*Ibid.*

• In new technology development, design away from energy-based processes because of anticipated escalating energy costs.

• Measure performance in real terms by converting operating results via use of GNP deflator and wholesale price index."[6]

In addition to giving increased attention to internal efficiency and to obtaining such price increases as may be possible on the open market, Simmonds Precision Products is trying to "do more with the customers' money—more down payments, more progress payments, and more milestone billings against major long-term contracts."[7] This strategy of making existing resources stretch further seems to be typical of many managements' financial strategies.

Unfortunately inflation's impact on the availability and cost of capital has made it difficult for many companies to obtain external financing. Consider the following experience during the last half of 1979 and the first half of 1980. First the securities market shifted from equities to long-term debt financing because of the high cost of equity financing. When the bond market fell out of bed in the fall of 1979, short-term borrowing was left as the only external financing vehicle available. However, when the prime bank rate soared to 20%, even the cost of this external source of financing became prohibitive.

Capital Expenditure Evaluations

Several management accounting issues are associated with the evaluation of capital expenditures in an environment of uncertain, but perhaps significant, inflationary expectations. The key question is how should inflation be dealt with in the determination of the amount of expenditure, forecasting prospective revenues, expense and cash flows, the estimation of residual values, the development of capital expenditure hurdle rates, and the annual budgeting of capital expenditures? For example, should a constant rate of inflation be used or should different rates be used each year for each element of revenue and expenditure? Related issues pertaining to foreign projects include the determination of the currency and tax rates to be used to evaluate capital investment projects.

Despite the many variables involved, three general, alternative approaches seem to predominate:

1. Use nominal dollars and incorporate anticipated inflation on a specific basis in all significant elements of cash flow for each year of

---

[6]*Ibid.*

[7]Geoffrey R. Simmonds, "A Corporate Strategy for Combating Inflation," *Managing in Inflation,* The Conference Board, 1978, p. 11.

the project. Compare the internal rate of return on the project with, or compute the present values of future cash flows based on, an inflation-adjusted cost of capital or hurdle rate.

2. Incorporate anticipated inflation in some of the elements of cash flow for each year of the project. For example, some companies include anticipated cost increases in determining the amount of the capital expenditure, but use constant dollars to project cash flows on the premise that cost increases will be offset by revenue increases. Other companies provide a contingency allowance for increases in the cost of the prospective capital expenditure. Many companies do not adjust residual values for inflation. Some companies adjust for cash flows for anticipated changes in specific price levels, but they do not adjust the hurdle rate.

3. Project all expenditures and other elements of cash flow in constant dollars, and compare the result with a cost of capital that excludes inflation.

Based on his comprehensive study of the capital expenditure evaluation practices of 25 large Canadian companies, John Boersema concludes that while all companies reflected inflation in their capital budgeting calculations:

"1. Operating cash flows should not be adjusted for inflation without also adjusting the hurdle rate.

2. The hurdle rate should not be increased to offset inflation without also reflecting the effects of inflation on cash flows.

3. A general rate of inflation should not be used to adjust all cost and revenue items.

4. The estimate of capital investment should be separated into major categories, and appropriate price factors should be applied to restate the amount to future dollars.

5. Contingency allowances are frequently used to cover expected price increases in capital items; this practice should, however, be discouraged.

6. Working capital terminal values should be explicitly adjusted for inflation. . . ." [8]

Debra Raiborn and Thomas Ratcliffe advocate testing the sensitivity of the project's acceptance to different general price level changes. They recommend converting inflation-adjusting nominal cash flows to "real" (constant dollars) cash flows by dividing nominal flows by the index applicable to each year. Real cash flows are then discounted to yield a net present value. [9]

---

[8] John M. Boersema, *Capital Budgeting Practices Including the Impact of Inflation*, The Canadian Institute of Chartered Accountants, 1978, pp. 196, 223.

[9] Debra D. Raiborn and Thomas A. Ratcliffe, "Are You Accounting for Inflation in Your Capital Budgeting Process?" *Management Accounting*, September 1979, pp. 19–22.

One danger in using real cash flows is that fluctuations in inflation rates are not considered. For example, two projects may have identical expected returns given the projected rates of inflation over the life of the projects. If one project is in Switzerland, where the inflation rate fluctuates within narrow limits, and the other in Peru, where rate fluctuations have been severe, the relative risk is much different. To properly incorporate the effects of inflation into the analysis, the stability, as well as the magnitude, of inflation must be considered.

The issue of which measurements to use to evaluate prospective capital expenditures, how to measure sensitivity, and how to analyze risk should also be considered. While the resolution of these issues may not be dependent on inflation per se, consideration of the variability and unpredictability of inflation adds to the usefulness of internal rate of return, present value, and payback measurements and creates additional variables that should be included in sensitivity and risk analyses.

Increased Cost of Capital

Each firm's perception of its cost of capital provides the rationale behind the development of its capital expenditure hurdle rate and the allocation of resources to capital expenditures. Cost of capital can be particularly significant in the development of hurdle rates to assist in the screening and appraisal of prospective capital expenditures, marketing plans and alternative strategies. While hurdle rates do not necessarily equal the cost of capital, they are ordinarily related to the cost of capital and in theory are derived from the cost of capital.

As inflation increases, so ordinarily does the cost of the components of the cost of capital: interest rates increase, preferred and common stock yields increase, and stock market values decline. Accordingly, it may be helpful to review briefly ways that the cost of capital may be determined.

Several approaches have been advanced by financial academicians and practitioners. Despite a diversity of proposed methodologies there is general agreement that the cost of capital should be derived from a combination of the different sources of financing used by a firm. A cost of capital is calculated by obtaining the current, after-tax cost of the individual components weighted in accordance with either the company's actual or its normative capital structure. To illustrate:

Source of Financing	Proportion Assigned	After Tax Cost	Weighted Cost
Debt	30%	6%	1.8
Preferred stock	10	10	1.0
Common stock including retained earnings	60	16	9.6
	100%		12.4%

The after-tax cost of the individual components can be determined by a number of different methods. Some of these methods are:

Methods for Computing Cost of Debt

1. Yield divided by actual or imputed market value of current debt adjusted for taxes
2. Incremental after-tax cost of obtaining new debt including flotation costs
3. Current "riskless rate" money costs, plus provisions for decreased purchasing power over term of loan, plus risk factor, plus flotation and administrative costs

Methods for Computing Cost of Equity

1. Reciprocal of average, or latest, price-earnings ratio of common stock based on market values
2. Estimated incremental cost of obtaining new equity including flotation costs
3. Risk-adjusted present value of future dividends and capital gains

Irrespective of which method of calculation is chosen, inflation increases the after-tax cost of the sources of financing. Moreover, over the long run the cost of debt will exceed the inflation rate, and the cost of equity will exceed the cost of debt.

If the cost of capital is based on market values or incremental costs, inflation will be reflected in lower market values. If the cost of capital is based on one of the theoretical models, a rate of inflation will be implicitly included in the calculation of debt costs and reflected in the present value of future cash flows in equity costs.

Operating Planning and Budgeting

The management accounting issues that pertain to operating planning and budgeting are similar to those that apply to strategic planning although the two processes are quite different.

As previously noted, operating plans and budgets differ from strategic plans in that the former usually cover only the current year and are primarily used for performance evaluation. As a result, they are generally detailed in nature, are numbers-oriented, and are organized by responsibility. Strategic plans, on the other hand, typically span over the life of the strategy (three to ten years), are action-oriented, are less detailed than operating plans and

EXHIBIT 6–1

Summary of Key Management Accounting Issues and Options

Resource Allocation Issues   Some Options

Planning or Budgeting

1. Frequency of update   Annually, bi-annually, quarterly, monthly, as required

2. Contents of plans   Income statement, balance sheet, funds statement, statement of distributable funds, trend analysis, productivity measurements, comparison with CPI, GNP deflator or other index

3. Specificity of projections   Single number vs. range forecasts

4. Inflation rate assumptions   Determined centrally, determined by local business unit, not determined

5. Unit of measurement   Nominal (current) dollars, constant dollars, both nominal and constant

6. Currency exchange rate   Determined centrally, determined by local business unit

7. Currency used in plans submitted to corporate headquarters   Local currency, U.S. dollars, both local currency and U.S. dollars

Capital Expenditure Evaluations

8. Measurements used for: Nominal (current) dollars, constant
   a. Amount of expenditure   dollars, partially each way:
   b. Working capital requirements   Constant dollars converted to
   c. Revenue and expense   nominal dollars
      projections   Nominal dollars converted to
   d. Residual values   constant dollars

9. Capital expenditure hurdle rate   Adjusted for inflation, not adjusted for inflation, not used

10. Content of contingency allowance   Provides for inflation, does not provide for inflation

11. Treatment of overseas affiliates   Local currency, U.S. dollars, both
    a. Currency reported   local currency and U.S. dollars
    b. Inflation rate applied   Determined centrally, locally

budgets, and are often organized by strategic business unit rather than by organizational unit.

Despite these differences, both types of plans are ultimately quantified in the form of market forecasts, financial projections, operating forecasts, and the identification of accomplishment milestones.

Operating planning and budgeting involves several inflation-related considerations as to the most appropriate management methodology to employ. For example:

1. How often should plans or budgets be updated in periods of significant inflation?
2. What form should plans and budgets take? What trend analyses, productivity measurements and comparisons with the CPI or other inflation indices should be used, and how should inflation-related information be shown?
3. Should sales and earnings budgets be single-number forecasts or shown in the form of a range?
4. Should inflation rate assumptions be determined centrally or by local business unit?
5. Should financial projections be shown in current (nominal) dollars, constant dollars, or in both current and constant dollars?
6. How should international affiliates be treated? Should currency exchange rates be determined centrally or by the local business unit? Should international affiliates' budgets be submitted in local currencies, U.S. dollars, or in both local currencies and U.S. dollars?
7. What can be done to improve the accuracy of inflation forecasts?

Summary of Key Issues and Options

A summary of key management accounting issues and options pertaining to resource allocation (planning and budgeting and capital expenditure evaluations) is contained in Exhibit 6–1 to help the reader focus on the material that has been discussed in this chapter. The issues and options that pertain to the area that we have defined as management control are discussed in Chapter 7.

Chapter 7

Management Control Issues

The management process is commonly viewed as consisting of a continuous planning and control cycle. In essence, plans are prepared and quantified, actions are taken to execute plans, results are reported in comparison with plan, performance is evaluated, and new plans are prepared and quantified.

In practice, planning and control activities are often performed together, and the distinction between where planning ends and control begins is often difficult to discern. Peter Drucker, for example, includes reporting as part of strategic planning. He says that strategic planning is "the continuous process of making present entrepreneurial (risk-taking) *decisions* systematically and with the greatest knowledge of their futurity; organizing systematically the *efforts* needed to carry out these decisions; and measuring the results of these decisions against expectations through organized, *systematic feedback.*" [1] While management accounting spans the entire process, in real life planning and control often do not break down into nice, neat packages.

Despite the blurred or possibly nonexistent boundaries between planning and control, we thought that it would help the reader consider the inflation-related management accounting issues if we divided them into two categories. Chapter 6 dealt with strategic planning and budgeting issues. The remaining issues have been identified as control issues and are discussed in this chapter. They include the following topics:

1. Product pricing
2. Standard costing
3. Inventory valuation
4. Management reporting and performance evaluation

Product Pricing

In most businesses competition is the primary determinant of product

---

[1] Peter F. Drucker, *Management: Tasks, Responsibilities, Practices,* Harper & Row, 1973, p. 125.

selling prices, and thus supply and demand and the impact of inflation on *competition's* costs probably have more to do with pricing than internal cost increases. Notwithstanding this reality, and the fact that prices are often subject to mandatory or voluntary regulatory constraints, price changes are usually based on judgment, and management accounting practices can have an important impact on how often, and how much, prices are increased.

For example, one controller of a large consumer products company said that while LIFO may not be the best way of valuing inventories and costing products from a conceptual standpoint, he found that it does have a salutory effect on maintaining profit margins at the business unit level. During the course of a discussion of the effects of inflation, another chief financial officer suggested "NIFO" (next in, first out) was even a more appropriate tool to use for costing products for purposes of evaluating selling prices.

The use of the NIFO concept is supported by John Flowers, manager, Corporate Credit and Collection, General Electric Company, who says:

"As a general principle, a seller should strive to place inflation risks with the customers. The idea is not to shortchange the customer, but rather to ensure that the seller receives values commensurate with products delivered . . . this would include basing prices not on FIFO costing and not on LIFO, but on NIFO costing. Pricing on NIFO is merely requesting the customer to restore the purchasing power consumed in fulfilling the order." [2]

One might ponder the impact of setting prices based on product costs that include current costs. Such a practice can add a new perspective to pricing decisions. For example, the principal elements of construction costs are usually materials, labor and equipment. A few large construction companies have placed their equipment into separate leasing subsidiaries that lease the equipment to the operating company for each project at a rate which is based on the equipment's current value. This practice assures that the profit on the equipment resulting from changes in price levels (holding gains) flows to the leasing subsidiary while the operating profit (or loss) is assigned to the project. Other construction companies, and some managers within the companies that follow this practice, object to this approach on the basis that their competitors own their own equipment and price their jobs accordingly. Thus leasing equipment places the lessee in a noncompetitive position if he is competing against an owner who does not appreciate the distinction between operating profit and holding gains.

The issue therefore, is what cost concepts are most appropriately used for product pricing decisions? Are standard costs based on historical data the most useful approach? Or should the concept of current costs (or even

---

[2] John F. Flowers, "Pricing and Payment Terms in an Inflationary Era," *Managing in Inflation*, The Conference Board, 1978, p. 17–18.

NIFO) be introduced to this decision-making process? Higher selling prices resulting from the general use of current costs would, on the one hand, have the effect of assisting with capital formation. On the other hand, the use of current costs in setting prices would tend to heat up the rate of inflation.

Standard Costing

In companies that use standard costs, inflation can have an effect on the development of standards because of the frequent changes that take place in the costs of the individual elements of the cost per unit. Three approaches to this problem are considered:

1. Incorporate inflation expectations for the year into standards that are established for the year. Do not revise standards during the year.
2. Use dual costing. Establish a fixed standard at the beginning of the year for inventory valuation and fiscal reporting purposes, but supplement this standard with current standards.
3. Include only known cost increases in standard costs, but revise standards during the year to reflect subsequent cost changes.

The first alternative is commonly used in a noninflationary environment and is the easiest approach to apply because standards are revised only once a year.

The second alternative is used in Brazil and other countries with chronically high inflation rates. This approach retains the administrative benefits of a base standard and the requirement that all standards be revised only once a year. It also provides for current information for product pricing and management control purposes as required.

The third alternative provides reasonable current product cost information for all items at all times for purposes of product profitability analysis and pricing. It is feasible to employ if the company has up-to-date bills of material, current time standards, and a computer-based system that allows it to recalculate component and product standards based on revisions to unit material costs, labor rates, and burden rates.

Inventory Valuation

In an inflationary environment management is prompted to confront the question whether or not to switch to the LIFO method of valuation. LIFO depresses earnings during periods of inflation by increasing cost of goods sold, but cash is conserved during periods of inflation because of reduced income taxes.

Under LIFO, costs of the latest purchases are the first costs charged to cost of goods sold. Costs of the earliest purchases remain in inventory. During periods of rising prices, the more recent inflated costs are matched with the inflated sales prices.

Though LIFO values can, under FAS No. 33, be used as a surrogate for computing current costs, points of view differ as to the effectiveness of LIFO as an inflation hedge. Herbert C. Knortz, executive vice president & comptroller of International Telephone and Telegraph Corporation, says: "Experience tells me that the only reason people move toward LIFO is to obtain tax advantages. The association of LIFO with inflation is not logically appropriate. Even at best LIFO only tends to improve the income statement by creating an exacerbated balance sheet."[3]

Some have argued that adoption of LIFO is a good adjuster for the effects of inflation, at least for inventory costs. James Don Edwards and John Barrack point out: "In a technical sense, this is a myth. LIFO does not effectively adjust for inflation; it simply postpones recognizing the effects of inflation. However, this postponement may be long term if prices continue to rise over a long period and the inventory is not liquidated."[4]

Ronald Copeland, Joseph Wojdak and John Shank conclude that in periods of rising inflation industry needs LIFO inventory valuation to shelter profits from taxes. They believe that many companies have an excellent opportunity to conserve corporate cash by adopting LIFO. Their conclusion is based on results of a study of the pre-tax corporate profits and profit differences among 20 manufacturing industries.

Size of inventories relative to profits is one of the two variables that significantly affects the size of a profit difference. The higher this ratio, the greater the impact a given change in inventory prices will have on reported profits. The other key is the rate of inventory price changes. By multiplying the average price inflation by the average inventory/profit ratio, one can compute the approximate profit differences in each industry.[5]

LIFO is not always beneficial, and the consequences of the prospective changes should be considered before switching. J. P. Saccone, of Berol Corporation, provides a check list for this purpose that includes the following questions:

"1. Are the inventory costs going to increase over a long period of time?

2. Can management live with the requirements that annual earnings must be

---

[3] Herbert C. Knortz, letter to author.

[4] James Don Edwards and John B. Barrack, "LIFO Inventory Valuation as an Adjuster for Inflation," *CPA*, October 1975, pp. 21–25.

[5] Ronald M. Copeland, Joseph F. Wodjak and John K. Shank, "Use of LIFO to Offset Inflation," *Harvard Business Review*, May-June 1971, pp. 91–100.

reported to the owners and creditors by use of a LIFO method of valuing inventories?

3. Is the company willing to accept the fact that once the election is made, it is locked in until permission to change is granted from the District Director of Internal Revenue?

4. Is the company willing to allow the revenue agent to come in, and during his audit, change the accounts so they reflect what he believes is the true inventory?

5. Is there any possibility that raw materials may be in short supply in the near future?

If the answers to these questions are all 'yes,' the company can seriously consider adopting a LIFO inventory system."[6]

Management Reporting and Performance Evaluation

In response to the question, "How has inflation affected your internal management reporting practices?", one financial executive replied, "Wrecked them!" While this may be an overstatement, the distortions caused by inflation have added a new dimension to management reporting and performance evaluation. There are at least six areas where inflation should be considered:

1. *Trend analyses* of revenues, costs, expenses and profitability by separating the inflationary component from dollar volume.
2. *Profitability reporting* by basing cost of sales on LIFO (or other current costs), depreciation on net replacement costs, identifying holding gains and losses, and by computing returns based on current costs or using constant dollars to measure business unit performance.
3. *Variance analysis* by separating the inflation component from the actual results reported or comparing actual results with a price-level adjusted flexible budget.
4. *Funds management* by placing increasing emphasis on funds flow.
5. *Productivity improvement* by developing measures of productivity for each business unit.
6. *Management incentive compensation* by basing incentives on inflation-adjusted performance measurements or funds flow.

Possibilities pertaining to each of these areas will be discussed in the remainder of this chapter.

---

[6] J.P. Saccone, "LIFO Fundamentals," *Management Accounting*, February 1976, p. 29.

Trend Analyses

It is a relatively easy task to compare historical results by business unit with the consumer price index, or some other more appropriate index, over a period of, say, five to ten years. This information can be presented in either a chart or tabular form although many companies have found charted information to be the more effective alternative. Such charts and tables offer the advantage of separating real growth from inflationary growth, thus providing a more meaningful perspective of growth trends.

The most perplexing problems connected with trend analyses seem to concern the determination of methodology used to separate real and inflationary growth and the selection of the most appropriate index to be applied. For example, should a measurement of the general price level be used, or would a specific cost measurement be better? Should actual results be restated in constant dollars or just simply compared with an inflation index? While the ideal solution may not be readily apparent, many companies have found that even a rough analysis is better than none because either approach calls attention to the fact that much reported historic growth is illusory.

Profitability Reporting

A principal issue in the area of profitability reporting is determining how profits should be reported by business unit and for the corporation for *internal* purposes. Should historical cost information be used exclusively, or should this information be adjusted to reflect current costs? If current cost information is used, should it be shown on the primary income statement or in some sort of supplementary schedule?

FAS No. 33 and the British approach provide models for adjusting internal historical results for inflation. It is noteworthy that both models make adjustments for inflation on a supplementary basis rather than as a substitute for historic costs. For example, inflation-adjusted profit contribution information might be presented by business unit (in comparison with other business units or plan) in the following manner:

Profit contribution based on historical costs	$500,000
Current cost adjustments:	
Depreciation	(70,000)
Cost of Sales	(40,000)
Current cost profit contribution	$390,000
Current cost contribution % historical cost	78.0%
Increase in value of net assets held	150,000
Net economic gain before taxation	$540,000

Experience in the United States with such restatements has been mixed. Lever Brothers applies this approach,[7] but our earlier research for the Financial Executives Research Foundation indicated that current cost information was really not being used by line management at Lever Brothers.

Carrying the concepts of reporting profitability on a current cost one step further, it is also possible to calculate returns on net assets employed on a current cost basis by business unit. As we said, the data base for this calculation will be available by business unit for many large companies in connection with complying with FAS No. 33. Return information might look something like this:

	Historical Cost Information	Current Cost Information
Net assets employed	$2,500,000	$4,500,000
Return		
Profit contribution	$ 500,000	$ 390,000
Increase in value of net assets held		150,000
Net economic gain	$ 500,000	$ 540,000
% Return on net assets		
Profit contribution	20.0	8.7
Increase in value of net assets held		3.3
Net economic gain	20.0	12.0

Similarly it is possible to restate business unit results on a constant dollar basis.

Many management accountants do not perceive that such information has much value except possibly from a strategic planning standpoint. For example, Louis Peloubet, controller of Union Carbide Corporation, states: "It is argued that calculating returns on a current cost basis would give a more accurate picture of where the firm's profitability really lies. Those areas within the company where yields fall below a certain standard might then be discontinued, divested or de-emphasized. Costs would certainly be shifted from divisions with lower proportions of fixed assets to those with greater proportions, but it is not clear what decisions would be made differently."[8]

---

[7] A. H. Seed, *Inflation: Its Impact on Financial Reporting and Decision Making*, Financial Executives Research Foundation, 1978, pp. 73–76.

[8] Louis G. Peloubet, "Adjusting Internal Reporting for Inflation," *Managing in Inflation*, The Conference Board, 1978, pp. 21–25.

Variance Analysis

Variance analyses are prepared in many companies to account for differences between actual and budgeted results. Sometimes such analyses are also prepared to account for differences between results of a current period and those of a prior period. The primary components of a typical analysis for a business unit are illustrated below:

Actual profit contribution	$127,000
Budgeted profit contribution	100,000
Variance in profit	$ 27,000
Analysis of variance in profit:	
Sales volume	$ 10,000
Sales price	6,000
Sales mix	(2,000)
Production performance (efficiency)	1,000
Costs and expenses	12,000
Variance in profit	$ 27,000

Inflation can have a significant impact on the sales prices, and cost and expense (price and cost) components of this analysis. Some price and cost variances such as basic materials and unit energy costs are caused by changes in the general price level and specific price changes which are beyond the control of management. Other price and cost variances such as product prices and internal labor rates are partially subject to management control. Because externalities have an important impact on business performance beyond the control of business unit managers, effective performance measurement suggests that business unit managers not be put in a position of being able to take credit for performance when inflation flows in their favor and to blame inflation for adverse performance.

Three methods might be considered for separating the noncontrollable impact of inflation from controllable operating results.

The first method is to identify the inflation component in the actual results reported. This is done by measuring the difference between assumed and actual price levels by: calculating total selling price, or cost and expense variances, as the case may be; determining the noncontrollable component of this variance by calculating the difference between assumed and actual price levels (indices); and identifying by elimination the remaining price, cost or expense variance as being controllable.

The resulting separation of controllable operating variance from noncontrollable inflation-induced variances is illustrated on the next page.

Controllable Variances:

Sales volume	$10,000
Sales price based on difference between specific prices and general price level	8,000
Sales mix vs. forecast	(2,000)
Production efficiency vs. standard	2,500
Productivity improvements vs. plan	(1,500)
Costs and expense based on difference between specific prices and general price level	2,000
Total controllable variance	$20,000

Noncontrollable Variance

General price level based on differences between actual and assumed inflation rates	7,000
Total noncontrollable variance	$ 7,000
Total variance in profit	$27,000

The second method has been referred to as a "price adjusted flexible budget."[9] This concept requires that the budget, not actual results, be adjusted for changes in price levels. The budget is first modified for volume to provide a flexible budget, a procedure with which most management accountants are familiar. The second step is to "flex" the budget for the change in price level by a factor calculated by dividing actual material supply costs by actual issues at budget price. The result is a new budget that has been adjusted for noncontrollable changes in material costs.

The third method is to analyze the impact of inflation on a supplementary basis. The supplementary analysis method, as described by Kentbourne McFarlane of Corning Glassworks, involves the following five steps:

1. Calculate the inflation rate of each component of cost (percentage of change in year-to-date cost to base cost).
2. Calculate the weight for each component of cost (ratio of year-to-date component unit costs to total cost).
3. Determine the percentage of product inflation. (Summarize inflation rate of cost component times weight of component unit cost in product.)
4. Determine amount of impact of inflation by component of product for period. (Multiply percentage component inflation by year-to-date unit costs of products produced.)
5. Determine dollar for product or plant. (Summarize impact of inflation by component of product by product or plant.)

---

[9] D.I. MacGibbon, "Why Not Price Adjust Your Budget?", *The Australian Accountant,* November 1979, pp. 686–687.

This methodology provides a period-by-period evaluation of the effect of each component of inflation on each product line (percentage of cost and amount).[10]

Funds Management

Our experience has shown that many companies are placing increasing emphasis on managing the flow of funds. This emphasis began with the credit crunch of 1974 and has tended to increase as inflation has increased. As the relative value of cash to an enterprise increases, funds statements are becoming more widely used at the business unit level. This is not to suggest that the income statement is being replaced by the funds statement, but the latter is certainly gaining in importance.

The emphasis on funds management follows from the principle that the present value of future cash flow is the best measure of economic worth. Similarly, strategic planning, capital expenditure evaluation and financial analysis methodologies are now generally oriented towards the measurement of the present value of the future cash flow.

Operating managers have also recognized that profitability measurement is not enough. Managers struggle with programs for cash management, inventory management, and other forms of asset management. Profitability management coupled with asset management in effect amounts to funds management because funds management combines the management of the components of net income with the management of the elements of the balance sheet.

The statement of changes in financial position (funds statement) prescribed by APB No. 19 is the accepted primary financial statement for measuring the flow of funds. Unfortunately, this document is often oriented for external reporting purposes and is not structured in a way that is useful from a management accounting standpoint.

The funds statement is usually reconciled to changes in working capital rather than cash. Working capital is an arbitrary accounting term, whereas many managers think in terms of cash and specific balance sheet items. Furthermore, funds provided by or required for operating purposes and controlled at the business unit level are not distinguished from financial sources and uses of funds, which are controlled at the corporate level. One of the requirements of effective management reporting is to separate results by area of responsibility. A statement that combines data controlled at the corporate level with data controlled at the operating level falls short of meeting this requirement.

---

[10]Kentbourne A.W. McFarlane, "Tracking Inflation in Your Company," *Management Accounting,* May 1979, pp. 42–45.

How should the funds statement be structured? Several academicians and practitioners, including this author, have addressed the issue. The author suggests the format shown in Exhibit 7–1. [11]

EXHIBIT 7–1

Restructured Funds Statement
(Thousands of Dollars)

Funds generated from internal operations		
Profit after taxes	$500	
Depreciation	220	
Cash flow		$720
Decrease in receivables		150
Decrease in inventories		200
Funds generated internally		$1,070
Funds generated from financial sources		
Increase in long-term debt		$400
Income taxes deferred		100
Decrease in prepaid expense		20
Funds from financial sources		520
Total funds available		$1,590
Funds invested, paid out and distributed		
Additions of property, plant and equipment		$700
Investments		200
Decrease in accounts payable		40
Decrease in current liabilities		10
Dividends		240
Total investments, repayments and distributions		1,190
Increase in cash		$ 400

Alfred Rappaport suggests that the distributable funds measurement is a useful approach to financial analysis in an inflationary environment. [12] This concept is based on the premise that a going concern perpetuates itself in business and has distributable funds available only after it makes provision to maintain that portion of its operating capability (business capacity) financed by equity. Distributable funds represent the maximum amount that the company can distribute to its stockholders during a period without im-

---

[11] Allen H. Seed, III, "Utilizing the Funds Statement," *Management Accounting,* May 1976, p. 17.

[12] Alfred Rappaport, "Measuring Company Growth Capacity During Inflation," *Harvard Business Review,* January–February 1979, pp. 91–100.

pairing its business capacity. This approach requires three measurements to arrive at distributable funds:

1. Funds required for increases in costs of productive capacity
2. Funds required for increases in net working capital
3. Funds available from increased debt capacity

Dividends are subtracted from distributable funds to arrive at funds available for expansion.

Productivity Measurements

Improving productivity is essential for controlling inflation because, according to the neo-Keynesians, one of the primary forces that creates inflation is the failure of productivity increases to offset increases in costs. In simple terms increased productivity is achieved through technological improvement and people working longer and harder. Regrettably, the latter ingredient appears to run counter to the social and cultural aspirations of many workers.

Henry Wilson, in an article for British *Management Accounting,* says: "There is an increasing need to measure manpower productivity, not in a limited sense of efficiency on the job, but in an overall sense within the economic environment of a business. This need arises partly from inflation and its effect on prices and pay demand, and from a social view that payment of employees should, in some way, be related to their total contribution in their organization." [13]

Arthur Andersen Partner James Ksansnak points out that a better knowledge of productivity in a company helps isolate the causal effects of productivity changes versus inflation in explaining profit trends. "There are three areas involved. The influence of inflation on cost rates and prices must be distinguished. The utilization of capacity, particularly in capital-intensive industries, has had an important bearing on productivity and profits. Finally, the efficiency and effectiveness with which people perform can have great impact on company growth." [14]

Many companies seek to improve productivity in order to enhance their competitive position and profitability. Indeed, there is usually general agreement that this is a desirable goal. However, our experience indicates that managers have varying perceptions of what productivity is and how it is

---

[13] Henry A.V. Wilson, "Added Value in Measuring Manpower Productivity," *Management Accounting,* (British), June 1971, pp. 168–170.

[14] James E. Ksansnak, "Measuring Productivity," *Management Planning,* December 1974, pp. 15–20, 34.

measured. An ability to measure productivity is important because measurements are needed to determine whether or not productivity goals are being achieved.

Productivity is often confused with performance measurement. The former is a measure of price level adjusted outputs divided by inputs. The latter is a measure of operating efficiency—e.g., standard man-hours divided by actual man-hours or standard yield divided by actual yield. While performance measurement is an element of productivity, it is not the same as productivity.

There are two kinds of productivity: total productivity and partial productivity. Total productivity is defined as total output divided by total input. Outputs of a firm are the number of units of physical volume, such as pieces, tons, feet or number of cars, *produced* by a firm in a given period. Inputs are ordinarily labor, capital, raw material, purchased parts and other miscellaneous goods and services. Partial productivity is total output divided by partial input. A familiar example is the output per man-hour ratio often called the labor productivity index.

Value added per man-hour is another partial productivity measurement. This measurement is based on the concept that value is added to products based on the expenditure of labor. A value-added ratio is therefore calculated by dividing the sales value of production, less materials consumed, by the number of man-hours expended to provide the production. This ratio is, of course, influenced by changes in price levels, product mix and capital investments as well as by the efficiency of labor.

The issue of incremental productivity might also be considered. If productivity increases, what caused the increase—the addition of capital (e.g., through the purchase of labor saving equipment) or labor efficiency? The answer to this question is difficult to determine because changes in productivity are usually based on both the expenditure of capital and the labor efficiency.

Effective productivity measurement requires that all inputs and outputs of a firm be stated in a common measurement unit (e.g., constant dollars). If constant dollars are used, all outputs for any year after (and including) the base year should be stated in base-year dollars. Economists refer to this restatement procedure as deflating the output and input factor.

Outputs are difficult to measure in many companies because they produce multiple product lines with different values and units of measure. One approach to the multiple product line problem is to assign a weighted value to each product line based on its relative selling price during a normal base year. Computing a weighted value requires selecting a base unit and factoring every other unit in relation to this base unit. Another approach is to ignore changes in product mix on the premise that changes in product mix reflect changes in productivity.

Output measurement is further complicated by the fact that even though outputs may have similar selling prices, they may offer different values in terms of quality and levels of service. Accordingly, some companies (such as Inland Steel) use output measurements that incorporate qualitative factors (e.g., shipping performance) as well as monetary factors.

Outputs are supposed to be based on the value of production rather than the value of sales. Sales should therefore be adjusted to reflect changes in the level of inventories between the beginning and end of the period. In the interest of simplicity, however, some companies (including GE) disregard the distinction between the value of sales and production and consider sales to reflect outputs.

Inputs (labor, capital, raw materials and purchased parts, etc.) are somewhat easier to deal with than outputs. The primary unit of labor, often a key input, is man-hours worked. Man-hours must be converted into dollars by multiplying total man-hours by an appropriate wage rate. The physical units of raw materials and purchased parts are tons, pieces, gallons, etc., which are multiplied by base-year material prices. Interest payments are not considered as an input. Historical depreciation generally is used as an approximation of the capital consumed in the production process. However, current cost depreciation or annuity values calculated for each asset on the basis of its base-year cost, productive life, and the firm's cost of capital, may be better measures. [15]

Donald Wait, of General Electric Company and chairman of the Subcommittee on Productivity of the Management Accounting Practices Committee of NAA, points out that the more one analyzes the subject the more problems appear to arise. He believes that an overall measure would be useful in many firms, but he suggests that the following questions be considered in the selection of productivity measurements:

"1. How complex a measure is needed or desired?
2. How will the impact of major resources be delineated?
3. How will the top level measures be tied to measures in operating functional components?
4. How will the measures be tied to profitability measures?
5. How are changes in capacity utilization to be reflected?
6. How are changes in the qualitative characteristics of products to be reflected?" [16]

Productivity measurements have often been considered the province of economists and industrial engineers. However, there are substantive meas-

---

[15] Charles E. Craig and R. Clark Harris, "Total Productivity Measurement at the Firm Level," *Sloan Management Review,* Spring 1973, pp. 13–27.

[16] Donald J. Wait, "Productivity Measurement: A Management Challenge," *Management Accounting,* May 1980, pp. 24–30.

urement issues that are clearly involved in the field of management accounting. If inflation continues, these issues will become increasingly important. Moreover, current management accounting practices usually require that management information systems contain the whole story and not be strictly relegated to the traditional financial books of account. Thus, it is desirable that management accountants familiarize themselves with the issues involved in the measurement of productivity and participate in the development of such measurements.

Management Incentive Compensation

Some commentators have implied that one of the reasons that business leaders have been slow to embrace inflation accounting techniques is that they fear that the application of these techniques will have an adverse effect on their compensation. For example, management consultant John G. Main says: "Management myopia in this area is caused by the entrenched position of historically based accounting. Not only is an intellectual wrench involved, but there are also functional reasons for executives' resistance—not the least of which is that compensation incentive structures are based on historical accounting, which in many firms drastically overstates management's achievements and inflates the rewards."[17] Despite Main's views, in our opinion it is also appropriate to suggest that financial executives and accountants resist inflation accounting because they think that historical cost models well serve their firm, they do not understand the newer concepts, and they do not really believe that inflation is here to stay.

Irrespective of what motivations are involved, inflation *does* distort historical results. The management accounting issue, in this instance, is the question of what to do about this distortion with respect to management incentive compensation.

One approach is to base management incentive compensation on profitability based on current costs. This approach offers the advantage of adjusting for inflation, but the disadvantage of linking the managers' compensation to inflation-influenced factors that they cannot control.

Another approach is to eliminate from all incentive compensation calculations the noncontrollable general price level variance referred to earlier in this chapter. In this case the manager would be compensated based on controllable factors, but these results are, by their nature, somewhat subjective in their derivation.

A third approach is to link incentive compensation to funds flow. This approach removes the influence of historical depreciation and focuses atten-

---

[17]John G. Main, "Inflation and Corporate Strategy: The Rashomon Effect," *Management Review*, May 1980, pp. 23–37.

EXHIBIT 7–2

Summary of Key Management Accounting Issues and Options

Management Control Issues	Some Options
Product Pricing	
1. Basis of operating costs for price and profitability analysis	Historical cost, LIFO or NIFO
2. Basis of depreciation	Historical cost, current cost
Standard Cost Accounting	
3. Standard revisions	Annually, semi-annually, as required
4. Contents of standard costs	Current costs, known cost increases, estimated cost increases
5. Methodology applied	Fixed standard, current standard, dual standards
Inventory Valuation	
6. Methodology applied	LIFO, FIFO, average cost
Management Reporting	
7. Trend analyses	Measure in constant dollars, compare with price index, select index
8. Return on investment	Adjust profit and/or investment for current cost; compute in constant dollars
9. Variance analysis	Eliminate inflation variance from actual results, eliminate inflation from budget, analyze impact of inflation on supplementary basis
10. Funds management	Separate funds flow by responsibility, reconcile to cash
11. Productivity measurement a. How measured	Total productivity, partial productivity, other measurements
b. Outputs	Constant dollars, physical units of measurement
c. Inputs	Man-hours, deflated labor costs, depreciation, annuity values of capital
Executive Compensation	
12. Executive compensation	Base on inflation-adjusted results; link to funds flow; or achievement of strategic objectives

tion on asset management. Interestingly, up to half of General Electric's key managers' incentive compensation is reportedly currently based on funds flow.

A fourth approach is to link incentive compensation to the achievement of quantitative strategic objectives (such as market position and new-product introductions). This approach tends to focus attention on the attainment of longer-term strategic objectives rather than shorter-term financial measurements that can be distorted by inflation. Santa Fe Industries and others have reportedly employed this concept.

Summary of Key Issues and Options

A summary of the key management issues and options discussed in this chapter is shown in Exhibit 7–2. Our next chapter describes the actual practices employed by 282 corporations in dealing with the issues that we have discussed.

Chapter 8

Planning and Control Practices

Inflation has not had a substantial impact on internal planning and control practices in the United States. While controls have been tightened and the focus of certain practices has shifted in many companies, new management accounting methodologies have not been employed to deal with inflation to any significant extent.

Many companies have switched to LIFO inventory valuation, capital expenditure hurdle rates have been increased, and increasing emphasis has been placed on the measurement and management of funds flow and productivity. Nevertheless, current cost and constant dollar accounting concepts such as those prescribed by FAS No. 33 have not been widely embraced for internal planning and control. This is the essence of the findings obtained from 282 responses to a questionnaire that was mailed to the chief financial executives of the 1,000 largest industrial companies listed in *Fortune* magazine.

Profile of Respondents

A letter and questionnaire (shown in the Appendix, pp. 229–239), with a self-addressed, stamped envelope, were mailed on March 31, 1980, to the chief financial executives of the *Fortune* 1,000 companies. The researchers received 282 responses (28% response rate) from this mailing.

Fifty-four percent of the replies came from industrial product manufacturers, 26% from manufacturers of consumer products, and 5% from oil and gas companies. Thus this extensive sample primarily involves the practices of large manufacturing companies. Practices of utility, financial service, retailing and transportation companies, and smaller companies, may vary from these large manufacturers, but we have no evidence to suggest that they do.

The median dimensions of the respondents were revenues of $590 million and total assets of $385 million for the latest fiscal year. The largest respondent had revenues of $85 billion and total assets of $49 billion. The smallest respondent had revenues of $50 million and total assets of $35 million. Replies were analyzed by size of company (larger or smaller than mean revenues and total assets).

Capital turnover rates (revenues divided by total assets) provide a measure of the capital intensity of each business. The median capital turnover rate of the respondents was about 1.5. Responses from companies with a relatively high capital intensity (lower than median capital turnover rate) were compared to those responses with a low capital intensity (higher than median capital turnover rate).

In comparing the responses from large and small or capital-intensive and nonintensive companies, we broke the entire group into two divisions— those above and below the median. This provided us with equal-sized samples in which we could examine differences in reported management accounting practices. Using the Chi-square statistic, we examined the differences between groups to determine whether practices varied by size and capital intensity to a degree that was statistically significant. Given the equal sample size with approximately one-half the respondents in each group, differences in the percentage response to questions on management accounting practices of around 10% between groups were generally statistically significant at the 90–95% level.

Most of the revenues of these companies were derived, and the assets were located, in the United States where inflation rates have been moderate in relation to certain other parts of the world. Forty-five percent of the respondents said that the approximate percent of revenues outside the United States was under 10%, and only 3% said that they were over 50%. Fifty percent of the respondents said that less than 10% of their total assets were outside of the United States, and only 2% said they were over 50%. Ninety-two percent of the respondents said that under 10% of their total assets were located in countries with inflation rates in excess of 30% per year (e.g., parts of South America). The practices of the companies that derive 30% or more of their revenues or have 30% or more of their assets outside the United States were analyzed separately.

Inflation Expectations

U.S. chief financial executives as a group seem to expect inflation (as measured by the Consumer Price Index) to subside. Ninety-eight percent of the respondents said that they expect the CPI increase to exceed 10% in 1980. This 98% drops to 63% in 1981 and 23% in 1985. Conversely 1% of the respondents expected a single-digit inflation rate in 1980, whereas 36% expect the CPI increase to be less than 10% in 1981, and 76% expect the CPI increase to be less than 10% in 1985. We found these inflation expectations to be consistent across the group as a whole, with no significant difference by size, capital intensity, industry or degree of foreign operations.

While the preceding pattern of responses reflects a disbelief that double-digit inflation is here to stay, we do not know the reason for this expectation. It may be caused by the anticipated impact of the current business recession and/or it may reflect confidence that governmental actions to stem inflation will be effective. On the other hand, a drop in the inflation rate expectation may reflect a degree of simple, blind optimism. The expectation that inflation will decline is borne out by the status of the long-term debt market where interest rates on long-term debt were, at the time of our survey, lower than the prime bank borrowing rate or the yield on short-term money market certificates. [1]

Decreased inflation expectations may partially account for why most financial and accounting executives are not employing constant dollar and current cost inflation accounting methodologies for internal planning and control purposes. Despite the expectation that inflation rates will decline to single-digit levels by 1985, it is interesting to note that only 3% of the respondents said that they expect this rate to be less than 5% by 1985. Such information suggests that most financial executives believe that inflation will be institutionalized somewhere in the 5% to 9% range.

As has been previously discussed, price levels of different elements of revenues and expense increase at different rates. These differences are supported by the replies that we received to the question, "For your company, do you expect the following rates of change of average prices to be higher, lower, or approximately the same as the Consumer Price Index?"

The predominant pattern of responses here suggests that for their company financial executives expect selling prices to increase at lower rates than the CPI; labor (including fringes), material, service, plant and equipment and tax costs to increase at about the same rate as the CPI; and energy costs to continue to increase at a higher rate than the CPI. Indeed, 88% of the respondents anticipate the energy cost increases will be higher than the CPI.

One exception to the general pattern is that most oil and gas companies expect their selling prices to rise faster than the CPI, consistent with the increase in energy costs expected by most respondents, including the oil and gas companies.

To the extent that one business's selling prices are another business's costs, the expectation that most costs will match the CPI is inconsistent with the expectation that selling prices will be less than the CPI. However, this imbalance could reflect expectations of a lag in selling prices of consumer products, improved productivity, or reduced profit margins. It could also

---

[1] In an inflation-free environment, prevailing interest rates on long-term debt are traditionally higher than those on short-term debt because of the additional risk entailed in the longer maturities.

reflect a psychological reluctance to believe that cost increases will be passed on in the form of higher selling prices.

Inflation expectation information is obtained from diverse sources. Twenty-six percent of the respondents do not assign responsibility for developing inflation expectations, 18% look to the planning manager, 16% rely on a corporate economist and 11% look to the treasurer. The controller is responsible for determining inflation expectations in only 4% of the cases.

Oil and gas companies and other large companies rely much more heavily on corporate economists than the total group of respondents. Fifty-seven percent of the oil and gas companies use a corporate economist to develop inflation expectations. The group of high revenue companies relies on corporate economists in 32% of the cases, with responsibility not assigned in 2% of the cases. For the smaller revenue group only 19% used economists, and in 33% of the cases the responsibility was not assigned.

Financial Strategies

Corporate financial strategies have apparently been affected by inflation only to a limited extent. Most respondents (63%) reported that capital expenditure hurdle rates had been increased because of inflation, and many respondents (46%) said that the timing of capital expenditures for cost reduction had been accelerated because of inflation.

Thirty-eight percent of the respondents said that short-term borrowing had increased because of inflation, and 31% said that long-term borrowing has increased. These figures probably reflect the impact of increased capital equipment replacement costs and the advantage of increasing monetary liabilities in an inflationary environment.

Thirty-six percent of the respondents reported increased dividend payments per share because of inflation, and only 9% of the respondents reported that dividend payments as a percentage of earnings increased. Most companies' dividend policies, it seems, are largely unaffected by inflation. As illustrated in Chapter 6, increased capital equipment replacement costs have surely impaired the ability of many companies to increase dividend payments as a percentage of earnings.

Most companies also reported that leasing, equity financing, corporate acquisitions and long-term purchase contracts are largely unaffected by inflation. Some writers have suggested that corporate acquisitions are stimulated by inflation because facilities can often be acquired less expensively through a corporate acquisition than they can be obtained by building new facilities. However, our sample showed that inflation has increased corporate acquisition activity in 7% of the cases, decreased it in 20% of the cases, and has not affected it in 69% of the cases.

Companies with high capital turnover rates were more inclined to increase short-term borrowing because of inflation than those with low capital turnover: 42% of the former increased activity as compared with 32% of the latter. Companies with low capital turnover were, however, more inclined to increase long-term debt, with 34% reporting increases as opposed to 28% in companies with high capital turnover. Companies with high capital turnover rates often have greater liquidity than companies with low turnover rates and are therefore better able to repay short-term debt. Capital-intensive companies (with low capital turnover rates) usually have substantial fixed assets and it is often more common for them to tend to borrow long than short.

Oil and gas companies, who have reported substantially increased earnings in this inflationary environment, differed from the group as a whole in several financial strategies. Leasing increased in 29% of oil and gas companies as compared to 18% of the group as a whole. Dividend payment per share followed profitability, increasing in 71% of oil and gas companies as opposed to 36% for the group as a whole. Similarly, the timing of capital expenditures for capacity was accelerated in 43% of the oil and gas companies as opposed to 19% overall. The differences between the oil and gas companies and the total of all respondents are probably accounted for by the above-average financial performance of the oil and gas companies.

Companies with heavy foreign operations were less inclined to accelerate capital expenditures than the group as a whole, with 14% accelerating capacity expenditures as opposed to 19% overall, and 29% accelerating cost reduction expenditures compared with 47% overall. The decreased impact on the capital expenditure programs of multinational companies as compared to all respondents may reflect a perception of increased worldwide business, political and financial risk, depressed economic conditions overseas, or a reduced financial capacity to accelerate capital expenditures.

Large companies, with sales higher than the median, were more apt to increase the capital expenditure hurdle rate than smaller companies. Sixty-nine percent of the high revenue companies increased their rate as opposed to 57% of the low revenue companies. This difference between larger and smaller companies may reflect a greater sophistication in the practices of larger companies.

Management Incentive Compensation

While 81% of the respondents said that management compensation is *not* based on inflation-adjusted performance measurements, 11% said that it was, and another 5% said that they were planning to apply this practice. Oil and gas companies proved an exception, as 43% either use, or plan to use, inflation-adjusted performance measures for management compensation.

Eighteen percent of the respondents said that management incentive compensation is based on cash flow, and another 5% of the respondents also said that they were planning to apply this practice. Basing incentives on cash flow focuses attention on asset management as well as removes the effect of recorded depreciation on incentive compensation.

Planning and Budgeting

The practice of planning and budgeting operations is indeed widely applied although the overwhelming acceptance of these practices can probably not be attributed to inflation. Ninety-eight percent of the respondents prepare strategic or long-range plans, and all respondents prepare current-year profit plans or budgets.

The most common practice appears to be to update strategic or long-range plans annually (75%). Only 15% of the respondents update strategic plans "as required." Budgets or profit plans are most commonly updated quarterly (39%) although of the respondents, 26% update budgets annually, 17% monthly, and 11% twice a year.

Strategic plans and budgets ordinarily contain an income statement, and balance sheet or statement of net assets. Surprisingly, however, 76% of the strategic plans and 88% of the budgets also contain a funds statement. The funds statement is a relatively recent development in the field of management accounting. In 1974 we conducted an informal survey of the practices of several companies and found that few companies used the funds statement for internal purposes. Although funds statements had been discussed in accounting textbooks for many years, they were not used generally. The widespread use of the funds statement reported by our respondents, therefore, apparently reflects a substantial change in practice.

Also surprisingly, because again the methodology is relatively new, a statement of distributable funds is prepared by 27% of the respondents in connection with strategic planning and by 32% of the respondents in connection with budgeting. Companies with revenues above the median and companies with high capital intensity were more likely to prepare statements of distributable funds, in 35% and 37% of the cases respectively for budgeting.[2]

Trend or ratio analyses are included in over 60% of the plans. Productivity measurements are included in strategic plans by 32% of the respondents and in budgets by 40% of the respondents. Companies with heavy foreign operations also place more emphasis on distributable funds and trend analysis, with 40% and 72% reporting their use, respectively. Companies with higher than median revenues are more likely to emphasize pro-

---

[2] It may be that this question was misunderstood and that respondents confused the term "funds statement" with the statement of distributable funds.

ductivity measurement, with 48% including them in the budgeting process. Twenty-six percent of these large companies also compare results with the CPI, as opposed to 9% of the smaller companies.

The vast majority of budgets (88%) and most strategic plans (58%) are in the form of single number ("best estimate") forecasts although a substantial portion (38%) of strategic plans are prepared on a hi-low range basis.

Inflation rates are ordinarily determined centrally, and financial projections are ordinarily shown in nominal dollars adjusted for inflation. Sixty-eight percent of the respondents said that inflation rate assumptions are determined centrally for budgeting purposes, and 67% said that they were determined centrally for strategic planning purposes. Fifty-eight percent said that nominal dollars are used for budgets, and 45% said that they were used for strategic plans. However, a substantial number of strategic plans (48%) and budgets (39%) contain constant dollar information either in addition to, or in lieu of, nominal dollars. Only 25% of the respondents said that they prepared strategic plans in both nominal and constant dollars and only 16% said that they prepare budgets both ways. Despite the relatively small proportion of respondents embracing this practice, as discussed in Chapter 14, preparing budgets both ways may be the most effective method of isolating the effect of inflation in the planning process.

All but one of the high-revenue companies prepared a strategic plan, and most prepared them annually. While the smaller revenue group also prepared strategic plans, many more of them were on an "as required" basis. The plans of the larger companies were generally more sophisticated than those of the smaller companies. Larger companies tended to place more emphasis on productivity and comparisons with the CPI or other inflation indices. Capital-intensive companies and large companies were more inclined to forecast in nominal dollars than smaller companies, who tended to use the less sophisticated and more easily applied constant dollar technique.

Currency exchange rates for international facilities are usually determined centrally, and the most common practice is to submit the plans of international affiliates to corporate headquarters in both the local currency and U.S. dollars. The practice of viewing plans and budgets in both the local currency and U.S. dollars reflects a need to view operations from two perspectives: local currencies for local resource allocation and performance evaluation, and U.S. dollars for corporate resource allocation and performance evaluation.

The preceding information coupled with the comments that we received in answers to the question, "What is the most important change that has been made in your planning and budgeting process as a result of inflation?", suggest that the most common impacts of inflation on the planning and budgeting process are:

1. Increased capital expenditure hurdle rates

2. Greater emphasis on funds planning and management
3. More frequent updates of plans and budgets and shortened planning horizons
4. More intensive review of plans, profit margins and prices
5. Increased uncertainty and more "what if" planning
6. Confusion as to how to project the rate of inflation
7. Some greater emphasis on "real growth," constant dollar comparisons, ratios, and productivity measurements

Capital Expenditures

The most commonly applied methodologies for evaluating capital expenditures are to include an allowance for inflation in the amount of the capital expenditure, include an allowance for inflation in the revenue and expense projections used to support the request, and allow for inflation in determining the cost of capital, but to ignore inflation in the calculation of residual values. Seventy-six percent of respondents allow for inflation in the amount of the capital expenditure, 65% of respondents allow for it in revenue and expense projections, and 50% of respondents include inflation in the cost of capital, but only 38% of respondents include inflation in the determination of residual values.

The practice of not adjusting residual values for inflation appears to be inconsistent with the prevailing practices of allowing for inflation in the other components of cash flow. Inflation certainly makes a difference in these residual value amounts as the appreciation of airplanes, real estate, and other items illustrates. Perhaps the prevailing practice of not adjusting residual values for inflation stems from the uncertain amounts involved, the relatively small impact of far-off future values discounted to the present, and the fact that financial conservatism prevails in many companies.

A significant number of companies (43% of respondents) are adjusting or considering adjusting the projected cash flow for projects to units of constant purchasing power. This entails restating (deflating) projected nominal dollars into constant dollars.

Both firms with significant foreign components and larger firms tend to adjust capital expenditure requests to include inflation to a greater degree than smaller companies, as 68% and 71% of the companies, respectively, have applied the practice on a long-standing basis. Expense and revenue projections in nominal dollars are more prevalent in oil and gas companies, companies with significant foreign investments, and larger companies.

Oil and gas companies, larger companies and those with significant foreign elements have long included inflation in the cost of capital (50%, 38% and 45%, respectively, compared to 33% overall). Smaller companies tend to budget an unallocated allowance for inflation at a higher rate than the average of all respondents (16% vs. 12%). This difference may be caused by the fact that oil and gas companies, large companies, and multinational companies have a greater stake in developing sophisticated capital expenditure evaluation methodologies than smaller companies.

Overseas investments by U.S. companies are most commonly evaluated in both local currency and U.S. dollars, and by using both the local and U.S. income tax rate. Despite the debate that we have encountered in many companies as to which path to follow, these prevailing practices seem to be consistent with the underlying financial and economic realities of overseas expenditures which must meet both local and corporate criteria.

Standard Costs

Standard costs are being revised more frequently as the result of inflation, and the impact of inflation is ordinarily reflected in standards. Seventy-nine percent of all respondents reported using standard costs. Most companies (57% of the companies that use standard costs) still revise standards annually though many companies (32% of the companies that use standard costs) revise them as required. Forty-six percent of the companies that use standard costs said that they revise standard costs more frequently as the result of inflation. Fifty-four percent of the companies that use standard costs said that they reflect cost increases resulting from inflation in standard costs on an anticipated basis, and 88% said that cost increases are included in standard costs when known.

In most cases (47% of the companies that use standard costs), standard costs are fixed for the year, but in 30% of the cases a current standard[3] is used, and in 22% of the cases dual standards are used. As discussed in Chapter 7, dual standards usually consist of a fixed standard for fiscal accounting purposes and a current standard for control purposes. The difference between the two standards is usually recorded as an adjustment to cost of sales.

Inventory Valuation

LIFO has become the predominant method for valuing inventories in large manufacturing companies in the United States. As a vice president of a leading bank commented during an interview: "We get a little concerned nowadays when a company is not reporting on a LIFO basis."[4] Sixty-one

---

[3] There is probably not much difference between revising standard costs as required and using the current standard cost methodology.

[4] Allen H. Seed, *Inflation: Its Impact on Financial Reporting and Decision Making*, Financial Executives Research Foundation, 1978, p. 78.

percent of the respondents now use LIFO as the primary method of valuation, 8% of the respondents said that inflation *will* lead to a switch to LIFO within the next three years and 11% of the respondents said that inflation *may* lead to a switch to LIFO.

If all these changes take place, 80% of the sample will be LIFO users. Non-LIFO users have become the exception. LIFO is particularly prevalent among oil and gas companies, with 86% reporting its use. Companies with significant foreign involvement more often used FIFO in the U.S. with 43% compared to 27% overall. This may be accounted for through the use of FIFO overseas and the desire for worldwide accounting consistency. LIFO is often not accepted in other countries for tax and reporting purposes.

Most of the switches to LIFO (47% of respondents) were made between 1974 and 1979. This recent wave of changes as inflation has heated up leaves little doubt that inflation has provided the primary impetus behind these changes.

While an equal proportion of firms in each class use LIFO, the larger companies changed over before the smaller ones. Few financial and accounting executives endorse LIFO based on its conceptual merits, but from our experience must seem to be conscious of the tax deferral benefits on cash flow.

Management Reporting and Performance Evaluation

The only inflation-related management reporting practices that most respondents said were regularly applied are:

1. Emphasis is placed on funds flow (76% of respondents).
2. Productivity measurements are more widely used (53% of the respondents).

In addition to the 53% that now use productivity measurements more widely, 17% of the respondents said that they *plan* to apply them more widely in the future.

From a standpoint of management accounting methodology, therefore, this information suggests that central issues are:

1. How to measure funds flow
2. How to measure productivity

Discussions with accounting executives, consultants and practitioners, and a review of the literature, suggest that no consensus has been formed as to what the best method is for accomplishing either of these tasks. Moreover, there is also considerable debate as to what "funds" and "productivity" really are.

Other possibilities for employing management accounting techniques to reflect the impact of inflation are applied, or are planned to be applied, to varying extents. Notwithstanding the current practices of the *majority* of the companies that responded to our questionnaire, a significant proportion of the respondents said that they regularly apply, or plan to apply, the following practices:

	Regularly Apply	Plan to Apply	Total
1. Use cost of sales based on LIFO (or other current cost) inventory values at business unit level to measure performance	48%	6%	54%
2. Measure business unit performance in constant dollars	25%	9%	34%
3. Calculate business unit return on investment based on current cost of assets	16%	10%	26%
4. Routinely compare business unit performance with CPI or other indices	16%	5%	21%

The preceding practices apparently indicate a desire by many companies to evaluate business unit performance on an inflation-adjusted basis. The following practices are *less* widely applied:

	Regularly Applied	Plan to Apply	Total
1. Separate a component for inflation in the analysis of variances from budget	14%	4%	18%
2. Restate business unit profits on a current cost basis for internal performance measurement	8%	9%	17%
3. Restate fixed assets on a current cost basis for internal performance measurement	6%	10%	16%
4. Compare actual results with price-adjusted flexible budget	7%	5%	12%

We cannot explain the inconsistency between how 26% of the respondents could calculate their business unit return on investment based on the current cost of assets while only 16% of the respondents restate fixed assets on a current cost basis for internal performance measurement. The current cost of assets is required to determine return on investment based on the current cost of assets. Perhaps our questions were misunderstood; or perhaps some companies calculate the return based on current costs but do not report the underlying detail by business unit.

In answer to the question, "How has inflation affected your internal management reporting practices?", over 25% replied: "Not enough," "Has not," "Not significantly," or "No effect yet, but considering ways of coping with inflation." These comments tend to support the observation that inflation has had a relatively minor effect on the management reporting practices in many companies.

Other respondents stated that various changes have been made in management reporting practices as a result of inflation, and that other changes are being considered. FAS No. 33 was specifically referred to by four respondents who said that this standard was influencing their thinking.

Some differences in mangagement reporting practices were observed between classes of companies. Smaller companies were more inclined to apply constant dollars in business unit performance measurement while companies with large foreign operations were less inclined to use this technique. Companies with significant foreign components were also less inclined to calculate business unit returns on investment using current costs of assets than other companies. Oil and gas companies were much more inclined to use LIFO inventory values to measure business unit performance and to base management incentive compensation on inflation-adjusted performance. Companies with revenues above the median were more inclined to compare business unit performance with inflation indices on a routine basis than the lower revenue group. These larger companies were also more inclined to separate a component for inflation in variance analyses.

Whether or not inflation *should* have a more significant effect is another issue. The fact that we have experienced double-digit inflation and the fact that inflation is expected to continue at levels in excess of 5% per year does not mean that existing management accounting methodologies are inadequate. The evidence suggests the contrary. Budgets, standards, and profit margins need to be reviewed more frequently; more attention needs to be paid to funds management, productivity measurement, and other ratio analyses; and formal management reporting needs to be supplemented with additional inflation-adjusted information by business unit.

In substance, the management accounting and reporting methodologies that are in place in most companies need to be fine-tuned and refocused to cope with inflation. The evidence suggests that these methodologies can be adapted to inflation. They do not need to be scrapped in the current inflationary environment. The chapters that follow provide case studies to show how certain leading companies have, indeed, fine-tuned and refocused their management accounting practices to deal with inflationary realities.

Section III

Company Case Studies

Chapter 9

Inland Steel Company

Inland Steel Company has been actively engaged in the development of inflation accounting techniques for external reporting purposes and is regarded as having one of the most advanced computer-based management accounting systems in its industry. However, the company relies on time-tested historical accounting concepts for planning and control and really does not employ constant dollar or current cost techniques internally. Accordingly, this case describes how a leading domestic steel company has adapted historical management accounting techniques to an inflationary environment.

Industry Situation

The U.S. steel industry is currently faced with serious economic and competitive difficulties. Some of these difficulties are shared with other capital-intensive, basic industries, while others are unique to the steel business.

According to the American Iron and Steel Institute, the key problems are:

1. Persistently low rates of return coupled with tax measures that fail to provide adequate capital recovery

2. Capture of a significant portion of the domestic market by steel imports at "dumping prices"

3. Government control and regulation which significantly increase steel-making costs and mandate the spending of funds that would otherwise be available for replacement and modernization of productive equipment

4. Reduced earnings as a result of price administration which has restricted the recovery of cost increases

5. Escalation of steel-making costs at a rate in excess of increases in steel prices [1]

---

[1] *Steel at the Crossroads: The American Steel Industry in the 1980s,* American Iron and Steel Institute, Washington, D.C., January 1980, p. 1.

111

Cost and price-level changes, therefore, are simply one of many external problems facing Inland and the industry. At the time of our field work, April 1980, the specter of slackening steel demand and a probable softening of prices far overshadowed the prospects of cost increases in terms of potential impact on profitability.

Notwithstanding this turn of events, in Inland's 1979 annual report to stockholders, Chairman Frederick Jaicks stated: "The twin problems of energy resources and inflation will require concerted national efforts during the Eighties. To dampen inflation, we must also sharply increase productivity. The obvious starting point is increased investment in modern machinery for greater efficiency and lower costs. . . ." [2]

Costs receive continuous attention at Inland because they are subject to control. Changes in steel demand and price levels may have a greater impact on profitability, but those external forces are largely noncontrollable.

At the time of our interviews, Inland's economist and comptroller expected inflation (as measured by the CPI) to range between 12%–15% in 1980 and to trail off after that. The company's construction costs, however, have been increasing at a higher rate than the Consumer Price Index, except in 1974 and 1979 when the CPI soared into double-digit figures.

Background of Company

Inland Steel Company was founded in 1893. Today it is the sixth largest steel company in the United States. Its 1979 sales were $3.6 billion, net income was $131 million (3.6% of sales), assets were $2.7 billion (at historical costs) and return on equity was 10.3%. The company enjoys about 6% of the U.S. domestic steel market. Steel operations ($2.4 billion sales) are integrated in the Great Lakes region.

All of Inland's steel-making facilities, the subject of this case, are located at Indiana Harbor, East Chicago, Indiana. The Works are enormous: approximately 350 acres under one roof, on 1,800 acres of land. Over 20,000 people are employed at the Works which operate around the clock, seven days a week. The Works were constructed at the turn of the century and began production in 1902. As a result a few of Inland's facilities date back to the early 1900's.

The Indiana Harbor Works are considered to be among the most efficient steel-making facilities in the world. They are supplied by ore boat and rail with raw materials from iron ore mines and limestone quarries in Minnesota, Michigan, Wisconsin, Ontario and Quebec, and coal mines in Illinois, Pennsylvania and West Virginia.

---

[2] Inland Steel Annual Report, 1979, p. 2.

The steel-making process begins when the ore is converted into molten iron in a blast furnace. Molten iron is later converted into steel by a variety of methods: open-hearth, basic oxygen furnace or electric furnace. Molten steel is continuously cast into slabs and billet shapes or is poured into ingot molds for subsequent processing into slabs, blooms and billets. Slabs, blooms and billets are then rolled into sheets, plates, bars or structural shapes. Some products are also galvanized, aluminized, or otherwise finished.

Inland is currently expanding its coke and hot metal production capacity which, when completed, will raise its annual raw steel capability by 4.5% to 9.3 million tons.

Because of the location of Inland's facilities and the relatively high cost of transporting steel, markets served are largely in the Midwest. Much of Inland's output is consumed by the automotive, appliance and farm machinery industries as well as by construction, steel converters, and other manufacturers of capital goods which are centered in the area. Seventy percent of the nation's steel market is located within a 500-mile radius, and 90% of Inland's product is sold within 150 miles of its plant.

The main thrust of the company's strategy seems to be: focus on the prime market; provide a wide range of basic steel products; maintain market share by being price competitive; operate facilities as close as possible to capacity; upgrade product and customer mix to the extent feasible, and be a low-cost producer through integration, automation, and efficient operation at a single location. Its financial goal is to achieve a growth rate with sufficient return on investment to attract investment capital and adequately reward its managers, employees, and shareholders.

Organization

The company is organized on a line and staff basis as summarized in Exhibit 9–1. Management accounting functions are highlighted to show their relationship to steel-making operations.

The comptroller reports through the vice president, finance to the vice chairman, and is in charge of systems and data processing as well as management accounting, external financial reporting, tax and audit functions. He is the prime mover behind Inland's management accounting systems.

The line management at Indiana Harbor Works reports through a vice president, steel manufacturing to the president. Both the president and vice chairman report to the chairman.

The controller, Indiana Harbor Works, reports through the assistant comptroller, accounting to the comptroller on a line basis and to the vice president, steel manufacturing on a functional basis. This arrangement apparently works well at Inland because the management accountants at the

EXHIBIT 9-1

Inland Steel Company
Management Accounting Organization—Steel-making

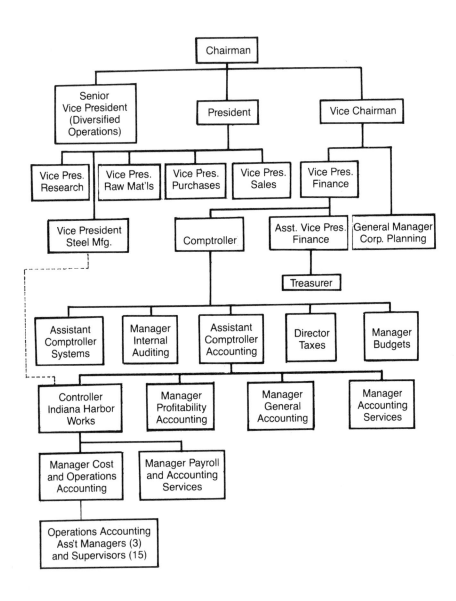

Works level operate as though they have two bosses: the comptroller and the line manager that they serve.

One of the keys to Inland's strong management accounting systems is a group of 15 well-educated operations accounting supervisors and three assistant managers who are assigned to various steel-making and mill processing activities. These individuals work closely with the mill superintendent or manager, monitor data, analyze and interpret financial results for him, and are the management accountants who are largely responsible for the effectiveness of Inland's steel-making control system. Altogether, some 400 persons are engaged in the accounting function at the Works level.

Status of Management Accounting Systems

Inland has well-developed management accounting systems. These systems cover corporate planning, financial modeling, budgeting, capital expenditure evaluation and control, product cost accounting, performance measurement, and management reporting.

Many of these systems are computer-based. Inland has a Systems Department staff of about 200 persons reporting to the assistant comptroller, systems of which some 40 are systems consultants, with the balance programmers, computer operators and keypunch and secretarial staff. Equipment for the management information systems, which include the management accounting systems, consists of two IBM 168 computers and one IBM 3032 computer which provides complete redundancy as well as adequate capacity for the rapidly growing MIS network. The computer units operate 24 hours per day, seven days per week. Materials management and production scheduling and reporting systems are considered to be optimum.

Current inflation-related refinements of these systems in process include:

1. Building nominal dollar information into the financial models used in the corporate planning and capital expenditure evaluation (resource allocation) process.
2. Tightening cost controls at the operations level through the emphasis on detail, more current information, and more analysis.
3. Developing a more extensive data base and more refined product cost information for sales, pricing and profitability analysis. While Inland has little control over price levels, management can control product mix.
4. Improving productivity. Methodology is not a "hot topic," but ways and means of achieving productivity improvements are.
5. Testing distributable funds flow techniques in corporate planning.

These refinements are discussed in connection with the practices described in the remainder of this chapter.

Resource Allocation

Considerable emphasis is placed on corporate (strategic) planning at Inland, and its system has been utilized for several years. As one participant responded, "Planning is taken very seriously in the company."

The objective of Inland's planning activities has been to identify the ways in which the company can most effectively employ its resources in order to maximize return on investment for its stockholders. Corporate planning has involved the coordination of market analysis, marketing strategies, facility planning strategies and financial strategies. Various options and combinations are assembled and subsequently analyzed by weighing the relative merits of one option against another.

Inland's current steel expansion program was undertaken with the expectation that demand for steel would increase in the 1980's and that Inland was in a good position to gain economic benefit from this increased demand. Because the steel business is capital intensive and most steel products are commodities, it appears that the planning process is largely oriented towards determining the timing and size of prospective facility expansions rather than to the development of marketing strategies. As a result, strategic planning is closely linked to facility planning and capital expenditure evaluations.

Corporate plans are supported by a sales forecast for each of 20 product lines, an income statement, funds statement, capital budget, and a schedule of operating statistics. These plans are prepared annually by year for a ten-year period. Projections are considered to be "satisfactory for the first two or three years," but they "become soft after that." The most critical requirements are to predict demand by product line, and prices and profit margins by product line and year for the span of the planning horizon. These predictions are, of course, complicated by inflation.

The basic technique which Inland has used in making financial projections in its long-range plans is to project all revenues and costs in constant dollars except for capital costs which have been shown in "escalated" dollars. [1]

Inland's computer-based financial model is constructed to forecast constant dollars. Cost changes are assumed to be offset by equal percentage price changes. Inland's 1979 strategic planning inflation assumptions state: "The current planning guidelines used in the development of the strategic plan are:

• Selling prices and operating costs are projected in current-year (con-

---

[1] "Escalated dollars" is a term used within Inland to refer to what we have referred to as "nominal dollars."

stant) dollars over the entire strategic planning horizon. Manufacturing margins are maintained and improved as volume increases and operating efficiencies are gained from new facilities.
• Capital expenditures are escalated (adjusted for inflation) at the rate of 6% per year."

The use of constant dollars for price and cost forecasts, and nominal dollars for capital expenditures, was adopted as the basis for planning projects. Inland's management believes that is a conservative approach which tends not to overestimate the ability of internally generated funds to support investment in new facilities. The effect of stating net income in constant dollars tends to understate the cash flow in terms of nominal dollars in periods of inflation. However, the use of constant dollars also has the effect of understating working capital requirements.

The planning organization has experimented with ways of supplementing constant dollar financial projections with forecasts showing all revenue and cost items in escalated dollars. They expect to continue these experiments in the future in an effort to provide more insight into the effects of inflation on their business.

The comptroller believes that inflation should be incorporated in the resource allocation process, but the question is, how? Should individual indices be established for each element of revenue and expense, or should a general rate be used? How should rates be established for each year?

A big obstacle to forecasting price levels has been an inability of management to estimate what future price actions will be feasible. The government has used de facto as well as formal price controls in the steel industry since World War II. Thus, the industry considers itself to have been in a price-cost squeeze and is uncertain as to what price increases can be expected. A possible solution to the difficulty of estimating future price levels is to provide a range of price/cost level assumptions and run the forecasts in the financial model on several different bases. From our interviews, we were left with the impression that this is the way the company is headed.

Capital Expenditures

Capital expenditure forecasts are prepared in inflation-adjusted (nominal) dollars. The inflation adjustment is based on Inland Steel's Internal Construction Cost Index prepared by the Engineering Department. The Construction Cost Index is based on a weighting of the actual engineering and craft labor and various material cost components. An internal index is considered to be more useful than an external index in Inland's case because an internal index more closely reflects Inland's own construction costs at its single location in East Chicago, Indiana. The components of this index and a comparison with other construction cost indices are shown in Exhibits 9–2 and 9–3. Note that the Inland index, 7.6% current annual rate, lags behind other construction cost indices and the current (1980) growth rate of the CPI (18% annual rate in April 1980).

Steel plant capital expenditures generally involve relatively long lead times and long economic lives. At the time of our interviews, in the spring of 1980, Works-level personnel were developing their 1982 budgets. Capital expenditure budget requests had already been submitted for 1981 and were being reviewed with IH Works management.

Cash flows used to evaluate capital expenditures are prepared in constant dollars. Constant dollars are used for this purpose (as they are for long-range planning) because of the uncertainties associated with the price and cost levels over the life of the project.

A departmental listing of projects is developed in the course of the capital expenditure budgeting process. This list is classified for review by management into the following categories:

1. Regulatory or agreement compliance (e.g., pollution control)
2. Risk to productivity capability (replacement)
3. Cost reduction—over 32% return on investment after taxes (IRR)
4. Cost reduction—under 32% return on investment after taxes (IRR)

The 32% return figure (roughly equal to a two-year payback) was established by top management as a cutoff point for screening or prioritizing steel division projects for inclusion in the annual capital budget. While this rate is influenced by inflation, it is intended primarily as a rationing mechanism. The requirements of Inland's expansion program strained its cash resources to the limit and it became apparent that funds available for other purposes would be meager. The company, in effect, establishes a fairly high hurdle rate at the Works level. Nevertheless, projects offering less than a 32% return are not necessarily cancelled, but rather are deferred to a later year if capital expenditure funds are limited.

At the corporate level, a 15% capital spending hurdle rate is used for other than steel plants. A 10% capital spending hurdle rate was increased to 15% in the early 70's when inflation rates escalated. Management notes that the 15% rate is equal to the two-decade average ROI achieved by all manufacturing companies in the United States.

Inland's management explains the difference between the 32% rate used in the steel division and the 15% rate used at the corporate level by the fact that each business segment has its own opportunity and risk characteristics and that this approach is used in establishing long-run return targets for each profit center.

Much of Inland's capital expenditure budget supports the company's

EXHIBIT 9-2

Inland Steel Company Construction Cost Index
Quarterly Roundup

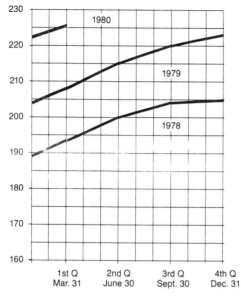

Average Annual Index

1968	= 100.0
1969	= 104.2
1970	= 112.7
1971	= 123.5
1972	= 129.2
1973	= 133.1
1974	= 149.6
1975	= 166.3
1976	= 174.5
1977	= 186.1
1978	= 200.5
1979	= 216.0

ESCALATION RATES

Current Annual — 7.6%
Year to Date — 8.6%

ISC Construction Cost Index	1st Q. 80 FINAL	4th A. 79 FINAL	3rd Q. 79 FINAL	2nd Q. 79 FINAL	1st Q. 79 FINAL
(1968 = 100)	225.6	221.4	219.8	215.1	207.8
COMPOSITE LABOR	192.1	192.2	193.4	191.1	180.6
Engineering	270.0	251.4	251.0	240.5	241.5
Craft Labor	255.8	255.6	255.6	252.6	235.1
COMPOSITE MATERIAL	253.2	245.4	241.5	234.5	230.4
Concrete	233.8	233.8	233.8	218.8	218.8
Steel	288.4	282.2	277.9	270.5	265.7
Mech. Equip.	247.5	238.2	231.9	226.9	221.7
Elect. & Equip.	193.4	181.7	180.4	174.4	171.5
Asphalt	185.5P	175.3	175.3	175.3	175.3
Refractories	299.0	262.1	262.1	262.1	262.1
Mobile Equip.	249.6	242.5	234.3	229.6	224.2
Other Business Indices					
ENR Constr. (1913 = 100)	3159.1	3140.1	3119.2	2982.4	2886.1
Chemical Engrg. (1957–59 = 100)	258.4P	247.6	243.4	237.2	232.5
Marshall & Swift (1926 = 100)	640.4	620.8	606.4	593.3	577.0
Mining and Milling	660.1	638.4	625.7	613.4	599.3
Consumer Price Index (Chicago Area, 1967 = 100)	239.8	228.4	221.3	213.5	206.6

119

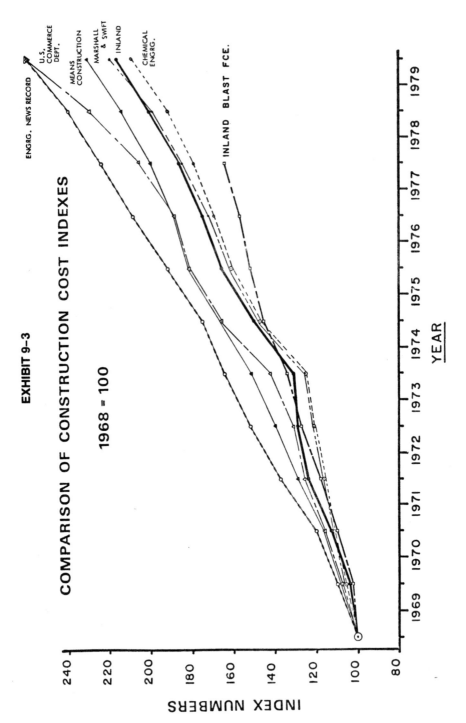

EXHIBIT 9-3

COMPARISON OF CONSTRUCTION COST INDEXES

1968 = 100

capacity expansion programs. The principal methodology employed for evaluating plant expansions is to establish a "base case" of production activity from a given sales forecast. "Expansion cases" with various operating options are evaluated. The facility plan is then prepared from this evaluation of alternative scenarios.

Demand expectations and technical considerations were the principal determinants in the decision leading to the current plant expansion program. The potential impact of inflation really did not affect this evaluation because at the time that the expansion program was planned, inflation was a relatively minor economic factor. The expansion program has been delayed somewhat, but only because of construction problems and labor and material shortages—not because of financial constraints caused by inflation. Inland still expects increased demand for steel in the 1980's partially as the result of the development of steel-intensive energy products.

Flexible Budgeting and Cost Control Reporting at Works Level

Inland Steel has a tight, computer-based cost control reporting system that covers the 500 cost centers at the Indiana Harbor Works. Standard and actual costs are reported by cost center. Accounting management believes that its system is adaptable to an inflationary environment.

Mill "turn" (shift) foremen are provided a predetermined schedule, machinery and equipment for a given steel-making operation, and a fixed crew. The key to cost control at the first-line production level, therefore, is to maximize throughput and yield because the turn foreman really cannot control his schedule and labor costs. While much of steel making has been systematized and computerized, there is still a lot of skill and art required in the process.

Unit standards are provided by industrial engineers for all direct operations including maintenance and material handling. These standards can be based on one of several determinants including machine hours, man-hours, tons produced, or hours operated.

Production reporting used to determine standard costs is keyed in on CRTs at the plant level at many key production areas and is monitored for accuracy by the operations accounting supervisors at each mill. Other production areas still use "paper copy" clerical recording, which is then key-punched into the management accounting system. The labor distribution used to determine actual costs is a by-product of the work assignment entered into the payroll system.

Data processing system outputs include weekly performance reports (in units), and monthly reports of actual (units and dollars) vs. budget. Cost center reports are summarized hierarchically, and variances from budget are analyzed by cause.

Operating variances (controllable) by cost center are separated from nonoperating variances (noncontrollable). Nonoperating variances include a provision for revising budget allowances for inflation. This is an application of the price-adjusted flexible budget concept discussed in Chapter 7. Programmed variances (e.g., wage increases) are budgeted. Cost center report formats also contain a provision for comments to explain major variances.

In order to monitor current monthly results, each Monday the operations accounting supervisors prepare a forecast of approximately 50 elements of costs and variances for each of their cost centers for the month. These forecasts are compiled into a weekly projection of costs and profitability for the Works and steel division. Thus the monthly reports, available on the eighth working day following the end of the month, largely represent a confirmation of previously projected information.

Annual results are monitored on a quarterly basis by updating cost and variance forecasts for the year.

Standard Cost System

Inland operates a computer-based, modified standard direct costing system that provides two measures of cost: "full cost" and "variable cost." As defined by Inland, full cost includes materials, conversion and plant-level overhead except depreciation, property taxes, and certain other minor costs. This standard is called "full cost." (Because depreciation is excluded from this definition, it is irrelevant whether it is computed on a historical cost or current cost basis.) Variable costs consist of the variable components of full costs. Some accounts have single determinants. Other accounts, such as maintenance labor and electricity, have more than one determinant.

Standards are revised once a year or whenever operating practices change significantly. Variances are applied to standard for purposes of profitability analysis. This means that the standard costs used to compute product profit margins are revised or adjusted to reflect changes in price levels as well as other influences on operations.

The company prepares a quarterly product profitability analysis for about 500 items. This analysis shows profit margins based on both full and variable costs including variances.

Inventory Valuation and Management

LIFO inventory valuation was adopted in 1949, the midst of the inflationary spurt following World War II. While income tax considerations reportedly motivated the conversion to LIFO, the comptroller is pleased with its present internal planning and control implications. He believes strongly that because of the complexities of accrual accounting and the distortions to historical accounting caused by inflation, cash flow over time is the best measure of performance. Management's objective should be to maximize cash inflows in relation to outflows, and the use of LIFO contributes to this objective. Moreover, LIFO is useful in helping to assure that current costs are used for profitability analysis and performance and valuation.

Inland's comptroller concedes that the understatement of inventories on the balance sheet is one of the penalties of LIFO. However, he suggests that this deficiency could be corrected by crediting the LIFO reserve to retained earnings if such financial reporting were allowed by the FASB and IRS.

Inland established a Corporate Inventory Control Committee in 1972 to manage inventories to avoid an inadvertent loss of LIFO reserves. The Committee consists largely of operating managers. Its purpose has evolved over time from being a watchdog over LIFO layers to conducting a broad, corporate-wide inventory management function. It now determines the inventory needed to support production, coordinates the flow of materials between mines and quarries and the steel division, and monitors investments monthly in inventories in relation to forecasts. Because of the time required between mining iron and coal and quarrying limestone, on the one hand, and shipping finished steel products, on the other, the work of the Inventory Control Committee required that Programs of Operations (budgets) be increased from a one- to two-year time span.

Productivity Measurement

With respect to the chairman's comments concerning the need to sharply increase productivity, Inland concentrates on dollar measures rather than statistical measures of total or partial productivity in the more traditional sense. Inland's approach to operational control is focused on its flexible budget and performance measurement systems (standard ÷ actual), and the persons that we interviewed said that these systems provide the basis for controlling the elements of productivity.

Notwithstanding its reliance on performance measurement against standard, Inland prepares supplementary statistical measures of productivity. Most of these measures have been used for several years, and more (e.g., energy consumption) were introduced to deal specifically with inflation. Nevertheless, Inland's performance measurements and all of its supplementary statistical measures eliminate the influence of inflation from the measurement of operations.

The principal measure at the Works level is bargaining unit man-hours per ton billed. This information is reported monthly by classification of product as shown in Exhibit 9–4.

EXHIBIT 9-4

Bargaining Unit Man-Hours Per Ton Billed
For the Month March 1980

	Year		1980
	1978	1979	Y-T-D
Primary			
Shapes			
Flats			
Operating Services			
Quality Control			
Miscellaneous	——	——	——
Total			

	Year		
Summary Statistics	1978	1979	1980 Y-T-D
Tons Billed			
B.U. Man-Hours*			

*Excludes: Back Pay; Work Orders; B.Fce. Reline;
Dismantling; Capital; Charges to Inv. Accts.

Other, more specialized productivity measures are also developed. Examples include:

1. Energy consumption per ton of raw steel produced and per ton billed
2. Delivery performance—percentage of product shipped on schedule, ahead of schedule, delinquent
3. Quality performance—percentage of nonapplicable steel produced and diverted to lower quality product

The company also prepares a weekly "Hours Worked Report" by department. This report shows:

1. Number of employees working
2. Hours worked
3. Labor index (manpower) this week, last week
4. Production index (tons produced) this week, last week

124

If the production index (tons) increases at a greater rate than the labor index (manpower), an improvement in productivity is indicated.

The application of the value-added concept (see Chapter 7) is also being considered by management accountants at the Works level.

Key Measurements

Key operating and financial performance measurements at the Works level were identified to be:

1. Safety—frequency and severity of accidents
2. Plant yield
3. Man-hours per ton billed
4. Quality performance index
5. Energy consumption—BTUs per ton billed
6. Delivery performance

Man-hours per ton billed, quality performance, energy consumption and delivery performance were discussed under Productivity Measurement. Profit vs. plan and percentage return on invested capital are computed at the steel division level. The steel division includes raw material operations as well as the Indiana Harbor Works; it is the lowest level at which profitability is measured.

This list of measurements may in itself tell a good deal about Inland's relative values and how the steel business is controlled on a month-to-month basis. Note the importance of safety, yield, productivity, quality, energy consumption and delivery performance—in addition to profitability—and how none of the former operating measurements is affected by inflation.

Budgeting and Profitability Accounting

Inland has a comprehensive budgeting and variance analysis program which is administered by the managers of budgets and profitability accounting at the corporate level. This program is structured so that anticipated price and cost changes are built into the budgets, and price and cost variances from budget are clearly identified.

Like many other companies, Inland has been faced with price level uncertainty. This uncertainty applies to the cost of certain major items such as coal, fuel oil, purchased power, and steel scrap. According to one Inland manager, "We don't know what's going to happen tomorrow. . . . We've been caught by too many surprises. . . ."

Selling price changes expected during the year are reflected in the Program of Operations (budgets). In estimating these changes, consideration is given to anticipated market conditions, projected costs, and applicable governmental regulations and guidelines. Inland's approach is to attempt to build inflation into the budgeting process through more careful analysis of historical cost data rather than by the application of a different methodology, such as constant dollars or current cost.

Programs of Operations extend over a two-year time span. Sales forecasts for about 125 products are developed by quarter by the end of October of each year. This forecast is used to develop a production forecast at the plant level for each of the 125 products and a raw material forecast in early November. Cost center budgets are also developed at the plant level by quarter. These budgets are related to ton, man-hour, and hours-worked determinants to calculate the standard allowances for the flexible budgets used in each cost center. Programs are also spread out by month.

Estimated cost of living adjustments (COLA) are built into the Program of Operations. Because anticipated increased labor costs are reflected in the budgeting process in this manner, variances arising from increased labor cost levels are limited to differences between assumed and actual cost of living adjustments.

By the 13th working day following each month, the manager, profitability accounting has prepared a comprehensive analysis of variance from "Program" for the preceding month. The package of analyses that are prepared includes:

1. Variances from program (budget)
2. Analysis of changes in manufacturing profit
3. Variances from program by type of product
4. Analysis of sales variances
5. Analysis of product cost variances

An example of the format used for the variances from program (budget) illustrates the extent of detail that is involved in this analysis and how price and cost variances are treated (Exhibit 9–5). Note that energy, raw material and other price variances are segregated as "Variance Not Directly Related to Operations." In this manner price level changes are identified separately and managers at the plant level are directed to "Variances Directly Related to Operations."

Inland also tracks costs changes on a monthly basis, comparing actual costs incurred with programmed costs. As part of the 1980 program submission, the 1979 actual cost per ton of steel shipped was reconciled to the projected 1980 cost per ton of steel shipped. This schedule shows the operations-oriented "cost and inflationary changes" applicable to fuel, wages and benefits, purchased material, alloys, ore and pellets, fluxes, outside processing, and the like.

126

EXHIBIT 9-5

Steel-making Manufacturing Profit Variances from Program

(In thousands)

	1980	
	March	Year-to-Date
Program Manufacturing Profit		
Seasonal and Revision Variances		
Variance Due to Difference Between Program and Refined Predetermined Costs		
Modified Program Manufacturing Profit		
Variances Related to Sales:		
Net Realizing Prices		
Volume		
Product Mix		
Under-Distributed Costs		
Budgeted Manufacturing Profit at Actual Volume and Mix		
Variances Directly Related to Operations:		
Processing Costs—Labor & Employee Benefit		
—Repairs & Maintenance		
—Energy Usage		
—Other		
Yield		
Material Usage		
Productivity		
Inventory Adjustment		
Product Flow		
Non-Normal Activity Level		
Budget Changes		
Variances Not Directly Related to Operations:		
Energy Prices—Coal		
—Fuel Oil		
—Purchased Gas		
—Purchased Power		
Raw Materials & Other Prices—Ores		
—Fluxes		
—Oxygen		
—Other		
Raw Material Mix—Ore		
—Coal		
—Coke		
Outside Processing		
Other		
Actual Manufacturing Profit		
Nonvariable Manufacturing Costs		
Contribution Margin		

( ) Unfavorable

127

Funds Management

Funds are managed at the corporate level under the direction of the assistant vice president, finance. While the company may be constrained in its rate of capital formation, inflation has not dramatically affected Inland's financial strategies.

Cash is, of course, monitored very closely as it has been for several years. Since 1974, Inland has prepared a monthly analysis of variances from financial plan for each subsidiary as part of its profitability accounting package. This analysis is used by top management to monitor the generation and use of cash by subsidiary. While Inland's emphasis on cash management was stimulated by financial needs rather than by inflationary pressures, a focus on cash is considered to be particularly useful in an inflationary environment. The format of this variance analysis is illustrated in Exhibit 9–6.

EXHIBIT 9–6

Analysis of Cash Variances

	$000's
Program net release (absorption) of cash	<u>500</u>
Variance due to:	
Higher (lower) net income	12
Noncash expense	(2)
Accounts receivable	30
Inventories	(20)
Capital expenditure	(100)
Federal income taxes	20
Accounts payable and other liabilities	<u>25</u>
Total variances	<u>(35)</u>
Actual net release (absorption) of cash	465
Dividends paid to parent company	<u>300</u>
Cash advanced to (or from) Inland	<u>165</u>

A source and application of funds statement is prepared quarterly for each subsidiary and is consolidated for the corporation as a whole. This statement is prepared in accordance with the traditional APB No. 19 format and is reconciled to working capital. However, the funds control system is really oriented around the variance analysis that was previously illustrated.

Because of pressures on liquidity stemming in part from inflation the comptroller perceives funds management as being an area that will receive increasing emphasis.

Experimentation with Inflation Accounting

As pointed out in the beginning of this chapter, Inland has been in the forefront of experimentation with inflation accounting techniques for the past several years. In 1975 Inland participated in the price level experiment of the FASB. The accounting department restated the entire company's results on a price level basis using the GNP deflator for the years 1972, 1973, and 1974. Fixed-asset records were reconstructed back to 1913.

The comptroller's organization found that the application of price level accounting techniques did not really have much of an effect on reported results except in the case of fixed assets and inventories. They incorporated monetary gains or losses into their profit calculations, but they did not agree with this approach because in their view the approach did not make sense. Monetary gains were perceived to be an unreliable measure of financial performance.

When asked what value this experiment had, the respondent replied, "Very little. Businessmen do not believe that price level (constant dollar) accounting techniques are meaningful. General management listened politely, but were skeptical of the conclusions that were reached. . . . It was a case of accountants talking to accountants. . . ."

The application of the replacement cost information required by the SEC under ASR No. 190 met with a similar reception. Inflation was of concern to top management, and the current cost concepts incorporated in ASR No. 190 were considered to be closer to the mark by Inland's financial management, but "we have not used this information internally. . . . Company management has not found this information to be useful. . . ."

In the course of discussing the current cost approach, one Inland accounting manager observed that depreciation is "the amortization of past costs as assigned to current products. Decisions for the future should be based on future costs, in which case past costs are irrelevant." This basic concept underlies Inland's practice of using historical costs for performance measurement and prospective costs for capital expenditure planning purposes.

Inland teamed up with Professor Alfred Rappaport of Northwestern University in experimenting with Rappaport's distributable funds approach (See Chapter 6). While a presentation of this approach was made to top management, "nothing came of it. . . . It more or less died. . . . Disposable funds seems to be more oriented to the needs of the financial analyst, rather than the needs of management."

The comptroller hasn't given up and is still searching for better ways to deal with inflation. He thinks that some form of inflation accounting will eventually be applicable internally. However, inflation accounting is still relatively new in this country. He feels that the accounting profession has not yet found a methodology which combines economically correct reporting with a degree of understandability that will encourage nonfinancial management to learn and use it. At the time of our field work he was inclined to explore further the application of the disposable funds concept. This may help solve what Inland's management accountants see as the big problems with inflation accounting: obtaining consistency of approach, reporting credible results, and getting management's acceptance of the value of new approaches to the solution of their planning problems.

Chapter 10

Acos Villares, S.A.

Acos[1] Villares is an example of a progressive, well-managed company in Brazil, a country that has recently been coping with inflation at a rate in excess of 75% per year. From all indications, the company's management accounting systems reflect the forefront of practice in Brazil.

In Brazil inflation ran wild in 1979 when the rate accelerated from a wild 30% to 40% range to over 75%. Increased oil prices and internal demands for higher wages are the principal reasons for this increase although much of the higher rate was caused by importation of inflation from other countries, such as higher prices on imports and interest rates on external debt. At the time of our research the Brazilian Government had taken steps to prevent the decline in the devaluation of the cruzeiro on the international market, peg the official ORTN (inflation-adjusted government bond) exchange rate, reduce currency in circulation, and tax imports in an effort to curb the rate of inflation.

Acos has installed many modern planning and control concepts and has adapted these concepts to the specific requirements of Brazilian corporation law and the ravages and unpredictability of inflation. Thus standard cost accounting, direct costing, flexible budgeting, responsibility accounting, strategic planning, return-on-investment analysis (partially based on current costs), funds flow management, and the evaluation of prospective capital expenditures based on their internal rate of return were installed in an existing inflationary environment.

The most important business problems faced by management at the time of this study were those of maintaining profit margins, improving productivity, and generating enough cash internally to support the expansion of the business. Construction of a new plant was largely financed by debt and internal funds. As a result, the company's remaining cash resources are stretched to service its debt, replace worn-out assets, provide machinery for productivity improvement, and furnish working capital to support increased sales.

---

[1] "Acos" is the Portuguese word for "steel."

Key management accounting issues are those of measuring the impact of inflation on operating results and developing appropriate performance and productivity measurements; the use of "constant" vs. "current" (nominal) cruzeiro measurements for planning and capital expenditure evaluations; and the integration and computerization of materials management, production and cost information systems.

Background of Company

Acos is the largest specialty steel producer in Brazil. Revenues are approximately $100 million (U.S.), assets are $170 million, and net worth is $110 million. The company is growing and is moderately profitable. After tax and monetary adjustment, profit margins in 1979 were 9% of sales, and the return on equity (based on the current cost of property, plant and equipment) was 7%.

Acos Villares is part of a group of Villares companies that were founded by Luiz Dumont Villares in the early part of the century. The other main companies are Industrias Villares, Equipamentos Villares, and Villares Industrias de Base, S.A. (VIBASA). While shares of Acos Villares, Industrias Villares and VIBASA are publicly-held, the group continues to be controlled and managed by the members of the Villares family.

Plants are located in Sao Paulo and Pindamonhangaba (Pinda), Brazil. The Sao Paulo plant was built about 40 years ago, but the Pinda plant is a "green field" development[2] that was started up in 1979. About 3,500 people are employed at the plant and office in Sao Paulo, and roughly an equal number will be employed in Pinda when this plant is fully operational. However, the Pinda plant will produce approximately four times the tonnage as Sao Paulo because Sao Paulo concentrates on producing specialized high and super alloy steels.

Acos has a broad product line of standard and custom-designed products including rolled and forged steel bars, heavy cast parts and rolls for iron and steel rolling mills. The process consists of a melt shop for melting steel scrap and converting scrap to ingot; and rolling mill, foundry, forge shop, machine shop and surface grinding facilities. The Pinda plant has an 8,000-ton press that is reportedly the biggest press in the Southern Hemisphere.

Acos primarily serves the Brazilian market, but about 10% to 15% of its steel products are exported to the United States and other countries.

---

[2] A "green field" development is a term used in capital-intensive industries to describe the addition of a new plant in a new location—e.g., a "green field."

Organization

The company is organized (in summary) as shown in Exhibit 10-1. Key management accounting-related positions have been highlighted to emphasize the relationships of these particular responsibilities.

The hierarchy of the organization consists of two corporations (Acos Villares, Sao Paulo and VIBASA, Pinda), a division (Villares Steel) and two plants (Sao Paulo and Pinda). Two corporate entities are required, even though the two plants are operated as one division, because different external investors participate in each plant. The Pinda plant was partially financed by the Brazilian government.

Management accounting is performed largely at the plant level although accounting policies and reporting formats for the division are specified by the corporate controller. Electronic data processing is performed at the group level (under the direction of the corporate controller), but functional specifications for new divisional systems are developed at the divisional level.

Strategic planning, and a new position, director of productivity, also report to the vice president, finance along with the corporate controller and treasurer. The division controller is currently responsible for strategic planning at the divisional level.

The vice president, finance, corporate controller, and division controller have been the prime movers behind the management accounting systems that are installed in Acos Villares.

Planning and Budgeting Systems

Strategic planning at Villares is in a relatively early stage of development. Strategic plans are "numbers-driven" forecasts rather than "strategy-driven" action programs. The strategic planning process at Acos consists of preparing an assessment of strengths and weaknesses accompanied by five-year, single-number forecasts (by year) of the profit-and-loss statement, balance sheet and funds statement. These plans are prepared in May-August of each year in *constant cruzeiros*. Thus inflation is not reflected in these financial forecasts.

Budgets by month for the following year are prepared in August-December for presentation to the Board of Directors in January (Villares' fiscal year ends on January 31). They consist of detailed sales and expenditure budgets at the divisional and plant levels and an income statement, balance sheet and funds statement at the corporate level.

Budgets are prepared in *nominal cruzeiros*. General inflation rate assumptions are provided to all members of the group by the corporation, but

EXHIBIT 10-1

Acos Villares Organizational Chart

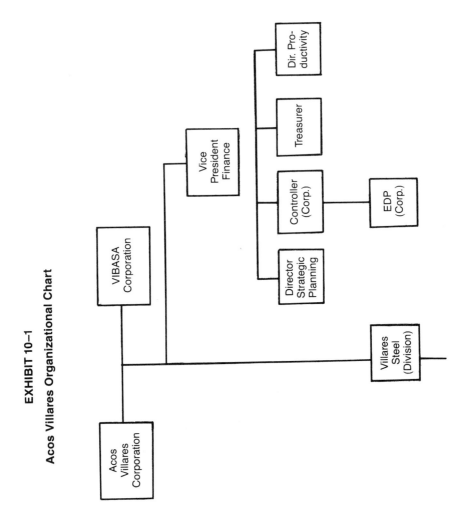

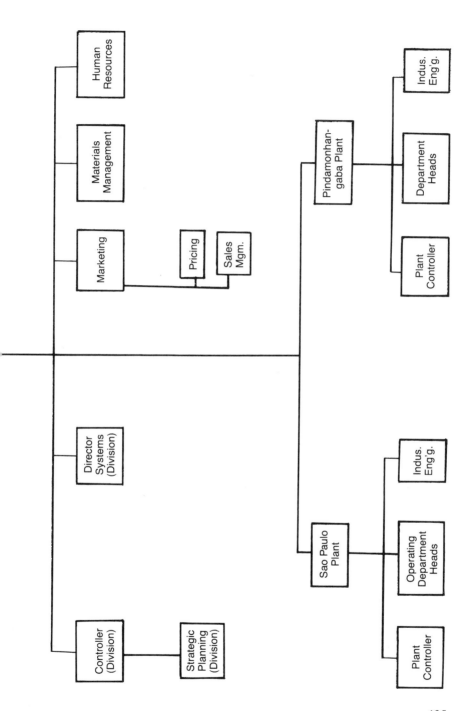

Acos estimates price and cost level increases for each type of material and major category of expense for budgeting purposes.

Budgets are prepared by department heads with the assistance of the plant or divisional controller. The plant controller works with the department heads that are associated with his plant, and the division controller works with the marketing, materials management and administration department heads at the divisional level. Department heads use constant cruzeiros to facilitate month-to-month and year-to-year comparisons, but the controllers adjust the constant cruzeiro amounts to nominal cruzeiro amounts before the budgets are submitted to senior divisional and corporate management for review. According to the divisional controller, the use of constant cruzeiros at the department head level is essential to analyzing operations on a real basis without regard to changes in price levels.

Budgets are revised in mid-year for the balance of the year. This revision provides for updating the budget to reflect unanticipated changes in price levels as well as other factors. However, the original budget is also still retained as a reference point so that results for the whole year may be compared with the original budget for the year.

Acos uses the price-adjusted flexible budgeting concept discussed in Chapter 7. Budgets are adjusted at the machine center level (Acos has approximately 120 machine centers in its Sao Paulo plant) to allow for variations in certain prices as well as variations in volume. Three types of costs are charged to machine centers: direct labor, assigned costs (maintenance, service costs and energy), and auxiliary materials (supplies and expense). Budgeted unit labor cost rates are adjusted to reflect actual labor cost per hour. Assigned costs of maintenance, service and energy are charged to each machine center at standard rates, and cost variances arising from changes in price levels are reported in the originating department. The actual cost of auxiliary materials is charged directly to the machine center that uses the material. As a result, cost variances arising from changes in prices at the machine center level are limited to auxiliary materials. "We only hold machine center supervisors responsible for the costs that they can control" is the principle employed here.

Differences between the price levels contained in the original budget and the price level adjusted budget used to compare actual cost with budget in the machine centers are ultimately reflected in a reconciling line item at the divisional level called "fiscal cost reconciliation." This concept will be discussed later.

Capital Expenditures

Capital expenditures are thoroughly documented, carefully analyzed, and closely controlled in the Villares group.

An investment proposal form is prepared for each expenditure. For investments above U.S. $15,000, the form includes the following information which is commonly found in proposals prepared in U.S. companies:

1. Description of project
2. Project classification
3. Project justification narrative
4. Investments required by type including working capital requirements
5. Economic life of assets
6. Payback period
7. Internal rate of return
8. Amount included in capital budget
9. Divisional and corporate approvals

The proposal is supported by forecasts of cash flows and other relevant information. The proposal is prepared by operating management, but the cash flows, the payback period, and the internal rate of return are computed by the plant controller.

The internal rate of return for most proposals is based on cash flows projected in constant cruzeiros. However, the Pinda plant expansion was recently projected in nominal cruzeiros (using a 40% per year inflation rate assumption) to fully reflect the working capital and financing implications of inflation on cash flow. Acos' division controller believes that nominal currencies should be used to reflect the impact of inflation and currency exchange adjustments on the company but that constant cruzeiros should be used to evaluate the merits of the project as such.

Because of the importance of government-subsidized financing for major new projects in Brazil, the investment decision often cannot be separated from the financing decision. Projected cash flows for major projects must therefore reflect the terms of the financing that will be available.

Acos has not calculated its cost of capital and does not use a capital spending hurdle rate. Management's philosophy is not to force managers to "compute the right answer" to obtain capital funds.

Cost Systems

Largely because of inflation, Acos Villares is in the possibly unique position of maintaining what amounts to four different (but related) cost systems:

1. Fiscal cost system used to value inventories and report profit in accordance with Brazilian corporation law

2. Standard direct cost system used to budget and control operations
3. Replacement (NIFO) cost system used to price new products
4. CIP (Interministerial Price Control) system used to adjust prices on existing products

The fiscal cost system is based on actual average direct costs plus depreciation (including monetary adjustments for increased depreciation based on monetarily corrected plant and equipment values) per ton of product and broad cost center (pool of machine centers). The standard direct cost system is based on budgeted costs of each product by specific machine center. The replacement cost system simply updates the standard direct cost system for current material replacement costs and labor rates. The CIP system is based on the actual historic cost of a sample of 36 products computed in accordance with government regulations. While the CIP system may not be considered as a cost system in a traditional sense, cost records must be maintained for the products included in the sample in order to comply with regulations.

A comparison of the components of Acos' fiscal cost and standard direct cost systems follows. While these two systems may have certain conceptual similarities, and the data incorporated in them come from the same general accounting systems and production reporting base, the systems differ in the respects shown in Exhibit 10-2.

As a general rule, fiscal costs are revised whenever variances from fiscal costs exceed 10% to 12% of standard. A 10% to 12% variation is simply a practical tolerance for determining when fiscal costs are probably outdated.

The difference between standard direct costs and fiscal costs is credited to the "Fiscal cost reconciliation" line item on the Profit-and-Loss Statement (See Exhibit 10-3). Profit (loss) from plant operations is based on fiscal costs. Other cost line items are derived from the standard direct cost system. The "fiscal cost reconciliation" line item therefore provides the bridge between the standard direct costing system that is used for control purposes and the fiscal cost system that is used for external reporting.

Product Pricing

Product pricing is a responsibility of the marketing department of the company. The pricing process in Brazil is similar to that in the U.S. except that prices on existing products in Brazil are subject to government control. The primary determinants of price, in order of importance, are:

1. Competition
2. Prices of comparable products

EXHIBIT 10–2

Comparison of Fiscal Cost and Standard Direct Cost Systems

Element of System	Treatment of Element	
	Fiscal Cost	Standard Direct Cost
Product detail	Type (grade) of product	Specific product
Cost center detail	Broad cost center (pool of machine centers)	Machine center
Primary unit of measure	Tons produced	Machine center standard machine hour
Conversion cost composition	Direct labor Indirect labor Maintenance Service costs Energy Auxiliary materials Depreciation	Same excluding depreciation
Treatment of variances	Included in cost	Excluded from cost
Material recovery cost credit	Actual recovery	Standard recovery
Raw materials valuation method	Average cost	Replacement
Term of application	Until revised	Six-month period
Frequency of revision	4 times in 1979	Once a year

139

EXHIBIT 10-3

	Results for Month			Accumulated to Date					Total for Year	
	Actual	Budget	Variance	Actual		Budget		Variance	Forecast	Budget
				Amount	%	Amount	%			
Sales (excluding IPI tax)					100.0		100.0			
Sales deductions										
Standard direct cost										
Margin										
Price and usage variance										
Loss on returned goods										
Plant operating expense										
Depreciation (including monetary adjustment)										
Plant administrative expense										
Sale of scrap										
Fiscal cost reconciliation										
Profit (loss) from plant operations										
Divisional marketing and administrative expense										
Profit (loss) from divisional operations										
General and administrative expense										
Interest and financial expense										
Interest earned										
Other nonoperating expense										
Profit (loss) before taxes										
Provision for income taxes										
Profit (loss) after taxes										
Results of monetary correction										
Results of equity adjustment										
Profit (loss) after correction and adjustment										

ACOS VILLARES, S.A.   MONTH   STATEMENT OF PROFIT AND LOSS   Pg. 2

3. CIP constraints
4. Replacement cost

The marketing department keeps track of competitive prices and the prices of comparable Villares products. Plant controllers furnish the marketing department with the CIP and replacement cost information needed for this decision-making process.

All prices are quoted subject to adjustment caused by changes in the CIP index. This means that price quotations are subject to change whenever the CIP index is revised. The CIP index was revised four times in 1979 and is expected to be revised twice in 1980 as part of the government's plan to stem the tide of inflation.

Management expects future price increases to lag behind cost level increases as measured by the CIP index. This lag means that margins will be squeezed unless productivity is improved. Thus increasing attention is being given to the improvement of productivity.

Top Management Reporting

Acos Villares reflects the effect of inflation in five parts of its top management reporting systems. These include the:

1. Structure of the Profit-and-Loss Statement
2. Computation of "return on invested capital" shown in the Summary of Significant Results
3. Format of Source and Application of Funds Statement
4. Preparation of a Cost of Production Statement (which appears to be unique)
5. Development of productivity measurements

Acos' practices with respect to each of these areas will be discussed in the remainder of this chapter.

Structure of Profit-and-Loss Statement

A translation to English of the format of the company's Profit-and-Loss Statement is shown in Exhibit 10–3.

Actual results for the month and year-to-date are compared with the budget, and variances are shown for each line item. Results for the year are forecasted and are compared with the budget for the year.

Cost and usage variances based on the flexible budget are shown as a single line item. Losses on returned goods are shown as an expense. Divisional "period expense" is segregated between plant operating expense, depreciation, and plant administrative expense.

Depreciation is monetarily adjusted, and this adjustment is allowed for income tax purposes. As described in Chapter 3, each year the government publishes indices for adjusting fixed and associated depreciation accounts. The methodology employed is similar to that used to recalculate the value of fixed assets on a current cost basis using the indexing method under FAS No. 33. Therefore profit (or loss) before and after taxes is based on historical costs plus the monetary adjustment for depreciation.

As previously noted, the line item "fiscal cost reconciliation" links the company's standard direct cost system with its fiscal cost system in the same manner that an "inventory adjustment" line item on many U.S. internal income statements links standard direct cost inventory values with full absorption cost inventory values.

The methodology employed in this reconciliation is illustrated below:

(CR$ Millions)

Beginning inventories based on actual average (fiscal) costs	$ 26
Actual costs of production	12
	38
Less ending inventories based on actual average cost	29
Fiscal cost of sales	9
Less cost of sales based on standard direct cost	11
Fiscal cost reconciliation	$(2)

Debts are "monetarily corrected" and this adjustment is included in the Statement of Profit and Loss in the "Interest and financial expense" line.

The "results of monetary correction" line item includes the monetary correction of plant and equipment, investments in subsidiaries, and net worth. Working capital is not monetarily corrected. Because net worth (assets less liabilities) exceeds plant and equipment and investments in subsidiaries (Acos has a positive working capital), monetary corrections for inflation result in a charge to the "results of monetary correction" account (and a reduction of profit).

The "results of equity re-evaluation" reflects Acos' share in subsidiaries' results, which have been monetarily corrected. The increased value of this investment results in a credit to this account (and an addition to profit). Acos' profit performance, therefore, is measured after giving effect to results based on fiscal costs and all monetary corrections and adjustments.

When asked how inflation had affected his reporting system, the division controller responded, "Inflation has not had any effect on our reporting system because this system was established to manage the business on the presumption that inflation exists. However, because of inflation, product pricing is based on replacement costs, and we are especially concerned with analyzing:

1. Price (cost or expense) variances
2. Fiscal cost reconciliation
3. Monetary corrections
4. Equity re-evaluations."

Computation of Return on Invested Capital

Return on invested capital is a key measurement that is used to evaluate all of the companies in the Villares group. It is based on annualized adjusted profit after taxes divided by the average amount of invested capital in the period. Adjusted profit after taxes (the numerator) is computed before interest and monetary corrections (net of taxes). Invested capital (the denominator) includes monetarily corrected long-term financing and net worth.

Inventories are always stated in the balance sheet on a historical average (fiscal) cost basis. Property, plant and equipment are monetarily adjusted for management reporting purposes. Acos' plant and equipment was revalued based on an appraisal two years ago, thus these values, as adjusted for inflation during the intervening period, are close to current cost.

In summary, some elements of the calculation of net worth (e.g., inventories) are based on historical costs while other elements (e.g., property, plant and equipment) are based on current costs. This means that despite Brazil's inflation rate and management's emphasis on return on invested capital, Acos does not compute a "real" rate of return on invested capital on a current cost basis. To do so, it would be necessary to divide profit based on current costs by the current cost of invested capital *including inventories.*

Funds Statement

According to the corporate controller, the most important impact of increased inflation on Acos has been the squeeze that has been placed on capital formation and the availability of external financing at an affordable cost. As a result, increasing emphasis has been placed on cash management, the projection of cash requirements, and the use of the funds statement.

Cash receipts and disbursements are forecasted monthly for the succeeding 12 months. Funds flows are budgeted, and are tracked, in the Source and Application of Funds Statement. This statement separates funds from operations from the corporate movement of funds as shown in Exhibit 10–4.

EXHIBIT 10–4

Source and Application of Funds Statement

Sources and Application of Funds	Year-to-Date Actual	Year-to-Date Budget	Forecast For Year
Division profit (loss)			
Depreciation and nonmonetary items			
Total sources			
Increases (decreases) in:			
Accounts receivable			
Inventories			
Cost of construction in process			
Other assets/liabilities			
Decreases (increases) in:			
Accounts payable			
Customer advances			
Total applications			
Nonmonetary adjustments			
Supply of funds			
Investments in fixed assets			
Net funds flow to (from) corporation			
Nonoperating profit (loss) of corp.			
Depreciation and nonmonetary items			
Capital increases			
Investments in subsidiaries			
Cash dividends received			
Financing received or repaid			
Interest on financing			
Dividends paid			
Other increases and decreases			
including nonmonetary movements			
Net movement in corporation			
Increase or (decrease) in cash			

Cost of Production Statement

The Cost of Production Statement is the principal report used by top management to monitor inflation on a year-to-date basis. This report is based on tracking the unit replacement costs of major elements of cost in accordance with Exhibit 10–5.

144

EXHIBIT 10-5

Cost of Production Statement

Principal Items Produced	Unit of Measurement	Month Quantity Consumed	Unit Price Current Month End	Unit Price Beginning of year	% Change
Primary materials— Domestic (14 types of material are listed)					
Primary materials— Imported (8 types of material are listed)					
Total primary materials					
Auxiliary materials (12 types of material are listed)					
Total auxiliary materials					
Energy Production hours	KWH hours				
Total change in cost					

Total actual, budgeted, and previous year cost increases are summarized on a Statement of Significant Figures.

The January 31, 1980, year-end Statement shows that the general price index increased by 81% as compared to a budgeted increase of 35% and a previous year increase of 41%. Most metal costs increased by over 100% in 1979, and costs of imported materials increased at a higher rate than domestic materials. Costs increased by 25% for the two months ended March 31, 1980.

Productivity Measurements

By hiring a director of productivity for the Villares group, senior management has explicitly recognized the need to improve productivity in an inflationary environment. Because of government policies Villares' top management believes that labor costs, materials, plant and equipment costs and taxes will increase at a faster rate than the general inflation rate. Selling prices, on the other hand are expected to lag behind inflation. This has left management with only one basic alternative: improve productivity.

Acos' management has been struggling with the measurement of productivity. Because of the multitude of products involved and variations in product mix, management has not established any plant-wide measurements of partial or total productivity. Such plant-wide measurements would require the calculation of meaningful "equivalent ton" or "constant cruzeiro" output measurements and the definition of input measurements for all items produced.

Productivity measurements[4] of a sort were established in 1979 for three major pieces of equipment (2,000-ton press, melt shop and rolling mill) that constitute the principal "bottlenecks" in the plant. These productivity measurements are indices based on consistent machine hour standards established by Industrial Engineering.

Three measurements are charted monthly (for the month and on a six-month moving average basis):

1. Percentage performance (standard machine hours ÷ actual machine hours)
2. Percentage utilization (actual machine hours ÷ total machine hours available)
3. Percentage productivity (standard machine hours ÷ total machine hours available). Percent productivity is the product of percent performance and percent utilization.

These charts show that percentage performance tends to vary with percentage utilization. The busier the plant is, the higher its percentage productivity tends to be. Thus increased production has a double-barrelled effect on increasing productivity.

As in many U.S. companies, financial strategies and management accounting techniques for coping with the impact of inflation are in a state of flux at Acos. Operating and financial management are not satisfied with their current systems and are continually striving to modify these systems to better deal with the realities of Brazil's business and inflationary environment as well as the company's internal planning and control needs. How these systems will evolve is unknown. From all indications, however, it appears that management intends to develop and install productivity measurements, make more use of current cost rather than constant cruzeiro information, and computerize the data processing that is required.

---

[4] Although these may not be productivity measurements in the traditional sense, Acos' management refers to them as such.

Chapter 11

Shell Oil Company

Shell Oil Company is recognized as one of the leading oil and gas producers, refiners, and petrochemical manufacturers and is one of the largest marketers of gasoline in the United States. Because petroleum prices have recently increased at rates that exceed general price levels, oil companies are affected by inflation differently from other businesses. Nevertheless, Shell shares many inflationary problems with other capital-intensive companies and has therefore adapted its business strategies and planning and control practices to deal with these challenges.

Because of the substantial investments required in the oil and petrochemical business, inflation has probably had its largest impact on planning and control practices in the areas of strategic planning and capital expenditure planning and control.

Shell pioneered in reporting its results to the public on a price level adjusted basis. Despite the use of constant dollars for external reporting, however, the company relies primarily on traditional management accounting tools for internal reporting and profitability and performance measurement.

Background of Company

Shell reported revenues of $14.5 billion and net income of $1.1 billion on shareholders' equity of $7.0 billion and total assets of $16.1 billion in 1979. While these reported results represent a 30% increase in revenues and a 38% increase in net income over the preceding year, 12% of the increase in revenues and 9% of the increase in net income (exclusive of purchasing power gains on net assets) resulted from inflation when measured in December 1979 constant dollars. Moreover, an 18.4% historic return on shareholders' equity is reduced to a 10.9% return on a constant dollar basis.

The company is engaged in two major business functions: oil and gas exploration and production, and oil and chemical product refining and marketing. Exploration and production accounted for about two-thirds of net income in 1979, and product refining and marketing accounted for the remaining third. In the past few years the emphasis in exploration and production has been the search for oil and gas, while in oil and chemical products the focus has been on efficiency and productivity improvement.

In 1979, Shell's expenditures for exploration and production projects were $5.2 billion, which included $3.6 billion for the purchase of Belridge Oil Company. Shell's planned 1980 capital and exploratory spending for exploration and production is about 70% higher than its 1979 (excluding the Belridge acquisition) expenditures for new exploration and production projects. In exploration and production a high priority objective is to bring Belridge reserves up to maximum sustainable production as quickly as possible. In chemical products Shell is adding capacity, and in oil products the company is seeking to become the most efficient large-volume marketer.

Along with other oil companies, Shell is faced with foreign supply and pricing pressures (which have, of course, recently benefited the company), increasing exploration and production costs and uncertainties, and adverse regulatory and taxation constraints. The energy shortage, increasing OPEC prices and the resulting windfall profits tax have been the most visible manifestations of these external forces. Increased costs, coupled with environmental constraints, have driven up the cost of drilling and production.

Because of the size and nature of the business, the business strategies that have been adopted, and the external forces referred to above, the principal management accounting issues at Shell relate to strategic planning, capital expenditure control and productivity improvement. It is natural, therefore, that these areas receive considerable internal attention.

Organization

Shell Oil Company's operations are decentralized to its two main functions: exploration and production, and oil and chemical products. While the vice president, finance, and the controller are responsible for external reporting and internal accounting policies, management accounting techniques and management reporting formats are prescribed largely at the function level.

The finance manager in exploration and production and the general manager, finance, in oil and chemical products are functionally responsible to the corporate financial organization but report on a line basis to the executive vice president for their respective functions.

Highlights of this basic organization are shown in Exhibit 11–1. This is not a complete organization chart; it is simply intended to show the relationship of selected key operating and financial executives.

The corporate financial and administrative organization is structured as shown in Exhibit 11–2. This is also not a complete organization chart; the

EXHIBIT 11–1

Shell Oil Company Organization

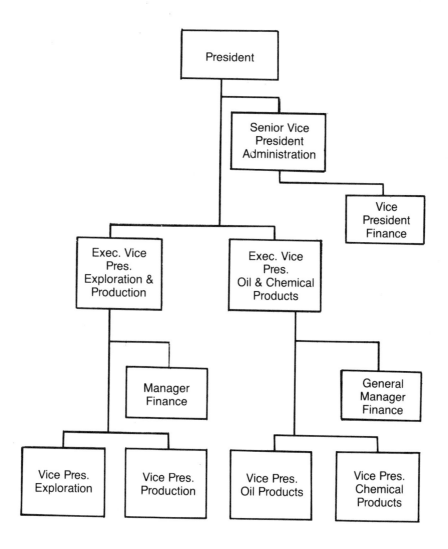

EXHIBIT 11–2

Shell Oil Company
Corporate Financial Organization

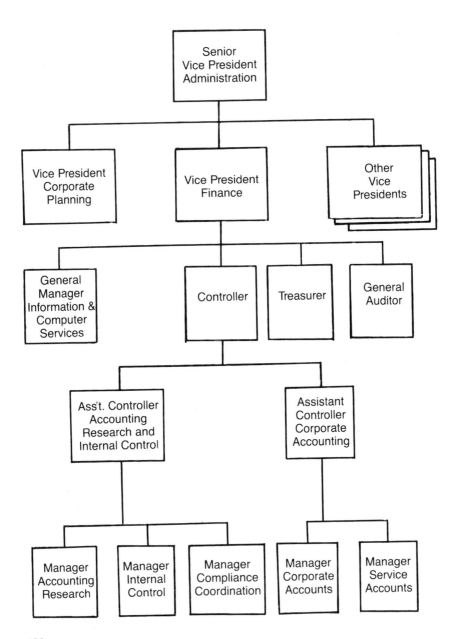

intention here is to show how the corporate accounting function is organized.

Shell's financial reporting and consolidation accounting information flow is portrayed in Exhibit 11–3.

EXHIBIT 11–3

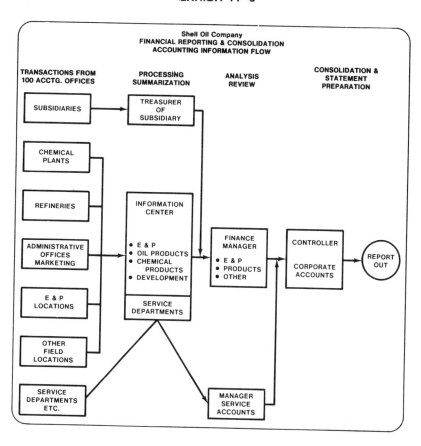

Source: W.J. Ihlanfeldt, "Shell Oil Company's Approach to Internal Control," *Financial Executive*, July 1979.

Information and computer services operations are centralized and provide services to the entire corporate organization. Budgeting is administered by the separate functions and is coordinated by corporate planning. Corporate planning is responsible for coordinating functional strategic planning. The treasurer is responsible for managing all of the funds of the corporation. Much recent attention has been directed towards raising new capital.

The general auditor is an important position at Shell as it is in most oil companies. He has both operational and financial auditing responsibilities.

Shell's style of management is conservative, and decisions are made on a participative basis. Employees typically are recruited out of school and remain with the company for their entire working careers. While senior executives are seasoned by progressive responsibility within the Shell organization, they are nevertheless encouraged to adopt ideas from outside the company. As a result, planning and control techniques at Shell evolve slowly, but they are generally innovative and apparently represent the state of the art in the industry.

Strategic Planning

Inflation is one of many variables considered in the strategic planning process, but it is by no means a driving force. As a senior financial executive acknowledged, to a certain extent oil companies are inflation-proof. No matter what rate of inflation is incurred, energy costs are not likely to decline. A planning executive pointed out, "We really do not know where inflation is headed. Our planning methodologies, therefore, must be designed to accommodate varying inflation premises."

"Base planning premises" are promulgated by the corporate planning department in January of each year. These premises cover crude oil supplies, economic growth and anticipated price and regulatory actions in addition to inflation. Also, several "derivative premises" are developed from the base premises. Examples of derivative premises include the unemployment rate, housing starts, number of automobiles and miles driven.

General inflation premises are based on the GNP deflator rather than the Consumer Price Index. Shell's GNP deflator inflation rate premises in 1980 ranged downward from 8.5% in 1980 to 6.5% in the late 1980's. These premises are based on several economic models and are predicated on the judgment that a conservative political tide in the United States will bring about an amelioration of inflation. Shell also uses "cost index" forecasts for certain categories of activity.

Shell's planning process consists of short-term operating plans (STOP) and long-range plans (LRP) that are prepared by each function. Short-term plans are prepared in the fall of each year and include a forecast for each of the next three years. The first forecast year of the operating plan is, in effect, the budget for the coming year. Long-range (strategic) plans extend over a 20-year horizon with the first five years being shown in detail.

The long-range planning process is built around the concept of alternate scenarios. Scenarios are developed for the base premises, as well as for two or three sets of alternatives in order to ascertain the potential impact on the company of various likely technical and economic variables (including price levels).

152

Plans are prepared in both current and constant dollars. Forecasts are developed in nominal dollars but are deflated back into constant dollars because it is "a lot easier to think of the world in constant dollars. . . . Inflation at a 7% to 8% rate over ten years 'boggles the mind.'" Plans prepared in both current and constant dollars allow management to "unclutter its thinking."

Four or five strategic options are developed for each business unit. Strategies are selected from these options on a participative basis. Strategic plans are presented to top management by the business unit manager at a corporate strategy conference which is held each June.

The oil and chemical products organization, for example, consists of growth chemical businesses and mature oil businesses. In making investment and pricing decisions, growth chemical strategies are focused on obtaining sufficient *real* profit margins and *real* rates of return. Oil product strategies, on the other hand, are focused on cost reductions, productivity improvements, and energy cost savings in order to sustain the buying power of cash generated from the business.

"Action items" are developed for each strategy. Action items are periodically reviewed, but a routine reporting system has not been developed for this process.

The planning process at Shell provides for the following financial schedules and five-year projections:

1. Use of funds
2. Source of funds
3. Capital expenditures
4. Real net income
5. Financial ratios based on historic costs including:
   a. Net income to total capital (excluding deferred taxes)
   b. Net income to equity investment
   c. Net income to total capital (including deferred taxes)
   d. Cash flow from operations to gross investment (before depreciation)
   e. Capital expenditures to cash flow from operations
   f. Debt to total capital (excluding deferred taxes)
6. Cash position (funds statement)
7. Financial (debt service) and dividend requirements (disposable income)

In addition, 20-year projections are prepared of:

1. Funds flow (in both nominal and constant dollars)
2. Balance sheet
3. Capital expenditures (in both nominal and constant dollars)

4. Net and cash income
5. Corporate ratios
6. Financial (debt service) and dividend requirements

The 20-year projections are supported by a summary of the premises that are applied.

Another integral part of the strategic planning process in the products group is the intensive business review. These studies are conducted on a periodic basis by multidisciplinary teams appropriate to each business unit. Such studies involve an in-depth review of the business, its plans, and the strategic options available.

Especially high stakes are involved in the development of strategic plans for exploration and production. This process involves different premises with respect to the price of crude as well as different general inflation rates. However, we were told that general inflation has a relatively minor impact on this process.

The oil and gas exploration and production cycle typically extends over many years as is illustrated in Exhibit 11–4.

Plans are prepared for each major geological province, e.g., the Gulf of Mexico. Alternate scenarios are developed for nontechnical considerations such as price levels and costs, technical considerations such as discovery volumes, the rate of development and production rates. A number of "what if's" are evaluated, especially for marginal projects which may, or may not, be profitable. Technical considerations, especially discovery volumes— rather than price levels—constitute the big unknowns and are the reasons why investments in exploration and production are so inherently risky.

Corporate Financial Strategies

According to Shell's treasurer, several corporate financial strategies have been affected by inflation.

Short- and long-term borrowing was accelerated largely to pay for the Belridge acquisition, but also to pay for the increased exploration, production and plant expansion costs caused by inflation. Shell's long-term debt increased from 20% of total capital at the end of 1978 to 34% of total capital at the end of 1979.

The treasurer observed that inflation causes financial managers to lean towards the increased use of leverage and a greater application of different kinds (short-, intermediate- and long-term) of debt providing that such debt can be obtained at a reasonable cost without jeopardizing the company's credit rating. He perceives that investors presently prefer short- and inter- mediate-term bonds and convertible bonds with "kickers." In an inflationary environment, bonds are repaid with cheaper dollars which prompted the treasurer to note that from strictly a company perspective, Shell has never sold a "bad bond" nor has it sold a "good stock."

Shell's capital expenditure hurdle rate has been boosted by inflation. Shell follows the practice of calculating an inflation-free (real) rate and an annual inflation-adjusted (nominal) rate for evaluating capital investments. The inflation-free rate is used for comparisons with deflated dollar projections, and the inflation-adjusted rate is used in conjunction with projections of current dollars. Both rates are used to prioritize investments in the capital allocation process. (Shell has reportedly emphasized the cost-of-capital concept routinely in investment evaluations since the mid-1950's.)

Capital expenditures for cost reduction have been accelerated as a result of inflation. This practice is in keeping with the company's emphasis on productivity improvement and with the practices of other large companies (see Chapter 8). Shell has not deferred any capital expenditure because of inflation.

Dividend payments per share have been increased because of inflation and the company's earnings record. However, the dividend payout ratio has not been increased because of Shell's increased capital requirements.

The use of long-term purchase contracts has also been increased because of inflation in order to obtain materials at predictable prices. Along with most of the oil and petrochemical industries, Shell values its inventories on a LIFO basis in order to conserve cash.

Inflation has also affected Shell's incentive compensation formulas which are partially based on inflation-adjusted net income. However, monetary gains or losses are not included in these calculations because such gains and losses are subject to swings which are not considered to be controllable by management.

Capital Expenditures

Shell undertakes several major capital projects each year. Because of the substantial funds involved in many projects over an extended period of time, Shell has developed sophisticated systems for planning and controlling capital expenditures. These systems allow for price changes and the impact of inflation on future cash flows.

Capital expenditure planning is performed on an iterative basis in increasing detail, and inflation is considered in each phase of this process. The basic steps of this planning process are as follows:

1. Long-Range Plan (LRP) estimate including preliminary outline of production process
2. Short-Term Operating Plan (STOP) estimate including final production process design

EXHIBIT 11—4

Characteristics of an E&P Cycle
Annual Expenditures

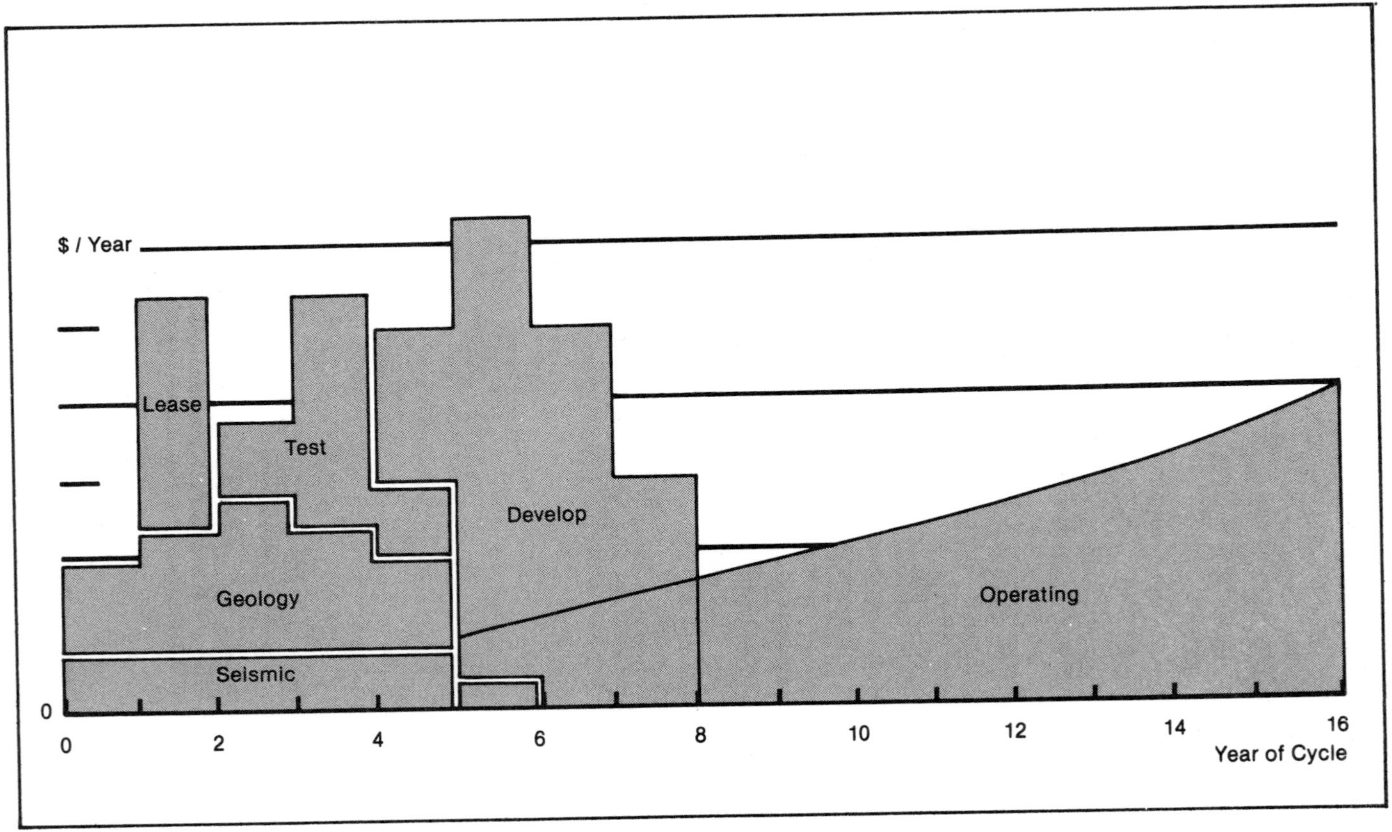

156

Characteristics of an E&P Cycle
Annual Expenditures

MMB & BCF / Year

Oil & Gas Production

Year of Cycle

3. Authority for Expenditure (AFE) including mechanical flow diagrams and scope specifications
4. Control estimate
5. Definitive estimate

Each step will be discussed in the paragraphs that follow.

Because approximately 70% to 80% of the projects included in the first three years of the LRP estimate are undertaken, the LRP is the critical point in the review process. Accordingly, projects are subjected to intensive review in the course of evaluating LRPs. Typically, several iterations are involved in an LRP estimate for different construction options, and the differences in cost caused by inflation (escalation) are tracked from estimate to estimate. Estimates are based on historical construction costs for similar plants adjusted for the specific size of the proposed plant, differences between construction costs by location, and cost escalation based on Shell construction cost indices for petrochemical and refining facilities.

Construction cost indices are developed for each element of cost (e.g., concrete, piping, steel, instrumentation and labor) by a multidisciplinary team of engineers. These indices are based on a three-year, detailed analysis of cost elements and a ten-year correlation of data. Indices are updated each six months.

Cash flow projections are made in both nominal and constant dollars, and returns are compared with both the nominal and real cost of capital. Sometimes the projection is made in constant dollars and then is converted to nominal dollars, and other times the projection is made the other way around.

Capital expenditures are undertaken for both economic and obligatory reasons. Projects are classified as "strategic," "tactical" (cost reduction) and "obligatory" (e.g., safety or environmental). Both the internal rate of return (IRR) and present value are used to evaluate strategic and tactical projects. Obligatory projects, accounting for about 20% of the dollars expended in the products function, are usually justified by noneconomic criteria.

The STOP project cost estimate for the following year reflects the final production process design and is prepared in more detail than the LRP estimate. By this time the plant sizing and options have usually been determined. The STOP estimate is also incorporated in the LRP as part of the iterative planning process.

The AFE provides the authority to commit funds to the project construction. It is generally supported by mechanical flow diagrams and scope specifications. (Shell follows the practice of estimating costs in detail *before* requesting bids from contractors rather than basing its estimate on contractors' bids.) Differences in construction costs between the estimates contained in the LRP and the AFE are analyzed to show the effect of specification changes and price escalation.

The control estimate is prepared in detail by work package[1] and type of cost. This estimate is used to control the actual costs of the project.

The definitive estimate is based on actual supplier quotations and is used to pinpoint completed construction costs. Inflation assumptions are monitored as bids are received and equipment is purchased.

About 20 to 40 major projects generally are in process at any one time. The financial organization reports and monitors costs; the engineering organization controls costs.

Inflation may defer new projects, but it does not delay projects that are already in process. Indeed, capital expenditures for cost reduction have been accelerated as a result of inflation as previously noted. Product function engineering executives said that they receive considerable pressure to complete cost reduction and high payout projects as quickly as possible.

Financial Reporting

Shell has been a financial reporting innovator. The company has publicly disclosed its financial results on a constant dollar basis since 1974 and was the first major U.S. company to provide such information. The vice president, finance, and the controller thought that inflation was an important factor and that the company would be correct in making this disclosure. Top management was supportive of this conclusion. No external pressures were involved.

Financial management evaluated alternative methodologies and decided that the general price level approach was the most appropriate. They reasoned that the price level approach is objective, and that since Shell was breaking new ground, the new disclosures should be highly credible. Shell's disclosure in its 1974 annual report, together with the inflation accounting information contained in its 1979 annual report, are reproduced in Exhibits 11–5 and 11–6 respectively.

The 1979 inflation-adjusted information goes beyond the minimum requirements of FAS No. 33 and includes balance sheet data and five-year comparisons of selected financial ratios. Note also that "Purchasing power gain on net monetary items" is added to "Income from continuing operations" in the constant dollar data comparison. (As indicated in Chapter 5, many accounting authorities disagreed with this practice.) However, the purchasing power gain on net monetary items has not been considered by Shell management in connection with the funds statement.

Shell's financial management was surprised that no one followed its lead in 1974 as inflation accounting had been the subject of considerable

---

[1]Work package is a term used in the construction industry to designate the smallest measurable component of the job.

EXHIBIT 11-5

Shell Oil Company Inflation Accounting Information Contained in 1974 Annual Report

(Millions of dollars except per share amounts)

	Current Dollars*			Historical Dollars		
	1974	1973	1972	1974	1973	1972
Summary Statement of Income						
Revenues	$8,866.7	$6,614.4	$5,876.1	$8,493.0	$5,749.6	$4,849.8
Costs and expenses:						
Depreciation, depletion, etc.	654.2	626.5	585.4	502.9	441.7	396.8
Income, operating and consumer taxes	1,320.2	1,236.2	1,163.6	1,264.5	1,074.6	960.4
Interest & discount amortization on indebtedness	63.5	69.9	72.0	60.8	60.8	59.4
Other costs & expenses	6,317.3	4,426.2	3,866.1	6,044.3	3,839.8	3,172.7
Income before purchasing power gain or loss on monetary items	$ 511.5	$ 255.6	$ 189.0	$ 620.5	$ 332.7	$ 260.5
Purchasing power gain (loss) on:						
Long-term debt	117.0	82.9	36.4	—	—	—
Other monetary items	(5.1)	(4.8)	2.2	—	—	—
Net income	$ 623.4	$ 333.7	$ 227.6	$ 620.5	$ 332.7	$ 260.5
Summary Balance Sheet						
Current assets	$2,161.7	$1,953.4	$1,925.2	$2,072.2	$1,713.1	$1,596.1
Investments & long-term receivables	129.5	110.3	106.1	116.0	91.7	84.1
Properties, plant & equipment (net)	5,146.6	4,906.7	4,923.3	3,905.3	3,526.9	3,438.9
Deferred charges	42.3	61.4	67.5	35.4	49.5	52.5
Current liabilities	1,272.6	1,097.4	1,113.4	1,272.6	981.6	928.2
Long-term debt	976.6	1,119.0	1,230.3	976.6	1,000.9	1,025.6
Deferred credits—federal income taxes	320.0	339.5	351.4	320.0	303.6	292.8
Shareholders' equity	$4,910.9	$4,475.9	$4,327.0	$3,559.7	$3,095.1	$2,925.0

Per Share Data†

Net income	$ 9.25	$ 4.95	$ 3.38	$ 9.21	$ 4.94	$ 3.86
Cash dividends	$ 2.56	$ 2.76	$ 2.91	$ 2.45	$ 2.40	$ 2.40

Ratios (see definitions on page 36)

Return on shareholders' equity	13.9%	7.7%	5.3%	20.0%	11.4%	9.2%
Return on total capital	11.7%	6.6%	5.0%	16.0%	9.2%	8.0%
Net income revenues**	7.7%	5.9%	4.6%	8.1%	6.7%	6.3%
Dividends: net income	27.7%	55.7%	86.1%	26.6%	48.6%	62.1%
Debt: total capital	16.6%	20.0%	22.1%	21.5%	24.4%	26.0%

*Based on purchasing power dollars at December 31, 1974.
†Per weighted average share outstanding each year.
**Excluding consumer excise and sales taxes.

EXHIBIT 11–6

Shell Oil Company Inflation Accounting Information Contained in 1979 Annual Report

Millions of dollars except per share amounts	Historical Dollars 1979	Dollars of Current Purchasing Power*			
		Constant Dollar Data		Current Cost Data	
		1979	1978	1979	1978

Summary Statement of Income

	Historical 1979	Constant 1979	Constant 1978	Current Cost 1979	Current Cost 1978
Revenues	$14,546	$15,374	$13,081	$15,374	$13,081
Cost and Expenses:					
Depreciation, depletion, etc.	704	1,107	1,015	1,219	1,217
Income and operating taxes	1,090	1,152	917	1,152	917
Other costs and expenses	11,626	12,337	10,545	12,362	10,684
Income from Continuing Operations	1,126	778	604	641	263
Purchasing power gain on net monetary items		337	236	337	236
Net income	$ 1,126	$ 1,115	$ 840		
Increase in current cost valuation of inventory and property, plant & equipment held during year				$ 2,149	$ 1,158
Effect of increases in general price level				1,754	1,176
Excess of increase in specific prices over increase in general price level				$ 395	$ (18)

Balance Sheet Data

	Historical 1979	Constant 1979	Constant 1978	Current Cost 1979	Current Cost 1978
Inventories of Oils and Chemicals	$ 520	$ 850	$ 890	$ 2,231	$ 1,557
Net Property, Plant & Equipment	$12,385	$16,043	$11,469	$17,178	$13,051
Shareholders' Equity	$ 7,004	$11,131	$10,257	$13,617	$12,505

Per Share Data†	1979	1978	1977	1976	1975
Income from Continuing Operations	$ 7.32	$ 5.06	$ 4.05	$ 4.17	$ 1.76
Net Income	$ 7.32	$ 7.26	$ 5.63	—	—

Five-Year Comparisons (In December 1979 dollars)

	1979	1978	1977	1976	1975
Revenues	$15,374	$13,081	$12,912	$12,551	$11,732
Constant dollar net income	$ 1,115	$ 840	$ 805	$ 778	$ 593
Cash dividends per share†	$ 2.22	$ 2.04	$ 1.98	$ 1.85	$ 1.80
Closing market price per share	$ 54.25	$ 36.54	$ 41.37	$ 52.02	$ 33.86
Consumer price index—end of year	229.9	202.9	186.1	174.3	166.3
Ratios:					
Net Income to Shareholders' Equity:					
Historical cost basis	18.4%	15.1%	16.2%	18.2%	14.4%
Constant dollar basis	10.9%	8.8%	9.1%	9.7%	7.7%
Income from Continuing Operations to Shareholders' Equity:					
Historical cost basis	18.4%	15.1%	16.2%	18.2%	14.4%
Constant dollar basis	7.6%	6.3%	7.4%	8.5%	6.0%
Current cost basis	5.1%	2.2%	—	—	—

*Current cost and constant dollar amounts are expressed in December 1979 dollars. Changes are measured by the Consumer Price Index.

†Per weighted average shares outstanding each year.

discussion among academicians and within the FASB. Moreover, the company received little reaction from users and does not know how to interpret this silence.

Shell's financial and accounting management continues to actively participate in the FASB's inflation accounting efforts and in the Financial Executives Institute's Committee on Corporate Reporting. The vice president, finance, concludes that the effect of inflation is not as well understood by operating people and investors as it ought to be.

Productivity Measurement

As a process manager put it on the way to the company from the airport, "The buzz word of the day is productivity. Everybody talks about it, but isn't sure what to do or how it should be measured. . . ."

Shell's president has emphasized productivity improvement in public statements, and the message apparently has reached middle management. This recent emphasis on productivity improvement at Shell has been largely inflation-generated.

The manager of production administration said that Shell has been performing productivity analyses since at least 1949. In the spring of 1980, however, Shell formed a 15-person multidisciplinary task force of senior people to develop a system to monitor productivity and to identify opportunities for improvements in productivity.

The manager of production administration believes that about ten indices will be required. He believes that any more than that number tends to confuse the recipient.

It is also noteworthy that, in keeping with Shell's decentralized style of management, the impetus for developing a productivity measurement system came from functional management rather than from corporate management. Shell has not promulgated any corporate guidelines as to how productivity indices should be calculated.

Profitability and Performance Measurement

Management performance at Shell is measured based on historical costs. Actual results are compared with budgeted (STOP) results by function and business center.

Product profit margin analyses are also based on historic costs. Standard product costs are reviewed annually and include an allowance for inflation. The controller noted that competitors also reportedly prepare their product profitability analyses on a historic cost basis.

164

Chemical plants, refineries and other operations are regarded as cost centers. Operations are controlled by comparing actual historic costs with budgeted (STOP) costs.

Funds management is more widely applied as a result of inflation, but none of the constant dollar or current cost concepts that are used for financial reporting is used for internal profitability and performance measurement. Current costs are used in the marketing function for determining exit values but not for profitability and performance measurement.

Despite proddings from the vice president, finance, operating management has really not bought constant dollar inflation accounting concepts. Because profitability and performance reporting at Shell originates at the functional level, it is unlikely that these concepts will be adopted for internal profitability and performance measurement until they are more widely understood. The problem of understanding and adoption is compounded by the fact that constant dollar or current cost income, divided by constant dollar or current cost capital employed, generally results in lower returns than historic cost income divided by historic cost total capital. Operating managers understandably tend to resist such reductions in performance measurement indicators.

Chapter 12

N.V. Philips

Inflation-adjusted accounting practices are not new to N.V. Philips Gloeilampenfabrieken, which has used the replacement cost concept for both internal and external reporting for many years. As a multinational firm operating in over 70 countries, Philips routinely deals with a multiplicity of inflation rates, interest rates and currency fluctuations. This case, therefore, describes the practices of a company that has dealt with inflation in several environments and has been in the forefront in developing management accounting techniques to deal with inflation.

Replacement cost accounting practices, which are described more fully in the section of this chapter on reporting, are used at Philips to provide management with a current "going-concern" valuation of assets and worth. By computing replacement costs for assets yearly, Philips' management can review the current economics of operations at any time without additional calculations of current asset values. Through the use of replacement cost accounting techniques, effects of changes in value of specific assets apart from general inflation can be isolated through discounting at an appropriate rate which considers both general inflation and interest components.

Company Background

Philips was founded in 1891 and has grown from a small manufacturer of light bulbs to one of the world's largest diversified electronics companies. Philips' worldwide sales in 1979 were Dfl 33,238 million (approximately $17 billion U.S.), making it the ninth largest non-U.S. company in the world. The company is headquartered in Eindhoven, Netherlands and employs 380,000 people worldwide.

The annual report for 1979 shows that Philips is organized into 14 major product divisions and has participations of importance in 66 individual countries (see Exhibits 12–1 and 12–2). The company's major emphasis is in Europe, where 290 of its 460 plants are located and 64.4% of sales were generated in 1979.

EXHIBIT 12-1

Philips in Individual Countries

The list of Philips participations of importance in individual countries as shown in the 1979 annual report includes:

Argentina	Malaysia
Australia	Mexico
Austria	Morocco
Bangladesh	Netherlands
Belgium	Netherlands Antilles
Bolivia	New Zealand
Brazil	Nigeria
Canada	Norway
Chile	Pakistan
Columbia	Paraguay
Costa Rica	Peru
Denmark	Philippines
Ecuador	Portugal
Egypt	Singapore
El Salvador	South Africa
Ethiopia	South Korea
Federal Republic of Germany	Spain
Finland	Sweden
France	Switzerland
Ghana	Syria
Greece	Taiwan
Guatemala	Tanzania
Hong Kong	Thailand
India	Tunisia
Indonesia	Turkey
Iran	United Kingdom
Ireland	United States of America [1]
Italy	Uganda
Jamaica	Uruguay
Japan	Venezuela
Kenya	Zaire
Lebanon	Zambia
Luxembourg	Zimbabwe

The company's activities can be classified into six business sectors which are similar in technology and market approach: lighting and batteries, home electronics, domestic appliances and personal care products, products for professional applications including computer products and systems, industrial supplies, and miscellaneous activities. The lighting division markets incandescent lamps, photo and professional studio equipment, batteries,

---

[1] Philips activities in the United States are being carried out by the U.S. Philips Trust.

EXHIBIT 12–2

Philips Product Divisions

Lighting
Audio
Video
Small Domestic Appliances
Major Domestic Appliances
Electro-Acoustics
Telecommunications and Defense Systems
Data Systems
Scientific and Industrial Equipment
Medical Systems
Elcoma
Allied Industries
Glass
Pharmaceutical-Chemical Products

lamp components, and chemicals as well as outdoor and indoor lighting and accessories. Home electronics for sound and vision include television, video long play (video disk), cassette and reel-to-reel recorders, car radios, as well as portable and main radios. Domestic and personal care appliances include washing machines, dishwashers, refrigerators and freezers, microwave ovens and coffee makers (well-known under the brand name Norelco in the USA).

The products and systems for professional applications sector includes telecommunications, cable products and systems, defense systems, small computer systems, word processors, and medical systems for diagnosis and therapy. The industrial supplies sector manufactures picture tubes and television glass, integrated circuits, transistors and diodes, passive (capacitors and resistors) components and materials, plastic and metal components, and welding products. This sector is a vertically integrated supplier to many other Philips groups.

Other products are grouped together to form a miscellaneous sector that includes pharmaceutical products for human and animal health, crop protection products, retailing and musical instruments.

Organization and Management Philosophy

Philips employs a matrix organization concept that provides for joint management responsibilities. The national organizations (listed in Exhibit 12–1), which may themselves consist of several companies, form one side of the matrix. The product divisions (listed in Exhibit 12–2) form the other side of the matrix.

Operations, including marketing and manufacturing, are controlled by the national organization of the country in which they are located. The product divisions determine product policy in consultation with the national organizations based on the nature of the market, products, and organization in each particular country. Thus, the national organizations are the "line organization" while the product divisions provide technical and functional coordination from Eindhoven. The Board of Management sets overall policy.

The overall organization of Philips is portrayed in Exhibit 12–3. In some instances Philips products are produced in one or a few locations for worldwide distribution. Because of their multinational character these International Production Centers (IPC), report to the product division as well as to the national organization.

EXHIBIT 12–3

Overall Organization

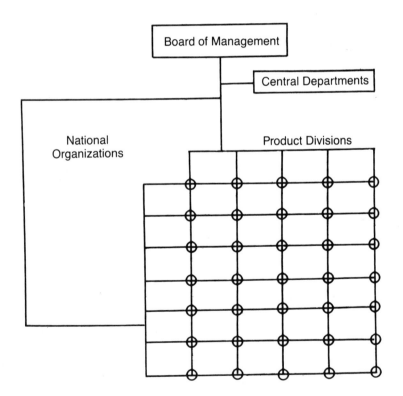

Corporate staff departments, listed in Exhibit 12–4, assist the national organizations and product divisions. They also provide coordination from a functional standpoint. The accounting department, for example, establishes corporate standards and procedures for internal reporting.

All of the functions normally associated with a company operating in that environment are contained in a national organization. The structures of the national organizations may vary slightly from one another to reflect the requirements of the country and local business community.

EXHIBIT 12–4

Corporate Staff Departments

Accounting Department
Building Design and Plant
    Engineering Division
Bureau Concern Committee
    External Relations
Bureau External Economic
    Relations
Central Development Bureau
Center for Technology
Concern Industrial Design
    Center
Concern Marketing Support
    Department
Concern Office The Hague
Concern Press Office
Concern Projects Group
Concern Quality Bureau
Concern Service
Concern Staff Bureau
Concern Standardization
    Department
Concern Strategic Planning
    Group
Direct Export
Engineering Works
Financial Department
Fiscal Affairs
Forwarding
Industrial Coordination Office
Information Systems and
    Automation
Internal Audit Department
Legal Department
Military Affairs (Military Defense
    Center)

Patents and Trademarks
    Department
Personnel and Industrial
    Relations Department
Plastics and Metalware Factory
Purchasing Department
Real Estate
Special Overseas Organization
Technical Efficiency and
    Organization

Regional Management Bureau

Research Organization

Product division organizations are concerned with the marketing, planning and production activities for a product, and may be quite different from one group to another, reflecting specific needs. A typical product division organization (in this case the Data Systems Product Division) is illustrated in Exhibit 12–5.

Much of the rationale for a matrix organization stems from Philips' multinational characteristics. Less than 10% of corporate sales are in its home country, the Netherlands. Consequently, Philips has created a concept

EXHIBIT 12–5

Data Systems Product Division Organization

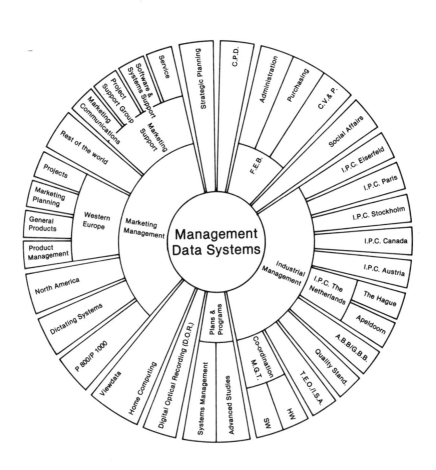

of a federation of companies serving a variety of consumer markets, with a cooperative nondirective posture taken in Eindhoven. One manager described the organizational style as "management by acceptance—you need to convince your counterparts, not overrule them." An example of cooperation is in the European television market, where the same television chassis is sold with a variety of cabinets differing by country to match the local culture.

The work atmosphere at Philips is informal. Employees are reportedly very loyal to the company, perhaps resulting from a paternalistic attitude by the company in the early part of the century. In looking about Eindhoven, one sees Philips' schools, Philips' parks and the Philips' soccer stadium. Perhaps the attitudes at Philips were best summarized by its Chairman Frederick Philips, who once stated, "Figures are important. People are more important."

Planning at Philips

Philips employs formalized, uniform, worldwide planning processes. Replacement cost accounting, rather than historical cost accounting, concepts are employed throughout the company. Planning starts with economic forecasting and includes annual four-year strategic plans and operating budgets.

Economic forecasting for the company is performed centrally in Eindhoven to provide a consistent set of economic assumptions for the strategic planning process. A working group, composed of members of the Finance Department and Marketing Support Department, publishes annual environmental information and five-year economic forecasts for use in the planning process. These forecasts cover real growth in GNP, developments in consumer prices and inflation, growth in private expenditures in durable goods, currency forecasts, and specific developments in various sectors of industry. Special country studies are also provided for 26 major countries, with particular focus given to consumer and investment expenditure trends in Western Europe and the U.S.

Because Philips operates in a large number of countries, currency exchange rate planning is a particularly important function. With floating exchange rates on the world market, differences in inflation between countries are often reflected in foreign exchange. Exchange rates are forecast by the Currency Committee, which consists of members of the Administration (Accounting), Auditing, and Finance departments. Internal conversion rates are established by this committee, which consults with the relevant national organization in the process.

Three types of "precalculation" (or planning as opposed to "postcalculation" or actual) rates are calculated, the "four-year plan rate," the "budget rate," and the "trend indication rate." Four-year plan rates are forecast earlier than budget rates, which cover only one year and are a more current estimate. The trend indication rate is used in the internal transfer pricing system to ensure consistency between countries in cost and price assumptions for intracompany transactions.

Strategic Planning—The Four-Year Plan

Strategic planning is conducted locally by the national organizations and is coordinated and consolidated for the company by the Strategic Planning Group in Eindhoven. The corporate group works with the organization to define strategic business units (SBUs) around which to plan, which is often difficult in a multi-tiered, vertically-integrated operation. Markets are often also unclear. For example, in the case of home computers, should they be included with small systems, home appliances or video markets for planning purposes?

After SBUs are defined, project teams are formed to conduct external and internal appraisals of the economic, social, political and technical aspects of the business. The external appraisal team, composed of both national organization and product division staff, focuses on the marketplace. Analyses of market share, industry attractiveness, industry maturity, business strength and competitive position are used to formulate a list of 20–25 important issues for management. This list of issues is used in a working session with the SBUs' top management to select a list of key criteria, usually about ten in number. Inflation and productivity vis-a-vis competition are two issues which often emerge from this process.

The internal appraisal is a more complex process. Management and the strategic planners work together to reach a consensus on the strengths and weaknesses of the business. Each of these items is used in formulating a "confrontation matrix" in which these strengths and weaknesses are contrasted with business opportunities and threats. Key issues from the internal appraisal are formulated from this matrix.

Using these strategic issues, alternative strategies are formulated, and forecasted results under those strategies are quantified for analysis. Profitability forecasts are made for major alternatives (perhaps a decision on whether to make or buy or what channels of distribution to use) and are modeled using Monte Carlo simulation techniques. While such forecasts are prepared in nominal guilders, specific prices and replacement values are projected to reflect inflationary effects. Sensitivity analyses are performed on the alternative profitability forecasts.

Decision analysis techniques are used to assemble sets of strategies. A portfolio selected through this process is translated into the four-year plan. This plan contains nominal guilder income statements and balance sheets,

174

prepared on a replacement-cost basis. After individual units have completed their four-year plans, they submit them to Eindhoven for review, particularly with respect to the question, "Can we finance it?"

One of the important and difficult issues with Philips is the coordination of forecasts between business units. A product division cannot plan sales without consulting the national organizations. In some vertically-integrated situations, the process must include the component plants, the IPCs, the product divisions and the national organizations to provide a complete picture, oftentimes through several countries with different inflation rates.

The accounting department at Philips is faced with the need to develop ways to flexibly reorganize information flows within the accounting system to provide consolidated information on product profitability on a concern-wide basis. Measuring concern-wide profitability in a large multinational company is a difficult problem because several different currencies and inflation rates may be involved. Nevertheless, this need is regarded as particularly important in times of inflation to ensure that the selling units fully pass through increased costs to the degree the market permits.

Operating Planning and Budgeting

After four-year plans are approved, management undertakes a more detailed budgeting process which formalizes the first year of the four-year plan in greater detail. The same types of information summarized at high levels in the four-year plan are budgeted in detail by smaller sub-units, departments and individual products.

The budgeting process at Philips is bottom-up, but with strong central review and a consistent set of assumptions and directions. General inflation assumptions are included in the annual instructions from the corporate staff in Eindhoven and are used in the process. Specific forecasts of product cost are available from the trend indication system, which is also used for transfer pricing and is described below.

Budgets are assembled and reviewed by two groups: the national organizations and product divisions. The national organizations prepare the budgets, and the product divisions review their technical marketing and functional aspects and coordinate differences among divisions. After the budgets have been reviewed, they are assembled into a corporate budget. Several iterations of the budgeting process may take place before a budget is approved.

Transfer Pricing

Because many products are transferred among national organizations and divisions, transfer pricing is an important element of management accounting at Philips. Division-to-division transfer prices use a unique "trend indication system" to reflect inflation in transfer prices. This system tracks the costs of products and provides an updated forecast of product cost each four months for the next 16 months. These trend indications project prices and provide a "cost price" on January 1, May 1 and September 1 for planning purposes. National organization-to-national organization prices are, however, at arm's-length market prices.

In principle, a cost price is established for each article only once per year and remains the same throughout the calendar year. This fixed price, called the "January price," becomes the transfer price for intracompany deliveries. It includes the expected price levels of materials, wages, salaries, etc., on January 1 of the current year based on expected production quantities. The January price (the technical cost price for a product) is built up from basic costs using replacement cost accounting principles and fits in the price structure as shown below:

Materials cost
+ Processing cost
+ Total labor costs

    = Manufacturing cost
    + Development cost

        = Technical cost price (used for intercompany transactions)
        + Concern costs (overhead)
        + Selling expenses

            = Commercial cost price
            + Profit

                = Net price
                + Trade discount

                    = Consumer price

The technical cost price includes, on a normative basis, all manufacturing costs, including materials, labor and tooling, plus an allocation of development costs on a unit basis. Overhead, selling expenses and projects are not included in this price used for division-to-division transfers. Because all of the elements of the cost price are accounted for on a replacement cost basis and therefore change frequently, and because inflation differs between elements of the cost price, a pre-calculated index for homogeneous groups of raw materials, semi-manufactured goods and finished products is computed monthly to adjust transfer prices. This index is applied to January prices to adjust such transfer prices to reflect forecasts of external price changes which will cause deviations from the January level. Trend indications for periods outside the current budget year cover both internal and external influences, including efficiency, in addition to rates of exchange, wages and material costs.

Capital Expenditure Planning and Evaluation

Philips uses the "surplus method" of net present value analysis as opposed to the annuity method (net present value of cash flows) to evaluate capital projects. The surplus method is employed to determine the point in time at which a project reaches its peak and whether it may no longer be economically justified. Under this method the net capital worth of a project is determined by discounting the annual excesses of the expected receipts over payments for the coming years. The excess of cash inflow over cash outflow of each year (annual surplus) is discounted to a value as of July 1 of that next year.

Annual surpluses are discounted to the first year of the project and added to form a cumulative surplus by using a discount factor based on the minimum required rate of return. At the point in time at which the cumulative surplus reaches a positive value, the project has reached its payback point for both the original expenditure and the required return on investment. The net capital worth of the project is the highest cumulative surplus. This corresponds in time to the economic peak of the project, after which negative results would be expected for the remaining life of the project.

One of the objectives of the surplus method is to determine if, and if so, when, the continuation of the project is no longer economically justified. Because it could occur at any time, the calculation of the annual surplus must include the net realizable value of assets at year-end. Thus, "alternative proceeds," the receipts which would come in at the end of each year if the assets on hand were sold at that time, are included as a fictitious receipt in one year and, consequently, as an identical fictitious expense at the beginning of the following year. Alternative uses for assets are considered in determining the level of "alternative proceeds." Universal assets (those with many uses) are valued at their book value which, at Philips, is replacement cost. Those which are specific are generally assessed to be lower in value.

A capital project is approved on the basis of its net capital worth (based on the surplus method) and subjective judgments of how well it fits with the business objectives. In addition, the larger projects are judged on a presentation of the financial projections and figures in the same format as the standard monthly reporting on results.

Investment in fixed assets is broken into two types, special investments and normal investments, with different approval procedures for each. Special investments include investments in land, buildings and equipment resulting from facility expansions, development of new products, and other situations of major consequence such as entering into joint ventures. Normal investments include replacement and overhaul of capital equipment and routine computer hardware acquisitions. Special investments must be specifically applied for and approved by the Board of Management, accompanied by a more detailed economic evaluation than for normal investments. Normal investment requests are made and approved through the annual budget process.

The capital project review process at Philips does not end with the approval process. A series of post-calculation and recalculation reviews are undertaken during the life of the project to provide updated projections and ensure continued profitability for the project. A flowchart of the post-calculation process is shown in Exhibit 12–6. Post-calculation at Philips looks at the actual results of a project and often includes more than accounting data. Market share penetration, technology and expected product life are often considered in the post-calculation process as is profitability.

Post-calculation and looking at results of projects after the fact have been particularly useful in times of inflation, primarily because of the potential impact of inflation on the economic life of a product. Also, Philips occasionally recalculates rejected projects, which sometimes, through inflationary impacts, become profitable at later points in time. Through post-calculation and recalculation, estimates of results and residual values based on more recent information can be computed. Unexpected changes in the economic climate or inflation are routinely reflected in revised forecasts because of this process.

Recalculation, which is the production of a new set of projections using the most recent data, is usually done simultaneously with post-calculation. The revised forecast of project results, using the surplus method in the same manner as in the original calculations, can provide management with insight into potential problems. Using the post-calculation and recalculation results, management can determine whether corrective action is needed and reformulate plans accordingly.

In practice, one of the most difficult tasks is the collection of data to conduct a post-calculation. For this purpose, at the time the budget is approved, an ad hoc system is employed in which internal and external data which might influence the conclusions are collected and processed in such a way that evaluations of the starting points are facilitated. Accounting results are organized by reporting units, which may not match the organization of a project. As a result, allocations and estimates must be made, particularly when a vertically integrated project crosses several organizational boundaries.

Management Reporting

With the notable exception of the USA, Philips' internal reporting system, and external reporting in the Netherlands, uses the principles of

EXHIBIT 12–6

The Post-Calculation Process

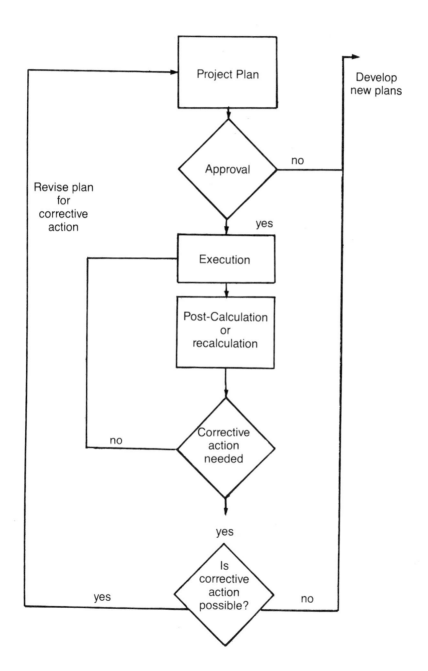

replacement cost accounting on a worldwide basis. This means that assets are valued on the basis of the specific replacement cost, which is also the basis for calculating depreciation and cost of sales. The difference between replacement value and historical cost at the moment of sale, or at the balance sheet date, is not treated as a profit or loss but instead is added to the shareholders' equity interest, after deduction of latent taxes. Adding increases in replacement costs to shareholders' equity allows the relationship between operating results and assets employed to be articulated on a consistent and current basis.

Several methods are used to determine the replacement cost of property, plant, and inventories at Philips. Building cost indices are available from several external publications and are supplemented by Philips' engineering department. Machinery cost data are available both from the marketplace and Philips' internal operations. The price levels of raw materials, semi-finished products and finished goods are followed closely in the marketplace by purchasing and accounting staffs, and appropriate adjustments are made. For internal transfers of goods, the trend indication system is used to provide current price levels.

No adjustments are made at Philips for purchasing power gains and losses from monetary items. Because Philips generally has greater monetary liabilities than assets in times of inflation and would show a monetary gain, the company has, conservatively, elected not to adjust for them.

Because taxes are normally assessed on the difference between fiscal income and historical costs, a tax is due on the difference between the replacement cost and historical cost valuation of assets. At Philips, a provision for those taxes is created at the moment the relevant assets are revalued. For example, suppose an item is purchased at $100. One month later the price rises to $120 and it is sold for $130. Under the replacement cost system, profit and taxes would be as follows:

Sales	$130
Cost of goods sold	120
Gross profit	$ 10
Taxes (50%)	5
Profit after taxes	$ 5

Using the government-required historical cost system for taxes, profit would be computed on the following basis:

Sales	$130
Historical cost of goods sold	100
Gross profit	$ 30
Taxes (50%)	15
Profit after taxes	$ 15

A tax difference of $10 is caused by revaluation. To compensate for this effect, Philips computes a latent tax on the differential gain at each revaluation. In this case it would be computed:

Replacement cost	$120
Historical cost	100
Differential for latent taxes	$20
Tax rate	× 50%
Latent taxes	$10

Operating results are reported by product groups using the replacement cost accounting principles. To facilitate this process, Philips has developed a computerized communications network from most of its national organizations into Eindhoven. For example, French operations and plants report their results to the French national organization headquarters, which serves as a collection point and forwards the results to Eindhoven. Summaries of results by product are extracted from the reports of the various national organizations in Eindhoven for use by the product divisions.

A standard reporting package must be transmitted monthly by each national organization. This package includes summaries of sales, cost of goods sold, operating expenses and interest costs to provide operating results before taxes. Schedules listing key management items (including inventory levels, assets employed, backlogs, personnel, and capacities) by product group supplement the operating statements. Reporting requirements for smaller countries, however, are not as detailed as those for larger countries. A summary report of results for the company and summaries of the main industry groups are prepared monthly in Eindhoven from these results.

Reports are submitted quarterly in more detail from each national organization. Additional information, including final asset replacement valuation and latent tax adjustments, is submitted at year-end for preparation of the year-end balance sheets and income statements.

Fiscal asset revaluations are normally booked only once a year. Stocks are revalued monthly using individual procedures for homogeneous groups. However, in countries with high inflation, such as Brazil or Argentina, revaluations of both inventories and fixed assets are booked monthly using an indexing system.

The consolidation process at Eindhoven takes nearly a month. Results are transmitted from the units by the 25th of the month. By the second working day of the month, consolidated sales figures are prepared. Final operating results by product lines and for the total corporation are usually produced in approximately three to four weeks after closing. Efforts are underway to further automate this process and improve the timeliness of reporting.

External reporting for local operations is done in several countries with annual reports published in accordance with the local format, such as in West Germany. Results for the company as a whole are published in Holland and include U.S. historical cost-based figures converted into the Dutch replacement cost method accounts.

Financial strategies and management accounting techniques for coping with the impact of inflation continue to evolve at Philips, and the practical application of replacement value accounting is constantly being refined. Operating and financial managers have lived with, and been evaluated on, replacement cost-based results for some time, and thinking in current value terms is said to be second nature to Philips' managers. How these systems will evolve further is uncertain. From all indications, Philips will continue to strive to provide managers with information for decision making based on what they consider to be sound economic principles using replacement cost accounting concepts.

Chapter 13

General Electric Company

General Electric Company (GE) has assumed a position of leadership in calling attention to the effects of inflation, developing inflation-adjusted management accounting techniques, and training its managers on how to cope with inflation. GE Chairman Reginald Jones has spoken to many groups and has written extensively about the impact of inflation. The company has developed unique internal planning and control practices that parallel the external financial reporting requirements called for by ASR No. 190, and more recently, FAS No. 33.

GE has conducted a series of training programs to explain these new techniques to its managers and to teach them how to better manage their business in an inflationary environment. This case study describes how GE has incorporated inflation adjustments into its planning, reporting and control systems and the extensive management education efforts currently being undertaken to ensure their success.

Company Background

From its incorporation in 1892, General Electric has grown to become one of the most diversified large industrial corporations. The scope of the company activities has broadened considerably from an initial thrust of manufacturing and marketing products for the generation, transmission, distribution, control and utilization of electricity.

General Electric is organized into seven major sectors: Consumer Products and Services, Industrial Products and Components, Power Systems, Technical Systems and Materials, Natural Resources, Foreign Multi-Industry Operations, and a wholly-owned credit subsidiary, General Electric Credit Corporation.

In the area of consumer products and services, GE manufactures, distributes, and services one of the largest and broadest lines of electrical consumer goods in the world. The Industrial Products and Components group produces a wide range of products serving several markets, from a variety of small and large electric motors and controls to diesel-electric locomotives. The Power Systems sector is primarily oriented towards electric utilities and manufactures components for the generation, transmission, and distribution of electricity, including steam turbine-generators, gas turbines, and nuclear power plants. The Technical Systems and Materials sector manufactures and markets a large variety of products including jet engines, high technology products for space and national defense, and specialized materials. The Natural Resources sector consists primarily of Utah International Inc., a subsidiary which mines coking coal, uranium, steam coal, iron ore, and copper, and which produces oil and gas.

The Foreign Multi-Industry Operations sector consists of international affiliates which operate as smaller versions of the parent and produce and market a wide variety of products and services. Principal multi-industry affiliates are located in Canada, Brazil, Venezuela, Italy, Spain and Mexico, along with a number of smaller affiliates worldwide. General Electric Credit Corporation (GECC) is an unconsolidated, wholly-owned subsidiary engaged primarily in consumer, commercial and industrial financing.

GE is the ninth largest U.S. corporation. Its 1979 revenues by segment were as follows:

	($ Millions)
Consumer Products and Services (incl. GECC)	$ 5,447.7
Industrial Products and Components	4,802.8
Power Systems	3,564.4
Technical Systems and Materials	6,060.8
Natural Resources	1,260.3
Foreign Multi-Industry Operations	2,900.5
General Corporate Items and Eliminations	(1,056.5)
Total Revenues	$22,980.0

Net earnings for 1979 were $1.4 billion. Because each sector would in itself be a large company, GE's corporate strategies focus on each of the sectors being a strong competitor in the markets in which it operates. Under this philosophy each effectively operates as an independent business.

Management Philosophy

GE is an example of a large company that has blended the needs for centralization and decentralization in its organization and management philosophy. In short, GE's philosophy calls for, at the operating-unit level, full decision-making responsibility and full autonomy to carry out plans within a framework of strong central financial planning, control and bottom-line accountability.

184

GE's management philosophy is evidenced in its management reporting and control systems. Each operating unit may operate a different general ledger or management control and reporting system and use its own chart of accounts for internal reporting. But each unit must also convert the required data into the corporate format for monthly consolidation and review and prepare strategic and profit plans in accordance with corporate requirements.

Internal reporting requirements imposed on the sectors by corporate headquarters at GE have consistently followed the external reporting trends in industry. In 1974, when general purchasing power adjustments were a controversial topic, they were introduced internally. When ASR No. 190 was issued by the SEC in 1975, its requirements were adopted internally and superseded general purchasing power adjustments as the internal standard. Following the publication of FAS No. 33 in 1979, GE adapted the requirements of Statement No. 33 to its internal planning and control system.

GE's rationale for adapting FAS No. 33 for its internal planning and control system was explained by GE Chairman Reginald Jones to company executives at the kickoff of the internal coping-with-inflation training program: "If you want to succeed, and if you want General Electric to succeed, you will have to understand inflation, realize how it distorts financial data, learn how to minimize the damage, and learn how to take advantage of the opportunities it presents."

Organization

GE is organized by business sector. Three vice chairmen, each with two business sectors, report to the chairman. The organization structure is illustrated in Exhibit 13–1. Each sector is also organized into strategic business units (SBUs) which are organized into departments, divisions or groups. SBUs, which may differ from organizational entities, are defined as separate businesses which can be evaluated in their own competitive environment, and SBUs vary widely in size. The key concept for SBU definition is that they can be evaluated, and planned for, as a logical or natural grouping of businesses in a competitive environment. The Finance, Legal, and Executive Manpower staff components report to the chairman; other staff components report to the vice chairmen.

The reporting structure varies by sector; in some cases departments may report to the sector executive, and in others departments may report through division and group structures. A typical sector reporting structure is illustrated in Exhibit 13–2.

The board of directors has charged the corporate senior vice president of finance, as chief financial officer, with the responsibility for accounting and financial reporting and with the safeguarding of the assets of the corpo-

185

EXHIBIT 13–1
Top-Level GE Organization

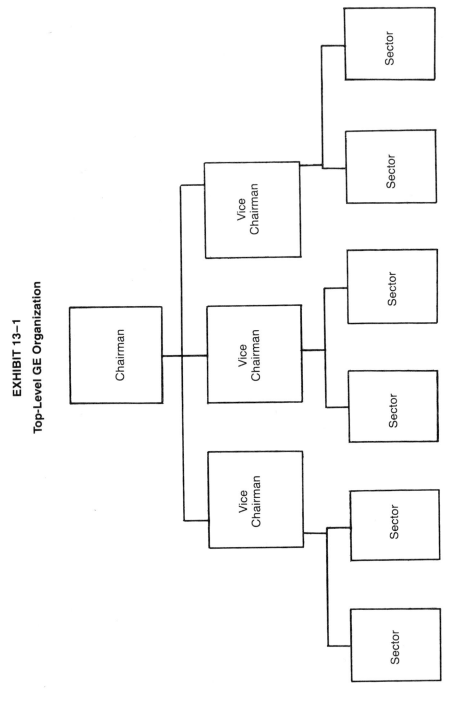

EXHIBIT 13–2
Organization

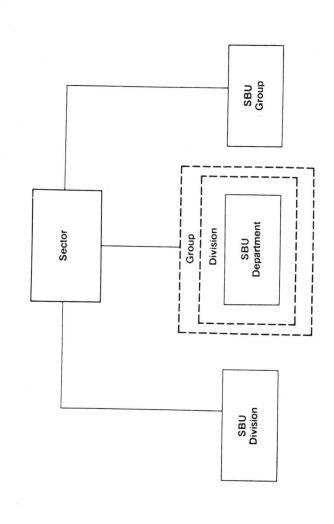

ration. Because of the fiduciary role of the chief financial officer, a financial executive in an SBU can be hired by the general manager of the SBU only with the approval of the chief financial officer. An SBU financial executive can be removed by either the SBU manager or the corporate chief financial officer. Thus, the corporate finance function has a strong role in establishing and enforcing policies through all levels of the organization.

GE employs about 8,000 people in the finance function, with the vast majority in the operating units. The corporate finance staff is organized into five areas, as illustrated in Exhibit 13-3. The vice president and comptroller is responsible for accounting services, corporate computer planning, general and cost accounting, personnel accounting and tax accounting. The corporate treasury function includes banking and corporate finance, corporate credit and collection, foreign financing, insurance and treasury operations. The vice president of trust investments is responsible for pension and other trust investments. The corporate financial administration group includes a variety of functions, from internal audit and financial planning and analysis to corporate business development activities. A manpower inventory for the financial function throughout GE is maintained by the corporate financial manpower group, which conducts the financial management program and covers development activities.

Management Practices

Inflation and its impact on GE have been taken seriously at the highest levels of the corporation. Top management's concern with inflation has been manifested by an extensive training program and an important addition to the primary set of corporate objectives. Like many companies, GE has objectives dealing with profitability and earnings growth. Unlike most companies, however, the company added the phrase "after recognizing the effects of monetary inflation" to its profitability goals for 1980. Concern about the financial effects of inflation led to the formation of an "Inflation Council" at GE several years ago to deal with the problem. One of the approaches developed by the Council was an extensive education program to ensure that management had not only an understanding of the financial effects of inflation, but also knew how to cope with inflation or develop strategies to minimize the effects of inflation on the business.

Management Education

Management education is not new to GE, particularly in the financial area. Over the last five years, several courses involving thousands of participants have been held, including a course on effective cash management and a course on managing in an inflationary environment.

EXHIBIT 13–3
Corporate Finance Staff

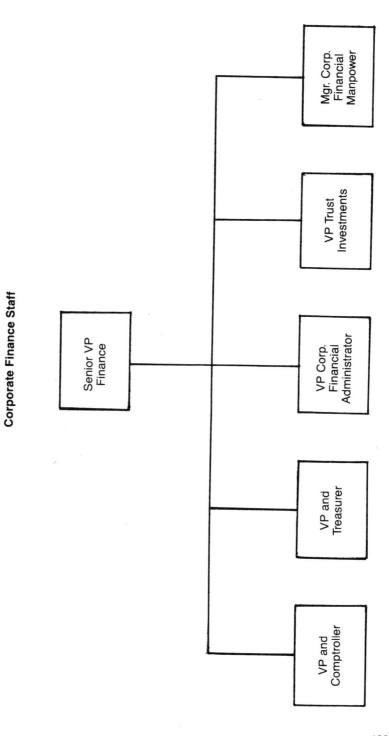

A new course, with an acronym COIN (for Effectively Coping with Inflation), was designed to bring an understanding of the effects of inflation on the traditional internal performance measures, introduce new measures and educate managers in the concept of dealing with units of constant purchasing power (called, at GE, "thinking real"). At the time of our field work, September 1980, the course had been given to the top 1,000 managers at GE, and presentations to another 5,000 managers and specialists had been planned.

Top management support was viewed as essential in making the course a success and was instrumental in both the development and presentation of the course. Instructors were provided from both outside and inside the company, but primarily were senior level GE officers explaining the impact of inflation on almost every facet of GE. Faculty included GE's chairman and chief executive officer, chief economist, senior vice president, finance, vice president and comptroller, staff executive-strategic planning, and other senior staff members. The outside instructor rounded out the accounting and reporting discussion while providing overall integration of the presentation. Exhibit 13-4 lists the topics covered in the course.

EXHIBIT 13-4

Topics Covered in COIN Course

FASB No. 33
Inflation's Challenge to Management
Economic Outlook and Background on Inflation
Inflation's Impact on GE
Inflation's Impact on the SBU and Investment Criteria
Price and Wage Controls
Effective Cash Management
Strategic Responses to Inflation
Coordinated Resource Management and Productivity
Productivity Case Study
Marketing Strategy
Wrap-up and Challenge

While much of the content of the COIN course relates to the procedures used internally at GE to cope with inflation and report results from operations on an inflation-adjusted basis, a large part was of more general interest. Reginald Jones, chairman of the board, spoke on inflation's challenge to management early in the program and set the tone for the course. Notwithstanding a belief that inflation is here to stay, he noted that "instead of wrestling inflation down, everybody's taking the path of least resistance." Because of this belief that inflation is not going away, Jones mapped out an action-oriented philosophy for GE. His charge was clear: "Let's not settle for coping with inflation; let's master it and bring it into our daily thinking and our planning until we accept it for what it really is—a problem, yes—but also an opportunity for those individuals who know how to handle it."

The background session on the history of inflation emphasizes the protracted extent of inflation in the United Kingdom and USA. A graph of U.S. inflation since the Civil War (Exhibit 13–5), along with a graph showing the history of inflation in the UK from the 17th Century, were used to show that high rates of continued inflation are a new phenomenon in the U.S., demonstrate the scope of current inflation in the U.S. and project the likelihood for it to continue.

Along with this background, the course documented the specific steps GE is taking to cope with inflation. These steps will be discussed in the latter portions of this chapter.

Strategic Planning

Much of the foundation for the modern practice of strategic planning was developed at GE. The company introduced the strategic business unit concept and developed the sector concept for the management of similar business units.

SBUs are categorized using a matrix approach around two axes: industry attractiveness and business strength. The positions of strategic business units in the nine-cell matrix, illustrated in Exhibit 13–6, are affected differentially by inflation.

Industry attractiveness considers several variables in arriving at a relative strength positioning for an industry. Factors traditionally considered include industry size, growth rate, profitability, cyclicality, and world scope. A new category, inflation recovery, was added to the attractiveness profile in 1980. Inflation recovery is the percentage of cost inflation recovered by both price and productivity. (Inflation recovery is explained further in the productivity measurement discussion.) In addition, industry profitability statistics are also now adjusted for inflation by converting to constant dollars.

The assessment of business strength is based on market share, competitive position and relative profitability. For 1980, the relative profitability of GE's SBUs was also computed on an inflation-adjusted basis.

Based on the findings from these analyses, several strategic thrusts have been defined by GE to cope with inflation. For example, GE has found that aged plant and equipment is a liability in times of inflation. The company also found that short product development cycles mitigate the risks associated with unanticipated changes induced by inflation and that inflation clearly increases the need for growth, price leadership, and cost control.

GE has developed a number of "active repositioning" strategies to lessen inflationary impacts, or leverage inflation, to improve the competitive position of SBUs. Several strategies can lessen the impact of inflation. Ex-

191

EXHIBIT 13–5

Inflation in the United States
Consumer Price Index 1967 = 100

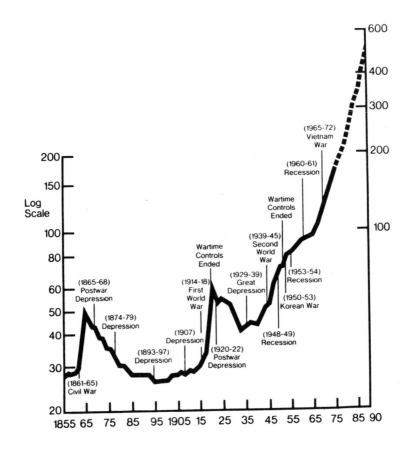

EXHIBIT 13–6

GE's Strategic Planning Matrix

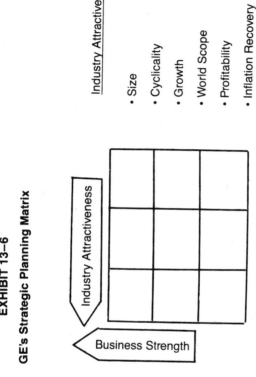

Industry Attractiveness

Business Strength

Industry Attractiveness

- Size
- Cyclicality
- Growth
- World Scope
- Profitability
- Inflation Recovery

Business Strength

- Market Share
- Competitive Position
- Relative Profitability

193

amples of these strategies are diversification of markets, specialization in a highly profitable niche, and restructuring manufacturing practices for increased productivity. A strategy to leverage inflation is "selling and practicing productivity."

Selling and practicing productivity can be accomplished through increased application engineering (working with the end customer to customize installation) and the development of proprietary products for specific customers by the sales force. Increasing manufacturing productivity through operating on a world scale, increasing backward integration or carefully staging capacity increases on the production side can also ease inflation-caused cost pressures.

Management notes that inflation necessitates higher returns in business development situations and brings increased risks to internal development. GE, like others, has found that acquisition and other external development strategies are appropriate to the current inflationary environment. Through the use of current cost and constant dollar techniques, GE is actively searching for strategies to combat the effects of inflation.

Capital Expenditure Evaluations

GE's financial analysis of proposed capital expenditures includes a review of internal rates of return and payback periods. However, financial results are not the sole decision criterion. Capital projects are also compared with the strategic plan as an integral part of the review process. The capital expenditure request normally includes a narrative description of the rationale for the project as well as other alternatives considered.

Capital projects over $1 million are reviewed at the sector level and projects of over $2 million are reviewed at the corporate level. One effect of inflation has been a recent increase in the review limits. A set of standard required projections and calculations of project cash flows must be submitted upward through the levels of management for approval and review in the capital expenditure process. Until 1980, these projections involved traditional nominal dollar cash flows, including operating savings, and discounted-cash-flow rates of return for the project. Now these projections must be supplemented by inflation-adjusted figures, including forecasts of constant dollar cash flow and rate-of-return calculations.

Calculation of Inflation-Adjusted Results

GE management feels that restatement of operating results using current costs is more meaningful than restatement using constant dollars. Although results using both approaches are reported externally, only current cost is used for internal reporting and measurement purposes. However, when comparisons are made with other periods, current cost results for all periods are converted to dollars of equivalent purchasing power using the Consumer Price Index (i.e., trend data are presented in current cost/constant dollar terms). Corporate economists prepare detailed economic forecasts, including a forecast of the CPI-U. Current cost indices for property, plant and equipment are also forecasted at the corporate level. However, some businesses develop their own indices when the broader based corporate indices are not appropriate.

The approach used to calculate current cost operating results for internal reporting is consistent with the procedures described in FAS No. 33. Both the income statement and the balance sheet are adjusted. Monetary gains or losses are not reflected in income at the SBU level although their effects are considered in corporate-level reviews.

In the income statement, specific adjustments are made to cost of goods sold for the current cost of replacing inventories and depreciation for the current costs of plant and equipment. The cost-of-goods-sold adjustment is relatively small because GE uses LIFO extensively. For those segments of the business using LIFO, an adjustment is required only if a quantity decrease in inventory has occurred. In those cases, any income effect from restoration of a portion of the LIFO reserve is eliminated. Segments not using LIFO, principally foreign affiliates, are required to make an adjustment to reflect the current cost of goods sold as if the LIFO method had been employed. Current cost depreciation is determined by applying accounting depreciation rates (generally modified sum-of-the-years'-digits) to the restated value of the assets.

The balance sheet is also adjusted to reflect the current cost of inventories and plant and equipment. Key operating measurements, including return on sales and return on investment, are calculated using current cost data.

In capital budgeting GE adjusts the nominal dollar cash flows from the project for each year to constant dollars using the CPI-U forecast. The nominal dollar cash flows include projected selling price and cost increases for the project. The adjusted cash flows are used to calculate the inflation-adjusted internal rate of return. These CPI-U conversion factors are also applied to residual value calculations by adjusting the remaining net book value of plant and equipment by year of acquisition using an appropriate CPI-U factor. (Although the assumption that residual values will appreciate at the CPI-U rate is widely used, supplemental computations are sometimes furnished for capital budgeting when residual values are expected to appreciate at a rate substantially different from the CPI-U.)

Key ratios, including return on sales, return on investment, discounted internal rates of return and payback, are computed on a current cost basis at GE for use in the capital expenditure review process. A chart of cumulative funds flow on both a reported and constant dollar basis is also provided. If these results meet general investment guidelines (ranges) and match the goals in the strategic plan, the expenditure is generally approved.

Planning and Budgeting

The planning process at GE is principally bottom-up through the build-up of operating forecasts from SBUs to business sectors to the total corporation. Long-range forecasts are prepared in detail by July of each year as part of the strategic planning process for each sector. Sector plans generally span five years for short-cycle business and 10 years for long-cycle business such as steam turbine-generators.

Long-range forecasts at GE include: operating data summaries, projection of funds flows, projected quarterly income statements for the next year and annual projections for the remaining years, summaries of programmed capital expenditures, plant appropriation approvals and expenditures for the next two years, productivity measures, and inflation-adjusted sales and earnings by SBU. Details and narrative descriptions of international operations, market position, research and development activities and technological expenditures are also included in the long-range forecast.

The degree to which an inflation adjustment has been included in the planning and budgeting process is illustrated in the management summary of the long-range forecast. In this summary, basic operating data, including net income, return on sales and return on investment, are shown on both an "as reported" and "inflation-adjusted" basis. The productivity measurements used at GE for many years have been augmented to include a "Percent of Total Inflation Recovery" statistic. This measurement will be described later in this chapter.

An exhibit titled "Operating Results Adjusted for Major Effects of Changing Prices and Inflation 1976–1986" has been included in the 1981 long-range forecast package, as shown in Exhibit 13–7. This form has evolved in recent years from a general price level statement through a replacement cost statement (corresponding to ASR No. 190) to the present form which corresponds to FAS No. 33 requirements.

Sector plans and budgets ordinarily are revised after they have been reviewed by corporate headquarters. After several cycles of planning, including iterations and revisions of SBUs' forecasts, a final sector plan is developed.

Detailed operating plans (budgets) are prepared for the first year. SBUs prepare detailed monthly budgets for each line item on the monthly operating report. After sector review and negotiation in the late fall, these become the SBU measurement budget for the next year. Budgets are fixed and cannot be modified during the year. They represent the performance commitment of SBU management to the corporation for the year.

EXHIBIT 13-7

1981

Operating Results Adjusted For Major Effects of Changing Prices and Inflation 1976–1986

(Dollar amounts in thousands)

Actual						1981		Budget 1982	Forecast			
1976	1977	1978	1979	1980		Budget	Estimate		1983	1984	1985	1986
					Net Sales Billed							
					As reported							
					Constant dollar							
					Net Income							
					As reported							
					Inventory output adjustment—current cost							
					Under-depreciation—current cost							
					Current cost							
					Current cost/constant dollar							
					Average investment							
					As reported							
					Inventory adjustment—current cost							
					Plant & equipment adjustment—current cost							
					Current cost							
					Current cost—constant dollar							
					% Net Income To Net Sales Billed							
					As reported							
					Current cost/constant dollar							
					%Operating Margin To Net Sales Billed							
					As reported							
					Current cost/constant dollar							
					% Return On Investment							
					As reported							
					Current cost/constant dollar							

1976–1980			1980–1986	1976–1986
_____%	**Average Annual Growth Rates** **Net Sales Billed**			
	As reported			
_____	Constant dollar	_____%	_____%
_____			
_____	**Net Income**	_____	_____
	As reported		
_____	Constant cost/constant dollar	_____	_____

Note: Constant dollars represent dollars of average year 1981 purchasing power

Date issued:

197

Performance Reporting

GE is the only U.S. company that we are aware of that currently reports both historical cost and inflation-adjusted results on a regular basis by business unit. It introduced quarterly performance reporting using the current cost/constant dollar methodology from FAS No. 33 in the first quarter of 1980 to supplement traditional historical monthly reporting.

One week after the close of the quarter, all reporting units submit inflation-adjusted results through the computer-based corporate time-sharing consolidation system. Reports summarize net sales, net earnings, return on sales and return on investment on both as reported, and inflation-adjusted basis for each reporting unit. As one financial executive put it, "At GE, with the new quarterly reports going to top-level management, inflation-adjusted reporting won't be just supplemental. There are likely to be questions from top-level management to explain results on an inflation-adjusted basis."

Variances are computed and reported on both a monthly and a year-to-date basis from historical cost results rather than current cost/constant dollar measurements. Estimates of total year results are also prepared, and variances from budget are forecasted for the year. These estimates for the year require management review if they vary significantly from budget, and they represent a revised commitment of performance from SBU management to top management. Nevertheless, the original commitment is not forgotten, especially in the course of performance reviews.

Productivity Measurement

GE has measured productivity formally since 1955. However, as a result of inflation and a strategic effort by top management to improve productivity, several changes in the productivity measures have recently been made. GE measures total cost productivity on a year-to-year basis. It uses the formula:

$$\text{Total cost productivity ratio} = \frac{\text{Total sales (constant dollars)}}{\text{Total cost of operations (constant dollars)}}$$

Constant dollars, as used in this formula, are determined using specific price changes for the business being measured rather than the general inflation rate. A productivity ratio is calculated for each year in the series at prior year price levels. The percentage change in the ratio from the preceding year's ratio represents the increase or decrease in total cost productivity. The productivity index is the cumulative annual productivity changes from the base year.

For example, assume selling prices in the home electronics business were 227 in 1979 and 243 in 1980 (a 1980 increase of 7%) while costs were

250 in 1979 and 275 in 1980 (an increase of 10%). If sales were $622,000 and $715,000, respectively, and total operating costs excluding financing $435 and $485, respectively, GE would measure productivity as follows:

$$
\text{Total cost productivity} \quad = \quad \frac{622}{435} \qquad \frac{715 \times \dfrac{227}{243}}{485 \times \dfrac{250}{275}} = \frac{668}{441}
$$

	1979 Nominal$	1980 Nominal$	1980 Inflation Index	1980 in 1979$

$$
= \quad 1.430 \qquad\qquad = 1.515
$$

$$
100.0 \qquad\qquad\qquad 105.9
$$

In the example, a 5.9% productivity gain would be recorded. Variable cost productivity is also measured by using variable costs only.

Productivity indices are part of the planning and control process at GE and are shown as a key statistic in the long-range plans along with operating results. Some special features of GE's approach to measuring productivity include:

• The calculation of productivity measurements on an aggregate basis for each business
• The inclusion of changes in sales volume and product mix as part of productivity
• The application of current cost depreciation in productivity measurements (beginning in 1981) to more accurately reflect the impact of inflation
• The calculation of an "inflation recovery" measurement

Inflation recovery is defined as the percentage of cost increases that have been recovered through price increases or increased productivity. Inflation recovery is tracked for each business and serves as a reminder to management that productivity increases are necessary in an inflationary environment.

Inflation recovery is computed by comparing the cost increases for each product group with the increases in selling price and productivity gains. Using the previous example, sales increased 15%, of which 7% was attributable to higher prices, while costs rose 11.5%, of which 10% was attributable to inflation. The productivity gain was 5.9%. Inflation recovery would be computed as shown on the next page.

$$\text{Inflation recovery} = \frac{\text{Productivity increase} + \text{price increase}}{\text{Inflation cost increase}}$$

$$\frac{5.9\% + 7.0\%}{10\%} = \frac{12.9}{10.0} = 1.29 \text{ or } 129\% \text{ recovery}$$

Using the same example, if selling prices had not increased, inflation recovery would be

$$\frac{5.9 + 0}{10.0}$$

or 59%, indicating only a partial recovery of cost increases.

Along with developing productivity measurements, GE's strategic thrust towards improving productivity includes task forces looking at robotics, materials substitution and CAD/CAM systems. GE also offers corporate consulting services in productivity improvement on a charge-back basis to business units needing assistance in implementing new programs.

GE's emphasis on productivity is, in part, caused by inflation because inflation reduces the effective life cycle for products and diminishes management reaction time. To ensure attention to productivity, business units annually forecast productivity trends and report on the programs they have developed on at least a qualitative basis in the strategic plan. These goals are later translated into specific action plans and are monitored through the budget and incentive compensation systems.

Six "P's" of Management in an Inflationary Environment

GE has made a major effort to modify its system of internal planning and control to reflect the effects of inflation. GE summarizes its COIN course material into what is called the "Six Ps" of managing in an inflationary environment:

- Possibility—inflation combatting strategies exist
- Positioning—is the key to success
- Price change accounting—is necessary for "real" measurement
- Productivity—is a major controllable element for management
- Prices—of goods coming in as well as those going out are key factors to profitability
- Payments—cash management is increasingly important in inflationary times

With top-management directives, new strategies, improved measurements and management tools in place, and broadscale training, GE management is striving to become one of the best-prepared U.S. companies to deal with inflation.

200

Section IV

Conclusions and Recommendations

Chapter 14

Conclusions and Recommendations

In the course of our research we reached certain conclusions as to how companies can deal with inflation more effectively in their internal operations. From these conclusions, and our professional experience, we have developed recommendations on how a company can better understand and deal with the planning and control issues that stem from inflation.

We recognize, of course, that there is no one "right" way to deal with the various management accounting issues that have emerged in an inflationary environment. Many companies are grappling with these issues, and the management accounting profession is a long way from developing a consensus as to what the most appropriate practices may be. A consensus may evolve eventually as more companies obtain experience with internal inflation accounting and individuals better understand what these measurements mean. But, as in the case of most management accounting practice, we expect that such a process will take several years.

Notwithstanding the rudimentary stage of development of many inflation-driven management accounting practices, we thought that our conclusions would be useful to the reader and would contribute to an evaluation of what practices might be most effectively applied in his or her own situation. We do not pretend that our views are unique because they are largely influenced by the experience of others. Nevertheless, we think that such experience can provide a practical foundation for determining which courses of action might be most appropriate in many business situations.

All of our recommendations are based on the premise that inflation will continue to fluctuate in a 5%–20% per year range around a 10% embedded rate. Regrettably, we believe that inflation is here to stay and that any notion that it will go away soon is wishful thinking. There are just too many political and institutional forces (such as OPEC oil price increases and legislated entitlements) at work that suggest that inflation is now built into our society and economy.

Significant Focal Points

We believe that there are three significant points where inflation should be considered in the field of management accounting:

1. Management education
2. Strategic management including forecasting, monitoring and productivity measurements
3. Operating management control including budgeting, standard costing, and management reporting

The distinction between strategic management and operating management control is emphasized because, in our opinion, an entirely different approach to dealing with inflation is needed in the strategic planning and control process than is required for operating planning and control.

Management Education

One of the major reasons that very little is done to deal with inflation in the internal planning and control processes is a lack of knowledge. A large number of accountants and managers do not really understand inflation accounting techniques, how inflation affects their business, and what the implications of inflation are from a strategic and operating standpoint. A major educational undertaking is required.

New planning and control techniques are seldom widely accepted unless the users of the technique thoroughly understand what they are all about. Through the years this has been the case with standard costing, flexible budgeting, direct costing and contribution accounting. A need for understanding is no less applicable to inflation accounting with its many implications.

It is a waste of time to introduce constant dollars and current cost concepts if only a few persons understand what these concepts mean. It is similarly pointless to factor inflation-related measurements into strategic plans, capital expenditure evaluations and internal rate-of-return calculations if the concepts and arithmetic that are applied are not widely understood. Recent MBAs and accounting and finance majors may understand these concepts, but many other managers have difficulty understanding even how income is determined on a historical basis. The starting point, therefore, lies in the educational arena.

General Electric has recognized the need for management education and is doing something about it. It has a head start on many other companies because most of its managers have a solid financial and strategic planning background to begin with. Furthermore, for many years General

Electric has had a strong in-house management education program. However, other companies also have the capability of developing their own programs and following General Electric's example.

Several educational resources might be considered in order to help executives better manage in an inflationary environment: business schools and other educational institutions, accounting literature and programs conducted by the National Association of Accountants and other professional organizations, external seminars conducted by accounting firms and consultants and in-house seminars and workshops.

No one resource should probably be considered to the exclusion of the others. The foundation for most financial and accounting education begins in the undergraduate and business schools. Continuing education is now also widely accepted as an integral part of professional life. However, educational institutions tend to reach the practitioners and providers of management accounting information rather than users of this information. In order to reach users, we have found that external and internal seminars and workshops are usually the best alternatives available.

General Electric has also provided a model as to the essential ingredients for a seminar on planning and control in an inflationary environment. These ingredients include:

1. *The sponsorship and participation of top management.* There is no doubt that General Electric's chairman's introduction to the COIN program has had a good deal to do with the participants' interest in this program. It is axiomatic that middle management tends to respond to what they perceive to be of interest to top management.

2. *An understanding of historical cost, constant dollar, and current cost accounting concept fundamentals.* While FAS No. 33 may have been promulgated for external reporting purposes, the techniques that are used in various types of accounting should be understood by the participants. Such an understanding is probably best achieved by requiring the participants to work through examples of the application of the constant dollar and current cost techniques.

3. *A discussion of the effects of inflation on cash flow, capital recovery, disposable funds, and the cost of capital.* Many users of internal and external financial statements do not understand the concepts involved and how these elements are affected by inflation. This ingredient is perhaps more important in a capital-intensive business than it is in a business with substantial net monetary assets or a high rate of capital turnover.

4. *Relating inflation and inflation concepts specifically to the business at hand.* Conceptual discussions tend to fall flat unless they are

specifically related to the case in point. General Electric's COIN program, for example, focuses on relating the impact of inflation to most every facet of General Electric. From a manager's standpoint, the central question has to be, "How should I manage differently in an inflationary environment?" A seminar that does not contribute to the response to that question may not be effective.

One of the issues that has emerged in our own practice is "Which is better: external or internal management education on inflation-related management accounting issues?" We think that one- or two-day in-house programs are probably more effective vehicles for educating management than external seminars. It is easier to relate inflation accounting concepts and managing in an inflationary environment to the business at hand and to obtain top management participation in an internal seminar. However, the internal approach does not preclude the use of outsiders to set the stage and discuss the concepts involved.

Strategic Management

Constant dollar and current cost accounting concepts generally apply to strategic management processes, but they may be of limited use for short-term budgeting and operating management. "Thinking real," as General Electric puts it, applies to the selection of the most effective strategy for a business to pursue, and helps monitor the execution of this strategy, but it does not really help budget and gauge operating performance on a day-to-day basis. There are three reasons for our conclusions:

1. The most significant impact of inflation in most manufacturing companies is in the acquisition, disposition and valuation of the company's assets. Evaluations associated with such transactions are inherently largely of a strategic, rather than an operating, nature.

2. The competitive operating environment might limit the value of constant dollar and current cost measurements where historical accounting information is used for management decision making. While constant dollars and current cost data can help management understand how irrational other participants in the market may be, each company must adjust to competition's perception of economic reality.

3. Strategic management can be accommodated by broad, imprecise accounting measurements that extend over quarters and years. Operating management, as a practical matter, relies on the hard daily, weekly and monthly historical results that are lodged in the accounting records.

For purposes of strategic planning, we recommend that selected current cost information stated in constant dollars, or other constant units of measure, be developed by business unit, by year, in addition to historical cost information. Because of its external use, such data should be calculated by applying the methodologies contained in FAS No. 33. Selected data might minimally include:

1. Revenues in constant dollars
2. Depreciation based on current costs or constant dollars
3. Net income based on current costs and/or constant dollars
   a. from operations (after taxes)
   b. from holding gains or losses on net assets
4. Cash flow from continuing operations based on current costs and/or constant dollars
5. Net assets:
   a. based on replacement costs
   b. or disposal (exit) values, as applicable
6. Return on net assets based on current costs and/or constant dollars

The preceding information enables business managers to view the effects of inflation on the business as well as the business independent of the effects of inflation. It also provides the financial building blocks needed for forecasting and evaluating alternate strategies to assist with the selection of those strategies that offer the greatest real return.

The inflation recovery concept developed by GE should also be considered in the evaluation process. It is useful to restate historical data on a constant dollar basis to determine the percentage of cost increases that have been recovered through price increases or increased productivity. This information can help strategic managers rank business units in terms of their potential for offsetting inflationary cost increases and thus select the most promising opportunities for investment.

Forecasting

Long-range forecasts of future operations for strategic planning or capital budgeting purposes should be prepared on *both* a nominal and constant dollar basis and should, if possible, include a sensitivity analysis over a range of specific price change assumptions. While this practice involves more work than using either constant dollars or nominal dollars and a single forecast, it provides for a more realistic picture of prospective future operations and inflation's impact on these operations. Constant dollar forecasts are easier to comprehend than forecasts in nominal dollars; yet nominal dollar forecasts probably more properly reflect reality. As a result, both techniques are useful.

Varying inflation assumptions should be applied to specific elements of nominal dollar forecasts so as to evaluate the effect of the uncertainty of inflation. Unfortunately, experience suggests that specific inflation rates cannot be predicted in any one year with any reasonable degree of certainty. Therefore, we think that the only realistic solution to the problem of predicting inflation is to assume a range of probable inflation rates in the forecasting process. Of course, this type of analysis most likely requires the use of a computer-based financial model.

Residual values should be adjusted to reflect inflation in forecasts of future operations wherever they are significant because such residual values may have an important bearing on present values and the internal rate of return. The airline and construction equipment industries provide examples of how residual values can appreciate. Residual values of commercial aircraft, for example, often exceed their original purchase price. Residual values of construction equipment have increased at less dramatic rates than those of aircraft but are still substantially higher than they would have been without inflation.

Whenever practical, inflation, taxation and currency exchange rate assumptions should be developed centrally in order to provide for consistency in the assumptions applied to each business unit.

A firm's cost of capital should be adjusted to reflect inflation particularly if this cost is used as a basis for establishing a capital expenditure hurdle rate. Opinions vary as to the usefulness of capital expenditure hurdle rates. Many companies have found that hurdle rates can be a useful tool for screening capital expenditures providing that they are used in conjunction with other criteria for evaluating business strategies or potential capital expenditures, while other companies tend to avoid the use of such rates. When hurdle rates are used, however, it is appropriate that they be based on an up-to-date, rather than an out-of-date, determination of the cost of capital.

Monitoring Actual Results

Current costs expressed in constant dollars can be quite useful as a supplement to historical data for monitoring the achievement of strategic plans. The level of detail and the techniques employed to measure actual results should correspond with these utilized in the planning process, especially in the use of the same base year for constant dollar conversions. While this practice may seem obvious, the strategic planning function is performed independently of the reporting function in many companies, and these two functions are often not coordinated.

Business unit results should be calculated in current costs expressed in constant dollars and reported periodically, perhaps quarterly. Such data provide management with an opportunity to evaluate the extent to which the "real" goals contained in the strategic plans are actually being achieved. We emphasize, however, that it is not worthwhile to monitor progress in "real" terms unless management understands the concepts of inflation accounting and its implications with respect to the business, and the cost data are expressed in the same terms as they are in the strategic plan.

An example of the type of financial report that might be prepared to compare progress against a strategic plan is shown in Exhibit 14–1.

EXHIBIT 14–1

Example of Use of Current Cost Data Expressed in Constant Dollars for Monitoring Strategic Plan

	This Quarter/Year-to-Date/ Program-to-Date/ Projected for Program		
	Actual	Plan	Variance
Revenues	290,000	245,000	45,000
Cost and expenses:			
Costs and expenses excluding depreciation	200,000	190,000	(10,000)
Depreciation	55,000	50,000	(5,000)
Total costs and expenses	255,000	240,000	(15,000)
Income before taxes	35,000	5,000	30,000
Income taxes	25,000	3,000	(22,000)
Income after taxes	10,000	2,000	8,000
% of revenues	3.4	0.8	2.6
Increases in value of net assets employed	15,000	10,000	5,000
Net economic gain	25,000	12,000	13,000
% of revenues	8.6	4.9	3.7
Net assets employed at historical cost	150,000	140,000	10,000
Gain or loss in value of net assets employed	15,000	10,000	5,000
Net assets at current cost	165,000	150,000	15,000
Return on net assets employed	15.2	8.0	7.2
Funds from operations	65,000	52,000	13,000
(Increase)/decrease in working capital	(20,000)	(5,000)	(15,000)
Net funds from operations	45,000	47,000	(2,000)
Funds reinvested in business	60,000	50,000	(10,000)
Funds available for distribution	(15,000)	(3,000)	(12,000)
% of funds from operations	(23.1)	(5.8)	(17.3)

Productivity Measurements

Productivity and other operating measurements should be incorporated in the strategic planning and monitoring process. While such measurements are needed to track progress in any event, measurements that are not distorted by changes in the value of the dollar are especially useful in periods of inflation.

Shell Oil Company provides some ideas for developing productivity measurements. Different partial productivity measurements should be developed by the operating people for each business unit. Usually, only a few relatively simple measurements are needed, but they should provide a reasonably consistent long-term gauge of business unit productivity.

Total productivity measurement is an interesting concept, but we do not believe that total productivity measurements add anything that cannot be achieved by monitoring current cost data expressed in constant dollars. Thus we recommend the application of the concept of current costs expressed in constant dollars rather than total productivity measurements for purposes of tracking overall productivity.

Budgeting and Standard Costs

In our judgment, budgets and standard costs should always be expressed in nominal dollars, but they should reflect all anticipated price level changes for the period covered by the budgets or standards. In other words, budgets and standards should allow for the inflation expected in the period covered by the budget or standard. This conclusion does not represent a departure from the management accounting practices currently employed by many businesses.

As illustrated in the Inland Steel case study, the use of budgets and product standards that include anticipated price level changes in the analyses of product profit margins, coupled with the application of LIFO inventory valuation methods, provides an opportunity to review prices based on current costs. N.V. Philips' use of a trend indication system to project future costs has formalized the projection of anticipated price level increases. These approaches provide for current cost data for product profitability analysis and consistent yardsticks against which operating performance can be compared.

Inflation has two important implications in budgeting and standard costing. First of all, budgets and standard costs should be revised more frequently to reflect the effect of unanticipated price changes, and second, some provision should be made in the variance analysis process for segregating the effect of uncontrollable price level changes which constitute an inflation variance.

Of the alternatives that have been applied for segregating the effect of uncontrollable price level changes, we are attracted to MacGibbon's price-adjusted flexible budget approach described in Chapter 7 and practiced by Acos Villares. It seems to us that this is a practical approach for separating the effect of noncontrollable price level changes from the costs that an operating manager can control. It has the further advantage of not requiring the manipulation of actual historical results as reported or requiring supplemental analyses. We anticipate that this technique will be more widely applied in the future.

Management Reporting

Fundamental management reporting requirements are largely unaffected by inflation. Similar basic tools are needed for control and performance measurement in an inflationary environment as are needed in noninflationary times. Reports should be relevant, accurate, timely, uncluttered and organized by responsibility. Actual results should be compared with plan or budget; controllable results should be separated from noncontrollable results; and key results should be highlighted. These needs remain unchanged by inflation.

The most important shift in management reporting requirements caused by inflation is increased emphasis on the funds statement. We believe that this statement becomes even more useful in an inflationary environment because of its focus on cash and asset management and because it is largely unaffected by depreciation and certain other transactions not requiring the use of funds. Indeed, as our survey of chief financial executives showed, 76% of the respondents have placed increased emphasis on funds flow as a result of inflation. LIFO has become the rule rather than the exception, at least in big companies, and cash flow has joined return on investment and earnings per share as the most widely used measurements in financial and accounting management. We think that this emphasis on cash flow is constructive because it forces a stronger linkage between internal planning and control practice and the inherent long-range interests of the investor.

Summary

In general, we view the application of inflation-oriented management accounting techniques to internal planning and control as an evolutionary process. American business is still pretty close to the beginning of the road with companies like Philips and General Electric setting the pace. If inflation continues in the 5% to 20% range, and we think that it will, then it will be just a question of time before other companies catch up.

Management education is the key to adopting new accounting techniques to deal with inflation. Without an educational program these new accompanying techniques are not likely to be widely accepted.

The application of constant dollar and current costs methodologies is not a cure-all, and these methodologies are not replacements for historical costs. Constant dollar and current data, however, can be quite useful in strategic planning although they probably do not have as much application in the area of operating management and control. These limitations notwithstanding, there are still a number of steps that a company can take to sharpen its existing management accounting tools to deal more effectively with inflation. We hope that the conclusions and recommendations that have stemmed from our research will contribute to this end.

Selected Bibliography

Selected Bibliography

The following annotated bibliography is submitted for readers who are interested in current literature on the internal planning and control aspects of inflation accounting. While a few key publications pertaining to current cost accounting, constant dollar accounting, Financial Accounting Standard No. 33, external reporting and inflation accounting practices in other countries are listed, the primary focus here is on management accounting issues.

Literature is listed alphabetically by author for each of the following categories:

    I. Management and Management Accounting Issues
    II. LIFO Inventory Valuation
    III. Productivity Measurement
    IV. Inflation Accounting Concepts
    V. FASB Statement No. 33
    VI. Practices in Other Countries

More extensive bibliographies of literature on accounting for inflation, LIFO method of inventory valuation, and productivity may be obtained from the National Association of Accountants, 919 Third Avenue, New York, New York 10022.

I. Management and Management Accounting Issues

C. Wayne Alderman and J. Kenneth Alderman, "The Impact of Inflation on the Taxation of Capital Gains and Losses," *Management Accounting*, December, 1977, pp. 53–55.

Concludes that current tax treatment of gains and losses from the sale of capital assets results in tax inequities for companies that replace their capital assets.

Martin V. Alonzo, "Corporate Strategy for Combating Inflation," *Management Accounting*, March, 1978, pp. 57–60.

Discussion of investment, financing and operating strategies employed by AMAX.

American Appraisal Company, *Bibliography of Cost Indexes*, Milwaukee, August, 1976.

Name, compiler, location and frequency of issue, and description of key cost indices.

Kenneth S. Axelson, "Facing the Hard Truths about Inflation," *Management Accounting*, June, 1980, pp. 11–14.

Points to deficiencies of historical accounting and need to adopt strategies to cope with inflation.

Lawrence J. Benninger, "A Method for Integrating Materials Price Changes with the Operation of a Standard Cost System," *Cost and Management*, July/August, 1975, pp. 16–19.

Proposed procedure for adjusting finished goods inventory costs to reflect price changes.

John M. Boersema, *Capital Budgeting Practices, Including the Impact of Inflation*, Canadian Institute of Chartered Accountants, Toronto, Canada, 1978.

Compendium of practices employed by 25 large Canadian companies. Suggests approach to capital budgeting in inflationary environment.

David Dee, "Sales and Cost Deflators," *Management Accounting*, December, 1976, pp. 35–37.

Suggests techniques for determining the extra capitalization that a firm needs to keep pace with inflation.

David I. Fisher, Ed., *Managing in Inflation*, The Conference Board Report #750, New York, 1978.

Collection of papers excerpted from the Conference on Inflation and Corporate Management. Includes company programs to counteract inflation.

T. Goldschmidt and K. Admon, *Profit Measurement During Inflation*, John Wiley & Sons, Inc., New York, 1977.

Text covering various aspects of profit measurement. Includes chapter on Managerial Accounting Reports suggesting that results should be reported on "inflation free" basis.

Willis R. Greer, Jr., "Inflation and Asset Performance Measurement," *Management Accounting*, January, 1976, pp. 42–49.

Mathematical model for evaluating the impact of the misestimation of future inflation rates.

C. Lowell Harriss, Ed., *Inflation, Long-Term Problems*, Academy of Political Science, Praeger Press, New York, 1975.

A collection of essays including:

a. "The Economic Effects of Inflation," G. L. Bach—on the redistributive effects of inflation in income.

b. "The Causes and Effects of Inflation," C. L. Harriss.

c. "Management Decision-Making," William M. Peterson—on capital formation.

d. "The Brazilian Experience," Stefan H. Robzock—a history of inflation and government policy in Brazil.

e. "The German Experience," Ginter Schmolders—on hyper-inflation in Germany between the two World Wars.

Intercollegiate Case Clearing House, *United States Steel—Accounting for Capital Investments*, Boston, Rev. 1969.

Case study

J. Robert Killpack, "Planning in an Inflationary Environment," *Managerial Planning*, January/February, 1976, pp. 10–13.

Overview of planning practices at Eaton Corporation.

Pat Kirkman and Chris Nobes, "Dividend Policy and Inflation," *Accountancy*, October, 1976, pp. 71–76.

U.K. study that concludes that dividend policy was little affected by current purchasing power (CCP) accounting information, but that current cost accounting (CCA) on national scale must have significant effect on dividend payments.

Aivars Krats and Thomas Henkel, "Effect of Inflation on Discounted Cash Flow Rates of Return," *Managerial Planning*, November/December, 1977, pp. 21–26.

Recommends use of constant purchasing power discounted cash flow (CPPDCF) rate of return measurement for appraising capital investment projects.

Robert E. MacAvoy, "Strategic Planning," *Financial Executive*, June, 1980, pp. 36–40.

Advocates inflation-adjusted, stand-alone analysis of the corporation's operations in each different business.

Robert E. MacAvoy, "Business Strategy and Inflation: Finding the Real Bottom Line," *Management Review*, January, 1978, pp. 17–18, 20–24.

Discussion of impact of inflation on strategic management. Advocates inflation-adjusted analysis for business units and by project.

D.I. MacGibbon, "Why Not Price Adjust Your Budget?" *The Australian Accountant*, November, 1979, pp. 686–687.

Proposes adjusting budgets to reflect inflation.

A. W. Kentbourne McFarlane, "Tracking Inflation in Your Company," *Management Accounting*, May, 1979, pp. 42–45.

Suggests method for tracking inflation on supplementary basis.

John G. Main, "Inflation and Corporate Strategy: The Rashomon Effect," *Management Review*, May, 1980, pp. 23–28, 37.

Discusses varying viewpoints of inflation provided by different types of accounting data.

Grant U. Meyers, "Accounting Problems Related to Price-Level Changes," *Management Accounting*, November, 1964, pp. 3–6.

Discusses responsibilities of management accountants for dealing with inflation.

The Inflation Dilemma, National Association of Accountants, New York, 2 vols., 1975.
Vol. 1. Managing Price-Level Accounting.
Vol. 2. Management Reporting under Inflation.

Compendium of articles that appeared in *Management Accounting* over a period of almost 30 years. Topics including historical costs vs. current value; depreciation practices and inflation accounting; LIFO and inflation accounting; reporting under price-level accounting; effect of inflation on capital budgeting and accounting for inflation in multinational operations.

Debra D. Raiborn and Thomas A. Ratcliffe, "Are You Accounting for Inflation in Your Capital Budgeting Process?" *Management Accounting*, September, 1979, pp. 19–22.

Proposed technique for incorporating general price level adjustments into the present value model.

Robert F. Randall, "ROI and Inflation: U.S. Steel President Speaks Out," *Management Accounting*, February, 1979, pp. 12–16.

Interview with David M. Roderick.

Alfred Rappaport, "Measuring Company Growth Capacity During Inflation," *Harvard Business Review*, January–February, 1979, pp. 91–100.

Advocates distributable funds (DF) measure for more effective management control. Includes methodology for calculating DF.

Richard E. Rhodes, "Price Level Changes in Financial Analyses," *Managerial Planning*, May/June, 1976, pp. 19–21.

Procedures for dealing with price level changes in the financial analysis of long-term investments.

Allen H. Seed, III, *Inflation: Its Impact on Financial Reporting and Decision-Making*, Financial Executives Research Foundation, New York, 1978.

Research based on interviews with preparers and users of financial statements concluding that the funds statement should be restructured to make it a more understandable and useful document, the income statement should be broken down by type of cost, holding gains and losses should be separated by operating income and extraordinary items, and financial statements should be supplemented with unaudited information that shows the real impact of inflation.

Allen H. Seed, III, "Strategic Planning: Cutting Edge of Management Accounting," *Management Accounting*, May, 1980, pp. 10–16.

Discusses application of inflation-adjusted data to strategic planning process.

Allen H. Seed, III, "Utilizing the Funds Statement," *Management Accounting*, May, 1978, pp. 15–18.

Advocates changes to format of funds statement to increase its usefulness as a management accounting tool.

John K. Shank, *Price Level Adjusted Statements and Management Decisions*, Financial Executives Research Foundation, New York, 1975.

Study concluding that supplementary general price level adjusted financial statements would not be useful to financial managers in the decision areas tested.

Gordon R. Sharwood, "Liquidity, Inflation and Vanishing Corporate Profits," *Cost and Management*, March/April, 1977, pp. 6–17.

Impact of inflation on corporate profits in Canada.

Alan Teck, "Financial Planning in Nations with Fluctuating Currencies," *Management Accounting*, January 1970, pp. 25–28.

Guidelines for hedging against currency fluctuations.

Winston W. Tsui, "Inflation Accounting and Foreign Currency Translation," *Management Accounting*, September, 1979, pp. 23, 26–31.

Discussion as to whether domestic or foreign inflation rates should be used for adjustments to consolidated statement. Advocates translation and restatement of foreign currencies into units of current domestic purchasing power.

"The Uneven Impact of Price Increases," *Business Week*, February 11, 1980, p. 32.

News article discussing differences of impact of inflation among different industries.

Richard F. Vancil, "Funds Flow Analysis During Inflation," *Financial Analysts Journal*, March/April, 1976, pp. 43–56.

R. Allen Vaughn, "This Hospital Service Forecasts Inflation for Its Fiscal Health," *Management Accounting*, December 1978, pp. 44–47.

Application of inflation forecast model to hospital pricing policy.

II. LIFO Inventory Valuation

Ronald M. Copeland and Joseph F. Wojdak, "Use LIFO to Offset Inflation," *Harvard Business Review*, May/June, 1971, pp. 91–100.

Includes analysis of relative magnitude of potential profit differences in 18 manufacturing industries.

Robert DeWelt, "Using Standard Costs with LIFO and FIFO," *Management Accounting*, May, 1976, pp. 25–30, 37.

Technique for linking inventory valuation with standard costs.

James B. Edwards and Dean E. Graber, "LIFO: To Switch or Not to Switch," *Management Accounting*, October, 1975, pp. 35–40.

Includes methodology for determining how many years will have to elapse before total reported assets using LIFO will equal or exceed total reported assets using FIFO.

James Don Edwards and John B. Barrack, "LIFO Inventory Valuation as an Adjuster for Inflation," *The CPA Journal*, October, 1975, pp. 21–25.

Discusses considerations involved in evaluating LIFO. Concludes that LIFO is of limited usefulness as an adjuster for inflation.

Orville R. Keister, "LIFO and Inflation," *Management Accounting*, May, 1975 pp. 27–31.

Description of mechanics of change to LIFO; concludes that companies not electing to use LIFO in an inflationary environment are electing to pay higher taxes and receive inferior cash flow.

Herbert T. McAnly, "How LIFO Began," *Management Accounting*, May, 1975, pp. 24–25.

History of LIFO.

Ken Milani, "LIFO and Its Limitations," *Management Accounting*, December, 1975, pp. 31–32, 36.

Disadvantages are explained.

Dale Morse, "LIFO . . . or FIFO?" *Financial Executive*, February, 1980, pp. 14–17.

Discussion of advantages and disadvantages of LIFO and FIFO. Includes statistics on percentage of using LIFO and comparison of different wholesale commodity indices.

III. Productivity Measurement

Thomas S. Dudick, *Profile for Profitability: Using Cost Control and Profitability Analysis*, 253 pp., John Wiley & Sons, New York, 1972.

220

Contains explanation of productivity measurement technique.

Charles E. Craig and R. Clark Harris, "Total Productivity Measurement at the Firm Level," *Sloan Management Review,* Spring, 1972, pp. 13–27.

Explanation of steps required to compute total productivity index.

Bela Gold, "Practical Productivity Analysis for Management Accountants," *Management Accounting,* May, 1980, pp. 31–38, 44.

Approach to productivity measurement.

Frank W. Kolmin and Michael J. Cerullo, "Measuring Productivity and Efficiency," *Management Accounting,* November, 1973, pp. 32–34.

Procedures for measurement.

James E. Ksnasnak, "Measuring Productivity," *Managerial Planning,* November/December, 1974, pp. 15–20, 34.

Approach to productivity measurement.

Donald E. Law, "Measuring Productivity," *Financial Executive,* October, 1972, pp. 24–27.

Describes measurements of productivity.

Productivity: A Selected Annotated Bibliography 1965–71, Bulletin No. 1776, U.S. Department of Labor, Washington, D.C., 1973.

Bibliography of references for nearly 800 publications.

Donald J. Wait, "Productivity Measurement: A Management Accounting Challenge," *Management Accounting,* May, 1980, pp. 24–30.

Discussion of issues involved in productivity measurement.

Joseph W. Wilkinson, "The Meaning of Measurements," *Management Accounting,* July, 1975, pp. 49–52.

Guidelines for comprehensive set of performance measurement.

Henry A. V. Wilson, "Added Value in Measuring Manpower Productivity," *Management Accounting* (British), June, 1971, pp. 168–170.

Explanation of added value technique.

IV. Inflation Accounting Concepts

Accounting Principles Board Statement No. 3, *Financial Statements Restated for General Price Level Changes,* American Institute of Certified Public Accountants, New York, 1969.

Morton Backer, *Current Value Accounting,* Financial Executives Research Foundation, New York, 1973.

Sidney Davidson, Clyde P. Stickney, and Roman L. Weil, *Inflation Accounting: A Guide for the Accountant and the Financial Analyst*, McGraw-Hill Book Co., New York, 1976.

This book is primarily devoted to general price level accounting, but has brief discussions of current value accounting and price level adjusted current value accounting.

Edgar O. Edwards and Philip W. Bell, *The Theory and Measurement of Business Income*, University of California Press, Berkeley, 1961.

Comprehensive text.

Financial Accounting Standards Board, *Field Tests of Financial Reporting in Units of General Purchasing Power*, Research Report, May, 1977.

D. L. Gittes, "GPL Adjusted Income Statements: A Research Study," *Management Accounting*, October, 1977, pp. 29–33.

Contains general price level accounting comparisons for four steel companies.

Monroe Ingberman, "The Evolution of Replacement Cost Accounting," *Journal of Accounting, Auditing & Finance*, Winter, 1980, pp. 101–112.

Traces history and discusses theory of replacement cost accounting.

James A. Largay, III, and John Leslie Livingston, *Accounting for Changing Prices*, John Wiley & Sons, New York, 1976.

Explanation of how to adjust historical financial statements in order to reflect the impact of price changes.

Leonard M. Savoie, "Price Level Accounting, Practical Policies and Tax Relief," *Management Accounting*, January, 1977, pp. 15–18.

Contends that it is time to stop the debate and take the message of inflation to Congress.

Dr. George M. Scott, *Research Study on Current-Value Accounting Measurements & Utility*, Touche Ross & Co., New York, 1978.

Examination of current-value accounting under inflationary conditions.

Richard F. Vancil and Roman L. Weil, *Replacement Cost Accounting: Readings on Concepts, Uses and Methods*. Thomas Horton & Daughters, Glen Ridge, New Jersey, 1976.

Compendium of articles.

V. Financial Accounting Standards Board Statement No. 33

Arthur Andersen & Co., *Statement of Financial Accounting Standards No. 33, Financial Reporting and Changing Prices: A Guide to Implementation*, Chicago, 1979.

222

Arthur Young & Company, *Financial Reporting and Changing Prices*, New York, 1979.

Arthur Young & Company, *Financial Reporting and Changing Prices: A Survey of How 300 Companies Complied with FAS 33*, New York, August, 1980.

Ettore Barbatelli and Alfred M. King, "How to Comply with FASB 33," *Financial Executive*, March, 1980, pp. 19–26.

"The Closest Look Yet at Inflation's Corporate Toll," *Business Week*, June 16, 1980, pp. 148–149.

Coopers & Lybrand, *Accounting for Changing Prices—Constant Dollar Implementation*, New York, November, 1979.

Deloitte Haskins & Sells, *Financial Reporting and Changing Prices: Supplementary Disclosure Requirements of FASB Statement No. 33*, New York, 1979.

Ernst & Whinney, *Inflation Accounting: Implementing FASB Statement No. 33*, New York, December, 1979.

Ernst & Whinney, *FASB Inflation Accounting: The First Year*, 1980.

Financial Accounting Standards Board, *Examples of the Use of FASB Statement No. 33, Financial Reporting and Changing Prices*, November, 1980.

Financial Accounting Standards Board, *Illustrations of Financial Reporting and Changing Prices: Statement of Financial Standards No. 33*, December, 1979.

Financial Accounting Standards Board, *Statement of Financial Accounting Standards No. 33: Financial Reporting and Changing Prices*, September, 1979.

Peat, Marwick, Mitchell & Co., *Statement of Accounting Standard No. 33*, November, 1979.

Peat, Marwick, Mitchell & Co., *The New Inflation Data: A Survey of Annual Reports*, New York, June, 1980.

Price, Waterhouse & Co., *Financial Reporting and Changing Prices: A Guide to Implementing FASB Statement No. 33*, New York, 1979.

Touche Ross & Co., *Financial Reporting and Changing Prices: A Guide to Implementing FASB Statement No. 33*, New York, 1979.

VI. Practices in Other Countries

"Accounting for Inflation," *CA Magazine*, November, 1974, pp. 4–5.

Reports the issuance of guidelines for accounting for inflation which the Accounting Research Committee of The Institute of Chartered Accountants in Canada developed. The guidelines propose use of supplementary statements which adjust for price-level changes through application of the gross national expenditure explicit price deflator.

Arthur Andersen & Company, *The Brazilian Method of Indexing and Accounting for Inflation*, (pamphlet), Chicago, 1975.

In addition to "nuts and bolts" of accounting techniques, includes a brief description of the entire system of "monetary correction" including taxes, financial transactions, wage and price controls and the exchange rate.

W. T. Baxter, "Coping With High Inflation in Argentina," *The Accountant*, November 4, 1976, pp. 526–527.

Description of accounting practices in Argentina.

Bhuwan Bhushan, "Effects of Inflation and Currency Fluctuation," *Management Accounting*, July, 1974, pp. 17–19.

Description of strategies for coping with currency fluctuations in Argentina and Brazil.

Canadian Institute of Chartered Accountants, *Estimating Current Values: Some Techniques, Problems and Experiences*, Toronto, 1979.

Techniques for arriving at current entry prices and current exit prices, and at current values based on Canadian experience.

Robert W. Comer, "Brazilian Price-Level Accounting," *Management Accounting*, October, 1975, pp. 41, 42–46.

A brief explanation of Brazilian price-level accounting practices.

M. R. Da Cruz Filho, da Silva Machado and Robert Thompson, "Accounting for Inflation," *Financial Executive*, December, 1978, pp. 42–45.

Brazilian and United States practices.

D. W. Finnett and C. R. Horsley, *Current Cost Accounting*, The Institute of Cost and Management Accountants, 1979.

Introduction to production and interpretation of financial data in U.K.

John C. Getzelman, "Financial Analysis in an Inflationary Environment," *Management Accounting*, March, 1975, pp. 31–35.

Description of accounting and financial analysis practices in Brazil.

Bob Grimsley, *Practical Accounting for Inflation*, Gower Press, Great Britain, 1975.

Comprehensive text covering U.K. accounting practices. Includes chapters on pricing, cost finding, cost control, monthly management accounts, and financial forecasting in an inflationary environment.

Asim Kumar Sen Gupta, *Inflation Accounting in India*, Kalpa Printers & Publishers Private, Ltd., Calcutta, 1976.

Text dealing with inflation accounting in Indian context.

Alexandre Kafka, "Indexing for Inflation in Brazil," in *Essays on Inflation*, Giersch *et al.* American Enterprise Institute for Public Policy Research, Washington, D.C., 1974.

Description of the Brazilian economy and the system of monetary correction, (indexing). Twenty-year review.

P.R.A. Kirkman, *Inflation Accounting: A Guide for Non-Accountants*, John Wiley & Sons, New York, 1975.

Text describing inflation accounting practices and issues in the United Kingdom. Current Purchasing Power (CCP) Accounting is described in detail.

R. W. Maskell, "Inflation Accounting in Brazil," *Management Accounting*, (British), January, 1980, pp. 21–23.

Advocates adoption of Brazilian methodology in U.K.

"Profits and Inflation," *The Economist*, December, 4, 1976, pp. 109–111.

A report on the Morpath Committee.

F.E.P. Sandilands, *Inflation Accounting: Report of the Inflation Accounting Committee*, London, Her Majesty's Stationery Office, September, 1975.

The "Sandilands Report" that contributed to the evolution of inflation accounting in Great Britain.

Krojiro Someya, *An Introduction to Flow of Funds Accounting*, The Institute for Research in Business Administration, Waseda University, Tokyo, Japan, 1977.

Text covering all aspects of funds accounting and budgeting with transnational relevance.

R. D. Thomas, (Editor), "Research: Accounting for Inflation in Australia," *CA Magazine*, September, 1976, pp. 68–72.

Primarily an explanation of the exposure draft on current value accounting.

University of Illinois, Center for International Education and Research in Accounting, *The Impact of Inflation on Accounting: A Global View*, Urbana, Illinois, 1979.

Proceedings of seminar. Includes discussion of practices in Iran, Poland and Mexico.

Henk Volten, "Research: Accounting Developments in the Netherlands," *CA Magazine*, November, 1976, pp. 54–57.

Explains the suggestions of the Dutch "Tripartite Study Group" in several areas of accounting, including valuation.

C. A. Westwick, "How Companies Account for Inflation," *The Accountant*.
Part I. April 10, 1975, pp. 455–461.
Part II. April 17, 1975, pp. 496–500.

Survey of U.K. inflation accounting practices. Cites cases and examples.

John C. H. Woo, "Accounting for Inflation: Some International Models," *Management Accounting*, February, 1978, pp. 57–60.

A comparative analysis of financial statements reflecting the methods used in the United Kingdom, the Netherlands, and Brazil as compared to the historical method used in the United States.

Appendix

National Association of Accountants

919 THIRD AVENUE
NEW YORK, N.Y. 10022
(212) 754 9700

March 17, 1980

Mr. Robert L. Short
Lane Company, Inc.
Altavista, Virginia 24517

Dear Mr. Short:

In view of continuing inflation, the National Association of Accountants is conducting an important research study concerning the impact of inflation on internal planning and control. The principal researcher is Allen Seed of Arthur D. Little, Inc. This study is expected to provide information that will help financial and accounting executives deal with the management accounting implications of inflation.

The principal thrust of this research is to find out how inflation has actually affected planning and control practices in leading corporations. This includes behavioral effects as well as methodological effects.

In order to obtain factual information, we are asking selected chief financial officers to complete the enclosed questionnaire. Most of the questions simply require an "X", so the questionnaire should not take more than a few minutes to complete. However, the researchers would also appreciate your comments as to the issues involved, so if you choose to add them, they will be most appreciated.

Results will be tabulated by type of industry and size of company and will be incorporated into the research report. Individual company responses will, of course, be considered confidential.

Please send the completed questionnaire to Mr. Seed in the enclosed envelope. If you will clip your business card to your response, we will send you a copy of survey results.

Thank you for your cooperation.

Sincerely,

Stephen Landekich
Research Director

NATIONAL ASSOCIATION OF ACCOUNTANTS RESEARCH PROJECT
THE IMPACT OF INFLATION ON INTERNAL PLANNING AND CONTROL
QUESTIONNAIRE

% TOTAL DISTRIBUTION
282 RESPONSES

COMPANY BACKGROUND

1. What is your primary type of business?

53.9 Manufacturing – Industrial Products   25.5 Manufacturing – Consumer Products   5.0 Oil and Gas

3.5 Mining or Other Extractive Products   0 Financial Services   0 Transportation

0 Utility   0 Retailing   12.1 Other _____ Specify

2. Revenues latest fiscal year in $ millions   Median $590 Million

3. Approximate % revenues outside U.S.:

| 45.4 Under 10% | 32.6 10% to 29% | 18.4 30% to 50% | 3.2 Over 50% | 0.4 No Answer |

4. Total assets latest fiscal year-end in $ millions   Median $385 Million

5. Approximate % total assets outside U.S.:

| 50.4 Under 10% | 35.1 10% to 29% | 11.0 30% to 50% | 2.1 Over 50% | 1.4 No Answer |

6. Approximate % total assets in countries with inflation rate in excess of 30% per year (e.g., South America):

| 91.8 Under 10% | 3.6 10% to 29% | 0.4 30% to 50% | 0 Over 50% | 4.2 No Answer |

ASSUMPTIONS ABOUT U.S. INFLATION

7. What are your expectations with respect to the inflation rate in the U.S. (consumer price index) in each of the following years?

	CPI Increase Less than 5%	CPI Increase 5% to 9%	CPI Increase 10% to 15%	CPI Increase Above 15%	No Answer
a. 1980	0	1.4	75.2	23.1	0.3
b. 1981	0.4	35.5	61.3	2.1	0.7
c. 1985	3.2	72.3	21.3	1.8	1.4

8. For your company, do you expect the following rates of change of average prices to be higher, lower, or approximately the same as the consumer price index?

	Higher than CPI	Lower than CPI	About the Same as CPI	No Answer
a. Selling Prices	15.6	49.3	33.3	1.8
b. Labor Costs including Fringes	19.1	31.6	47.2	1.3
c. Material Costs	36.5	20.2	42.2	1.1
d. Service Costs	28.0	13.1	56.4	2.5
e. Energy Costs	88.3	1.8	9.2	0.7
f. Plant and Equipment Costs	34.8	14.5	49.3	1.4
g. Taxes	19.1	36.9	40.1	3.9

9. Who is primarily responsible for determining inflation expectations in your company?

16.3 Corporate Economist	3.9 Economic Service	17.7 Planning Manager
11.3 Treasurer	4.3 Controller	12.4 Other / Multiple Specify
25.9 Responsibility Not Assigned	6.7 Line Management, incl. CEO	1.5 Missing

CORPORATE FINANCIAL STRATEGIES

10. Since 1974 when the U.S. inflation rate increased to about 11%, how have your corporate financial strategies been affected by inflation?

	Increased or Accelerated Because of Inflation	Decreased or Deferred Because of Inflation	Has Not Been Affected by Inflation	No Answer
a. Short-term Borrowing	37.6	5.3	54.6	2.5
b. Long-term Borrowing	30.5	14.2	52.5	2.8
c. Leasing	18.1	5.7	72.3	3.9
d. Equity Financing	7.5	16.7	72.3	3.5
e. Dividend Payment Per Share	36.2	4.6	55.7	3.5
f. Dividend Payment % Earnings	8.9	9.2	76.2	5.7
Timing of Capital Expenditures				
g. – for additional capacity	19.1	24.5	54.3	2.1
h. – for cost reduction	46.6	8.5	46.1	1.8
i. Capital Expenditure Hurdle Rate	62.8	2.8	29.4	5.0
j. Corporate Acquisitions	7.1	19.9	68.8	4.2
k. Long-term Purchase Contracts	23.1	11.3	59.2	6.4

233

PLANNING OR BUDGETING

(Please check where applicable)

	Current Year Profit Plan of Budget	Strategic or Long-Range Plans
11. Plans or budgets are updated:		
a. Once a year	25.9	74.8
b. Twice a year	11.3	4.3
c. Quarterly	39.0	2.8
d. Monthly	16.7	0
e. As required	9.2	15.2
f. Not required	0	2.1
12. Plans or budgets routinely contain:		
a. Income Statement	99.6	89.0
b. Balance Sheet or Statement of Net Assets	91.1	80.5
c. Funds Statement	87.9	75.5
d. Statement of Distributable Funds	32.3	27.0
e. Trend Analysis (e.g., financial ratios)	62.4	66.0
f. Productivity Measurements	39.7	31.9
g. Comparison with CPI or Other Inflation Index	17.7	26.6
13. Sales and earnings projections are:		
a. Single Number Forecasts	87.9	58.2
b. Range Forecasts (hi—low)	14.5	37.9

14. Inflation rate assumptions are:

    a. Determined Centrally   68.1   67.4

    b. Determined by Local Business Unit   30.9   21.6

    c. Not Considered in Planning Process   7.4   7.1

15. Financial projections are shown in:

    a. Nominal Dollars Adjusted for Inflation   58.2   45.0

    b. Constant Dollars   23.4   23.8

    c. Both Nominal and Constant Dollars   15.6   24.5

16. Currency exchange rates for international affiliates are:

    a. Determined Centrally   65.6   56.4

    b. Determined by Local Business Unit   17.0   14.9

17. Plans of international affiliates are routinely submitted to corporate headquarters in:

    a. Local Currency Only   20.2   18.8

    b. U.S. Dollars Only   22.7   20.2

    c. Both Local Currency and U.S. Dollars   37.6   32.3

18. What is the most important change that had been made to your planning and budgeting process as a result of inflation?

235

CAPITAL EXPENDITURES

(Please check where applicable)	Practice Applied		Practice Not Applied		No Answer
	Long-Standing Practice	Recently Applied Practice	Considering Application of Practice	Do Not Expect to Apply	
19. Amount of capital expenditures included in request allows for inflation?	57.5	18.4	8.5	14.2	1.4
20. Revenue and expense projections used to support request include allowance for inflation?	42.9	22.0	12.1	21.6	1.4
21. Residual values in request include allowance for inflation?	26.1	12.1	12.1	43.6	5.6
22. Projected cash flows for project are adjusted to units of constant purchasing power?	19.5	6.1	17.7	50.7	6.0
23. Cost of capital used to evaluate project includes allowance for inflation?	33.3	16.3	15.2	31.9	3.2
24. Summary of capital expenditure projects (budget) contains unallocated allowance for inflation?	12.4	7.1	9.9	63.1	7.5
25. Overseas investments are evaluated in:					
a. Local Currency Only	8.2	0	0	4.6	87.2
b. U.S. Dollars Only	23.4	0.7	0.4	2.1	73.4
c. Both Local Currency and U.S. Dollars	41.5	3.9	0.7	4.3	49.6
26. Overseas investments are evaluated using:					
a. Local Income Tax Rate	15.8	0	0.4	3.2	
b. U.S. Income Tax Rate	38.8	0.4	0.4	3.2	
c. Both Local and U.S. Income Tax Rates	45.4	3.2	0.7	3.2	

STANDARD COSTS

78.7 Use standard costs

If standard costs are not used in your company, please check here ☐ and go on to question 31. Please check following questions as applicable.

27. Standard costs are revised:

44.7 Annually   **2.8** Semi-annually   **4.6** Quarterly

24.8 As required   **1.4** Other

28. Are standard costs revised more frequently today as a result of inflation

35.8 Yes   **40.8** No

29. Cost increases resulting from inflation are:

5.3 Not included in standard costs

30.1 Included in standard costs when known

42.6 Included in standard cost on an anticipated basis

30. Standard cost methodology primarily employed:

36.9 Standard cost fixed for year

23.8 Current standard cost used

17.4 Dual standards are used: base standard fixed for year; current standards are also computed

INVENTORY VALUATION

31. Predominant method of valuation applied in U.S.

27.0 FIFO   **61.0** LIFO   **7.8** Average Cost

4.2 Other   **0** Not Applicable

32. Inflation at rates assumed:

a. Has led to switch to LIFO between 1974 and 1979   **47.2**

b. Will probably lead to switch to LIFO within next three years   **7.8**

c. May lead to switch to LIFO   **11.3**

d. Is not expected to affect inventory valuation method   **29.1**

e. No answer   **4.6**

237

MANAGEMENT REPORTING AND OTHER MANAGEMENT PRACTICES

Please check how the following management reporting techniques are applied in your company.

	Regularly Applied	Plan to Apply	Is Not Applied	No Answer
33. Business unit performance is measured in constant dollars?	24.5	9.2	64.5	1.8
34. Business unit performance is routinely compared with CPI or other indices?	16.0	5.3	75.9	2.8
35. Cost of sales based on LIFO (or other current cost) inventory values are used at business unit level to measure performance?	47.5	6.4	45.4	0.7
36. Fixed assets are restated on a current cost basis for internal performance measurement?	6.4	9.9	81.9	1.8
37. Business unit profits are restated on current costs basis for internal performance measurement?	7.5	8.5	81.2	2.8
38. Business unit return on investment calculation is based on current cost of assets?	15.6	9.6	73.4	1.4
39. Variance analyses (between budget and actual results) separate a component for inflation?	14.2	3.9	79.1	2.8
40. Actual results are compared with price level adjusted flexible budget?	6.7	5.0	84.8	3.5

41.	Emphasis is placed on funds flow?	76.3	8.5	13.1	2.1
42.	Productivity measurements are more widely used?	53.2	17.0	25.2	4.6
43.	Management incentive compensation is based on inflation-adjusted performance measurements?	11.3	5.0	80.5	3.2
44.	Management incentive compensation is based on funds flow?	18.4	5.0	72.0	4.6
45.	How has inflation affected your internal management reporting practices?				

National Association of Accountants
Committee on Research
1980–81

Calvin A. Vobroucek
Chairman
Caterpillar Tractor Company
Peoria, Illinois

Henry M. Klein
General Instrument
El Paso, Texas

Ira Landis
Laventhol & Horwath
Los Angeles, California

Paul H. Levine
Magnetic Analysis Corporation
Mt. Vernon, New York

Jack E. Meadows
Combustion Engineering Company
Chattanooga, Tennessee

Thomas J. O'Reilly
Coopers & Lybrand
Cleveland, Ohio

Ronald J. Patten
University of Connecticut
Storrs, Connecticut

Howard O. Rockness
Dartmouth College
Hanover, New Hampshire

W. Peter Salzarulo
Miami University
Oxford, Ohio

Bruce T. Santilli
Abex Corporation
Winchester, Virginia

Fred S. Schulte
Tracor, Inc.
Austin, Texas

Henry A. Schwartz
IBM
Armonk, New York

Milton F. Usry
Oklahoma State University
Stillwater, Oklahoma

No. 81131-GP-7M-10/81

242